S/NVQ 2

Care

Health and Social

S/NVQ 2

Health and Social
Care

Lynda Mason
Janet Murdoch
Linda Lightfoot
Jane Makey

Hodder Arnold

A MEMBER OF THE HODDER HEADLINE GROUP

Orders: please contact Bookpoint Ltd, 130 Milton Park, Abingdon, Oxon OX14
4SB. Telephone: (44) 01235 827720. Fax: (44) 01235 400454. Lines are open
from 9.00 - 6.00, Monday to Saturday, with a 24 hour message answering
service. You can also order through our website www.hoddereducation.co.uk

If you have any comments to make about this, or any of our other titles,
please send them to educationenquiries@hodder.co.uk

British Library Cataloguing in Publication Data
A catalogue record for this title is available from the British Library

ISBN: 0 340 81577 9
ISBN-13: 978 0 340 81577 9

Hodder Headline's policy is to use papers that are natural, renewable and
recyclable products and made fromwood grown in sustainable forests.
The logging and manufacturing processes are expected to conform to the
environmental regulations of the country of origin.

Typeset by Servis Filmsetting Ltd, Manchester.
Printed in the UK by CPI Bath.

CONTENTS

CHAPTER 6   UNIT HSC223   CONTRIBUTE TO THE MOVING AND HANDLING OF INDIVIDUALS   179

CHAPTER 7   UNIT HSC218   SUPPORT INDIVIDUALS WITH THEIR PERSONAL CARE NEEDS   203

Introduction

Welcome to this book, which has been written with the care worker specifically in mind. If you work in residential, intermediate or domiciliary care, you should find this book both helpful and informative.

We have produced the information in a user-friendly format, so that if you are working towards your NVQ qualification, you should find it an invaluable source of support. The text closely follows the standards required for the successful achievement of the award.

The chapters in the book cover the four core units, which are:

- ❏ HSC 21 Communicate with and complete records for individuals (Chapter 1)
- ❏ HSC 22 Support the health and safety of yourself and individuals (Chapter 2)
- ❏ HSC 23 Develop your knowledge and practice (Chapter 3)
- ❏ HSC 24 Ensure your own actions support the care, protection and wellbeing of individuals (Chapter 4).

Three of the optional units are included:

- ❏ HSC 213 Provide food and drink for individuals (Chapter 8)
- ❏ HSC 218 Support individuals with their personal care needs (Chapter 7)
- ❏ HSC 223 Contribute to moving and handling individuals (Chapter 6).

We have also included an additional unit:

- ❏ HSC 241 Contribute to the effectiveness of teams (Chapter 5).

Working in teams is an essential element of the care worker's job role, even though it does not figure in the Level 2 award. However, the knowledge and skills which you will gain from reading the relevant chapter should prove useful to your daily work, and help to ensure that you function as an effective member of the team. Remember, if you should change your job role or perhaps become a senior carer, you could be asked to add this unit to the qualification that you already hold.

You only need to complete six units successfully to achieve your award.

Using the book

Perhaps one of the best ways to use this book is alongside the course information that you received from the organisation where you are sitting your NVQ. This could be your local college, your own workplace or another training provider.

Throughout the book we have included case studies of real life situations and reflective activities, and provided opportunities to discover new information. Each of these features is designed to encourage you to think about your own situation, the people you work with and the individuals you support and care for.

The final section of the book suggests some further reading and information sources, which you may find helpful as your studies develop.

Finally, we hope you find this book very useful, and wish you well in your studies and future careers.

Lynda Mason
Janet Murdoch
Linda Lightfoot
Jane Makey

Acknowledgements

The authors and publisher would like to thank the following for permission to reproduce material in this book:

Figures 1.1, 3.13, 8.2, John Birdsall; figure 1.3, Bernafon AG; figure 1.4, Alamy/Photofusion Picture Library; figures 1.16, 7.9, Lorna Ainger; figure 1.7, Rex/Shout; figure 1.9, Getty Images/ Matthew Antrobus; figure 1.12, Getty Images/Yoshikazu Tsuno; figure 1.17, Ingram; figure 1.18, Photolibrary.com; figure 1.20, Corbis/Brooks Kraft; figures 1.21, 4.9c, 5.1, Rex Features/Alix/ Phanie; figure 1.23, Photofusion Picture Library; figures 1.24, 2.1b, 4.2, 5.4, Sally & Richard Greenhill; figure 2.1a, Rex Features/Jonathan Hordle; figure 2.1c, Shout/John Callan; figure 2.2, Science Photo Library/AJ Photo; figure 2.3, Kidde Fire Protection Services; figure 2.4, Alamy/Stockbyte Platinum; figures 2.5, 7.14, Photofusion; figure 2.6, Science Photo Library/Lauren Shear; figure 2.7, Alamy/Crispin Hughes/Photofusion; figure 2.8, Science Photo Library/Faye Norman; figure 2.9, Rex Features/ Chat Magazine; figure 3.5, Alamy/Image Source; figure 3.6, Science Photo Library/John Cole; figure 3.8, Corbis/Jose Luis Pelaez, Inc.; figure 3.14, Rex Features/Sipa Press; figure 4.1, Photofusion/Paula Solloway; figure 4.4a, Photofusion/Paul Doyle; figure 4.4b, Rex Features/Nils Jorgensen; figure 4.4c, David Sanger Photography/ Alamy; figure 4.4d, Rex Features/Andrew Drysdale; figure 4.5, Alamy/Janine Wiedel; figure 4.6, © Commission for Racial Equality; figure 4.8a, Science Photo Library/Jim Varney; figures 4.9a, 4.9d, Science Photo Library/Dr P. Marazzi; figure 4.9b, Alamy/Malcolm Freeman; figure 4.10, Rex Features/E. M. Welch; figure 4.11, David Hoffman Photo Library; figure 5.5, Getty Images/Matthew Antrobus; figure 5.9, Getty Images/Andrew Yates Productions; figure 6.2, Getty Images/Gary Buss; figure 6.3, Rex Features/ Shout; figures 6.4a, 6.4b, 6.7, 6.8, 6.9, 7.7, Days Healthcare; figures 6.4c, 6.4d, Homecraft Ability One; figures 6.5, 6.6, images by kind permission of www.uk-shopability.co.uk; figure 7.1, Getty Images/Lonnie Duka; figure 7.8, Science Photo Library/Adrienne Hart-Davies; figure 7.4, Carlos Dominguez/Science Photo Library; figure 7.11, Science Photo Library/Oscar Burriel; figure 7.12, Getty Images/Sigrid Olsson; figures 7.13a, 7.13b, 7.13e, 7.13f, 7.13g, 7.13h, 7.13i, 7.15, www.Homecraftabilityone.com; figures 7.13c, 7.13d, Help the Aged; figure 7.17, Science Photo Library/Gusto Productions; figure 8.3, Photodisc; figure 8.6, Alamy/David R. Frazier Photolibrary, Inc.; figure 8.7, Sunrise Medical Ltd; figure 8.12, Science Photo Library/Josh Sher.

Every effort has been made to obtain necessary permission with reference to copyright material. The publishers apologise if inadvertently any sources remain unacknowledged and will be glad to make the necessary arrangements at the earliest opportunity.

The authors would like to thank their families and friends for their patience and support during the production of this book.

1

Communicate with and complete records for individuals

> ## → Introduction
>
> This unit looks at how all aspects of communication can help to build, develop and maintain good relationships. The development of relationships with others is essential when working in health and social care. In order to develop relationships successfully, care workers need to display good communication skills.
>
> Communication is the two-way exchange of information between at least two individuals. It requires all parties to take an active part and involves much more than just talking!
>
> Not all individuals communicate in the same way, and so by respecting individuality, working with local policies and procedures and by applying theory, health and social care workers can improve their professional practice.
>
> In this unit you will learn:
>
> ❑ how to work with individuals and others to identify the best forms of communication
>
> ❑ how to listen and respond to the individual's questions and concerns
>
> ❑ how to communicate with individuals
>
> ❑ how to access and update records and reports

★ KEY WORDS

APPROPRIATE PEOPLE	Those people from whom care workers need to gain permission to access records according to legal and organisational requirements.
ACTIVE SUPPORT	This encourages individuals to do as much for themselves as possible to maintain their independence and physical ability, and encourages people with disabilities to maximise their own potential and independence.
COMMUNICATION AND LANGUAGE NEEDS AND PREFERENCES	These are the individual's needs and preferences in terms of communicating with their care workers, and then the care worker communicating and responding back.

INDIVIDUALS	These are the actual people requiring health and social care services. Where individuals use **advocates** and **interpreters** to enable them to express their views, wishes or feelings and to speak on their behalf, the term 'individual' within this standard covers both the individual and their advocate or interpreter.
KEY PEOPLE	These are the people who are essential to an individual's health and social wellbeing, and make a difference to their life.
RIGHTS	All individuals have the right to: • be respected • be treated equally and not to be discriminated against • be treated as an individual • be treated in a dignified way • have privacy • be protected from danger and harm • be cared for in the way that meets their needs, takes account of their choices and also protects them • access information about themselves • communicate using their preferred methods of communication and language.
SERVICE USER	An individual who receives care and support from your organisation.

Work with individuals and others to identify the best forms of communication

To help you meet the requirements for this section of the unit you will need to know and understand about:

❑ Seeking information about an individuals specific communication needs and preferences

❑ How to confirm with individuals about their preferred method of communication

❑ How to review your own communication skills

❑ How to record, report and share information

Seek information about the individual's specific communication needs and preferences

Care workers often take for granted that their service users can communicate their views, wishes and care needs effectively. In practice this is often not the case, and so it is important to find

Fig 1.1 Care planning meetings can be difficult for service-users.

the best way to communicate with a service user so that they can express their needs and preferences.

Due to physical, psychological, emotional and developmental reasons, service users may have difficulty in communicating, and may need to rely on others to assist them with passing on information about their care needs.

Examples of factors that can affect communication skills, abilities and development differences between individuals are:

❑ language used

❑ hearing loss

❑ visual impairment

❑ physical disability

❑ learning difficulties/disabilities

❑ dementia/confusion.

Other factors may relate not to the service user themselves but to wider issues, such as:

❑ physical environment – lighting levels, noise, temperature, distractions

❑ cultural differences

❑ care worker's attitude, manner and approach.

Confirm with individuals their preferred methods of communication

Once information about the service user's preferred method of communication has been obtained, it is essential that this is validated by confirming the information back to the person it came from. If this was not the service user, then it needs to be discussed and confirmed as accurate with them, if they are able to do so. By confirming the information received, it may prevent

CARE VALUES

All individuals have the right to have their views and opinions heard and considered when service provision is being planned and reviewed. If individuals have difficulty in communicating, it is important to find out the best ways their views can be expressed using their preferred communication method. To do this, the care worker will need to seek advice from people who may be able to assist.

Information can be obtained from a variety of sources, such as:

• the individual

• his or her notes and records

• relatives and guardians

• friends

• other members of the multi-disciplinary team

• colleagues

• advocates

• specialists who may be able to offer advice about specific communication devices or equipment that can assist in communication.

Fig 1.2 *Avoid external noise where possible!*

CASE STUDY

Eric is being encouraged to choose his own breakfast this morning. Since his stroke he has lost all interest in food and just eats what is put in front of him. Esmie asked Eric what he wanted and gave him a choice from the breakfast menu. He chose a 'full English' breakfast. 'Let me just check with you, Eric,' said Esmie, 'you want sausage, bacon and eggs for breakfast with beans and mushrooms and fried bread?' 'No, don't give me the beans,' said Eric, 'but I will have everything else, just make sure my egg is well done.' 'OK,' said Esmie, 'a full English without beans and with a well done egg.'

- How do you check with your service users that they actually mean what they say?

any misinterpretation and confusion. A good way to confirm the information that you have received is by paraphrasing; this means repeating the information in a different way. In other words, you repeat back to the individual what it is that you think they have said. They can then confirm this with you.

Communication is much more than the spoken word. It is a complex process of information exchange, and people communicate in many different ways.

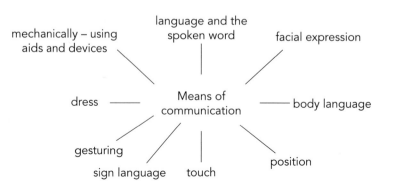

Fig 1.3 Hearing aids and devices need to be switched on to aid communication.

Reviewing your communication skills

Once the service user's preferred methods of communication have been established and confirmed, it is important that every care worker undertakes some form of self assessment in order to review their own communication skills.

Asking yourself questions can be a good way of identifying any shortcomings, prejudices, communication blocks and of course any training needs that you may have. Ask yourself the questions included here about your communication skills.

Communication involves the meaningful exchange of information between two or more individuals. If the views and wishes of the service user or your team members cannot be understood, it is unlikely that their needs will be met. This could leave everyone involved feeling frustrated and unsupported.

You could check your communication skills even further by asking your team members to observe your communication with an individual, and then give you feedback on your performance. You might like to link this kind of activity to Chapter 3, 'Developing your knowledge and practice'.

If you are experiencing any communication difficulties, either with service users or other individuals, it is essential that you seek support from within your workplace and if appropriate from external agencies and service users' family and friends. These people can often provide guidance and information that will enable you to develop more effective ways of communication. Do not assume you have to find all the answers to problems and difficulties yourself. It is very likely that other more experienced team members will have come across similar difficulties to those you might meet, and this makes them a valuable source of information and support for you.

REFLECT

How would you describe your ability to communicate with other people?

Do you:

- speak or use the same language
- use appropriate language avoiding jargon, slang or derogatory terms
- use appropriate questioning techniques
- make eye contact without staring
- actively listen
- paraphrase and reflect
- vary tone and pitch of your voice
- avoid raising your voice and shouting
- speak clearly without obstructing your mouth
- face service users when speaking to them
- adopt an open posture and avoid crossing arms and legs
- avoid excessive use of gestures which can appear threatening or distracting
- position yourself close enough without invading personal space
- avoid placing barriers and obstacles between you and your service user
- appear genuine, warm and understanding
- show respect for their views, opinions and culture
- give the service user time to finish their sentences
- spend time getting to know them and communicating with them?

REFLECT

Positive steps taken to promote better communications might involve:

- employing staff who can speak in a service user's preferred language
- providing leaflets and information that has been translated into the service user's first language
- carers learning some key phrases of their first language
- carers learning to use Makaton or British Sign Language (BSL)
- an organisation providing picture cards/boards to explain key terms
- an organisation providing training sessions for staff
- seeking help from external agencies, eg GP, audiologist, optician
- providing advocacy support
- providing interpreters in the caring environment
- providing appropriate places for communication to take place.

Have you or your organisation been involved in any of these services? If so, how did they help improve communication?

It is the professional responsibility of each care worker to seek support if they are finding it difficult to communicate effectively. It is also the responsibility of your workplace employer to provide equipment and training to develop the skills of their care staff further in order to improve communication between themselves and the service users.

Record, report and share information

Information about an individual's preferred methods of communication needs to be recorded in his or her notes. The information recorded may be as simple as their preferred name, or the way they like to be addressed. However, it could also be quite complicated and involve notes that explain that the individual is hard of hearing, that their hearing is better on the right side, and that they need to use a hearing aid.

Some service users, especially those with specific communication difficulties, may need very specific details to be recorded in their notes. Other service users may find that gestures and touch can be threatening, or that eye contact is intimidating for them. If this is the case, the result could be the displaying of challenging behaviour or a complete communication shut down. In cases such as these, it is absolutely essential for all caring individuals to share this information through the service user's notes and records. Clearly, failure to pass on such important information could have serious consequences for the caring relationship.

However, it is important to recognise that sharing such information needs to be handled sensitively, with confidentiality in mind. Not everyone needs to know everything; the care

Fig 1.4 Speaking clearly without obstructing the face and mouth is essential.

team needs to decide who should be told what information, in order for staff to be able to perform their duties safely and efficiently.

The service user's right to confidentiality and security of information must also be respected, and therefore before any information is disclosed, their permission must be sought. If the service user is not able to give such permission, this should be obtained from their guardian or representative if possible.

Listen and respond to the individual's questions and concerns

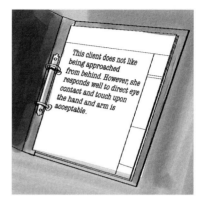

Fig 1.5 Record information!

To help you meet the requirements for this section of the unit you will need to know and understand about:

❑ Listening and responding to individuals appropriately

❑ The importance of position during communication

❑ Using appropriate body language, eye contact and methods of listening

❑ Seeking advice and support

Before any communication can successfully take place, it is important for the care worker to check that the service user has all the support they need to be able to express their views and wishes. To do this, you may need to use specific mechanical devices such as picture and word cards, or you may need to use the expertise of other professionals such as an interpreter or advocate.

Unless this support is available, the service user will not be able to listen and ask the questions that are important to them. In other words, they will not be able to have a meaningful two-way exchange of information. This could lead to feelings of disempowerment and frustration, which could result in a downward spiral of poor communication, frustration and anger.

Abraham Maslow put forward a theory about human needs. He identified that the goal of human life was personal growth in order to reach personal potential. However, before an individual can do this, their basic needs must be met first. These are represented by the pyramid, with the first, most basic needs placed at the base. In order to have their needs met, a service user must be able to express openly what their needs are and to be able to state how they would like them to be met. Therefore, adequate, effective two-way communication is vital if they are to succeed in meeting their daily needs and improve their quality of life.

> ## REFLECT
>
> • How do your service users like to be addressed?
>
> • How do you establish a trusting relationship with them?
>
> Initially, many older individuals like to be addressed as 'Mr' or 'Mrs' etc, especially by younger care workers or until a trusting relationship has been built up.

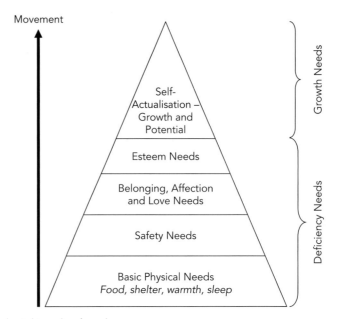

Fig 1.6 Maslow's hierarchy of needs.

As a carer, you will be only too aware of the different ways in which an individual or their family members communicate with you or your organisation. It is important that you feel confident and can demonstrate competence in listening and responding to requests, questions and concerns. These questions and concerns can come from:

❏   service users

❏   team members

❏   line managers

❏   health professionals

❏   family members

❏   social care workers

❏   many other people.

Wherever the questioning comes from, you need to be able to respond in a professional and effective manner.

Skills required for responding correctly

Using the telephone

Virtually all of us have to use the telephone somewhere within the caring process. For example, you may need to make a

Fig 1.7 The telephone is an important tool which aids communication – use it wisely.

doctor's appointment for a service user in their own home; or your line manager may need to telephone you during your daily routine as a home carer to ask you to change the time of a visit. No matter what the situation is, remember these points:

- ❑ Speak clearly and slowly.

- ❑ Paraphrase any information given to you.

- ❑ Make notes of the conversation.

- ❑ Fill in a 'communications' record as appropriate.

- ❑ Be clear about any action required of you or others.

- ❑ Follow up any actions by confirming with others that actions have taken place.

Listening skills

We have touched upon listening skills already and will do so again elsewhere in this unit. However, this is a useful place to reinforce the importance of listening. You will certainly fail to respond to questions and concerns if you do not listen to others in the first instance! Listening involves:

- ❑ being active – 'tune in' to what is being said

- ❑ weighing up the information – make a judgement

- ❑ maintaining attention – do not switch off

- ❑ making notes if necessary

REFLECT

Think about your own listening skills. How often have you 'tuned out' to an individual's repeated information? How often have you 'faked' listening? What action could you take to improve your listening skills?

If you interrupt a client or

speak over them . . . . . .

You are not listening!

Fig 1.8

❑   being motivated – listening really does make a difference

❑   avoiding distractions.

Responding to questions

Having good listening skills can take you more than halfway to creating effective responses for questions. To assist you with the difficult task of effective responses to questions and concerns, it may be helpful to remember the following points:

❑   Paraphrase the question back to the individual – confirm meaning and your understanding.

❑   Refer to any notes that you may have taken.

❑   Check that your information is accurate and up-to-date before you 'pass it on'.

❑   Be honest and truthful.

❑   Avoid ambiguity (double meanings).

As previously identified, some individuals may not be able to communicate their wishes easily, and so it is important that the care worker actively explores and promotes the best way for communication to take place.

CASE STUDY

Albert is 77 years old and is currently in hospital after having a stroke. This has left him with a severe right-sided weakness and no speech. Albert is struggling to communicate in several ways; he has poor vision, is deaf and now is unable to speak clearly or write. Prior to his admission, Albert lived alone in a terraced house and he was an active, independent gentleman.

There is due to be a team case conference, to prepare for his discharge and explore the options available to him.

Consider the following:

- Why is it important for Albert to be able to express his views and wishes at the case conference?

- If Albert was unable to do this himself, who could be contacted to act on his behalf and state his wishes?

- What equipment could be provided to assist Albert to hear and read the information that has been recorded from the case conference?

- What could be used to assist Albert to communicate his basic needs quickly for a drink, to use the toilet, to go back to bed, food, etc?

The importance of position during communication

To help maximise opportunities for successful communication, it is important to consider the environment in which the interaction is taking place and the position/s of those communicating. We are all probably aware that in some cases, care settings can be noisy and busy places (eg a hospital ward). These factors can lead to barriers which inhibit effective communication. Fortunately, there is much you can do to promote effective communication; eg:

- ❑ Reduce background noise.

- ❑ Minimise distractions around you.

- ❑ Minimise any possibilities of interruptions.

- ❑ Have a well-lit room.

- ❑ Have a comfortable room temperature.

- ❑ Provide ventilation.

- ❑ Ensure all parties are comfortable.

- ❑ Ensure all parties can see each other.

Fig 1.9 Comfortable furniture can promote positive communication.

To ensure good communication between you and others, including your service user, you also need to consider positioning. It is important that all parties are able to see each other so that they can monitor the non-verbal signals being given out, as well as being able to feel on equal terms and comfortable with one another.

When communicating with someone who is seated or in bed, it is very important for the care worker to position themselves at the same height level, or even a little lower. It is very intimidating if the care worker remains standing up, as the height difference can make them appear more powerful and domineering. It is also important to consider the position adopted by the individuals involved; the best position is often to be facing or at a slight angle, as this will enable all individuals to see each other's lips, eyes, gestures and facial expressions.

Proximity is the term that relates to the space between people or objects. It is an important concept in health and social care work and something you should be fully aware of. Everyone has a sense of personal space in which they feel threatened and uncomfortable if it is invaded or breached by someone they do not feel comfortable with. For most people, a comfortable communication space is when they are about 3–5 feet away from the others involved. The distances below are a guide to some of the different 'comfort' zones experienced by individuals:

❑   intimate zone = 1–2 feet

❑   personal zone = 2–4 feet

Fig 1.10 Expressions of power and dominance create blockages to effective communication.

- ❏   social zone = 4–8 feet
- ❏   public zone = 8 feet plus.

For example, when showing concern it is often appropriate to sit close to someone. The same applies when demonstrating love and affection. On the other hand, close proximity can also be threatening. Have you ever noticed the behaviour of people in a lift? In the main, everyone in the lift tries to find their own personal space and avoid touching anyone else.

☑ ACTION

The next time you are in a lift, watch the other people you are sharing the space with to see if you can note their reactions.

The positions which we adopt with line managers and team members can also affect our communication. It is now well established that team meetings are often more effective if all members sit on a comfortable chair in a circle with no single position dominating the meeting. This positioning encourages:

- ❏   team work
- ❏   open interactions

Fig 1.11 Personal space is important during communication.

- ❑ non-verbal signals
- ❑ equality
- ❑ participation by all.

Meetings held around a table can often be more inhibited as the table acts as a block between those involved. In fact it is now recommended that during communication, there should be no blocks between the people involved. The only places still adhering to blockages are those where employees may be in danger (eg banks).

Different cultures have different behaviours with respect to proximity. In the UK, the norm or accepted behaviour is that individuals should be quite close when conversation is with someone known to the individual and if it is emotive. It is also acceptable to greet individuals by shaking their hands or even giving them a hug. When communicating with strangers it is often the norm to greet them by shaking their hands and keeping apart by arms-length. When communicating with close friends, partners or family members, it is acceptable to become closer.

Careful positioning, often instigated by you, can facilitate communication and understanding between all parties. Equally so, a badly chosen position can inhibit good communication and reduce the opportunities offered to you for responding to

Fig 1.12 Communicating across a physical barrier can be difficult.

Fig 1.13 Invading personal space blocks effective communication.

questions and concerns, as service users and team members may not feel comfortable enough to approach you in the first place!

Reflect

Not everyone would want to shake hands on a first meeting. Use the internet to find out more about different greeting customs.

Use appropriate body language, eye contact and methods of listening

It should be clear by now that communication is much more than just talking. People communicate in a variety of different ways, using different methods including non-verbal signals (body language), such as:

- ❑ body position
- ❑ eye contact
- ❑ facial expression
- ❑ gestures
- ❑ sympathetic or empathetic noises.

Body language can be used by everyone to reinforce positively a message and convey interest in a particular topic. However, it can also be used to provide a different message from the one that is being spoken or signed.

Some people would argue that the non-verbal signals are even more important that the verbal messages being given out. In a health and social care setting, we often use non-verbals as the only means of communication with a sick or frail individual. Clearly then, it is important for us as carers to make sure that we have control over our non-verbal signals, and use our body language in a positive way during the caring process.

☑ ACTION

To recognise the importance of non-verbal communication, sit face to face with another person but do not speak to each other for the next two minutes. On completion of the time, discuss with each other what was being 'said' by both of you. What could you understand from the signals being given out?

The chances are that you noticed messages from:

- ❑ fidgeting
- ❑ smiles
- ❑ eye contact
- ❑ clothing
- ❑ body positions.

These messages may indeed be accurate, but remember that we are listening to our own 'inner voice', and unless we check with the other person involved, we could find that we have made wrong assumptions. This is a dangerous habit when working in health and social care. You might find that the laughter was not a signal for being happy, but rather a signal for embarrassment.

So how can we learn to use body language for the good of all involved? You will be pleased to note that much of our body language and the reading of other's body language comes naturally. It has been learned alongside our verbal communication skills, which of course means that there can be pitfalls along the way! Some people with learning disabilities, for example, may not have developed the skills to read or use non-verbal communication. You should be aware of this and not expect body language to confirm a situation or message. In these (and all other) cases, verbal communication must be explicit and clear.

Body language

The way in which the head is held, the sitting position and position and use of the arms and legs can indicate messages about whether the people involved in the communication are interested, tired, in agreement, disagreement, bored, tense, in pain, disbelieving, etc. Specific body language which is useful for a carer to note includes:

❑ leaning backwards – this can send out a message of being relaxed or bored

❑ leaning forwards – this can convey interest (think about active listening)

❑ folded arms – this can send out a message of negativity, anger or of not being interested

❑ crossed legs – this can indicate negativity and feelings of dislike, especially if they are 'wagging' a leg or foot up and down.

Facial expressions

Making eye contact is just as important as body language. The eyes have been described as the 'mirror to the soul'. In other words, they show our true feelings. This means that it is often possible to identify individuals' feelings and thoughts by the look they have in their eyes and on their face. For example, the pupils of the eyes become wider when excited or interested in someone or something.

Although it is important to make eye contact, it is very unnerving if eye contact is prolonged; it can become a stare which may

Fig 1.14 Positive body language is an essential part of good communication.

indicate a clash or conflict of interest. A fixed gaze or prolonged stare sends out a message of anger. Equally, you need to recognise that:

❑   looking away

❑   gazing vacantly at someone

❑   gazing into the distance

❑   the eyes darting around

❑   looking at your watch

❑   trying to read a paper or chart

can convey a message of being distracted and disinterested, although some people do look away when trying to remember something important or when pausing in a conversation. However, as you become more adept at reading an individual's non-verbal signals, you will be able to tell the difference.

Facial expressions can also have both positive and negative influences and effects on communicating messages. Smiles can be reassuring, conveying approval and happiness. A smile while trying to be stern, eg when scolding a young child, can confuse because they have received a mixed message. This can result in the child being more likely to do the same act again because they felt that the smile was reassuring and showed approval of their actions, even when the words did not!

Fig 1.15 What messages do these facial expressions convey?

Gestures

Gestures are usually hand or arm movements (sometimes the lower body can also be used) that can be used to reinforce a message and help understanding. For example, saying that 'he's over there in the corner' can be further reinforced if an appropriate gesture is included, such as pointing or waving the arm in the general direction of the patient.

It is interesting to note that many of our gestures are based on sign language; eg the gesture used for telephone, quietly, softly, walking, hearing, talking too much, etc.

Fig 1.16 The sign for 'telephone' is now a commonly used gesture.

☑ ACTION

Working with another person, create a list of all the gestures that you have used with either service users, team members or in a social situation. Do you both understand and use the same gestures in the same way?

Some examples of gestures include:

❑ pointing

❑ waving

❑ thumbs-up

❑ ok sign.

Warning: some gestures may carry a different meaning depending on the culture of the people involved. Check out the meaning of gestures before you use them!

👍 POINTS TO NOTE

It is extremely important for body language, facial expressions, position, gesturing and touch to match the verbal messages being spoken! Mixed messages confuse and lead to the breakdown of trust in a relationship.

CASE STUDY

Miriam, a service user, is very upset and turns to Danny, her care worker, for support and comfort. Danny sits down with his arms and legs crossed, and has a slight smile on his face. He looks ahead, avoiding eye contact (he thinks this will help) and says that he is worried and wants Miriam to share her emotions and feelings with him. Miriam is totally confused by the signals she is receiving from Danny; he says he is interested yet his body language is closed and negative! Miriam definitely feels that she cannot trust him.

- How would you advise Danny to behave, in order to create a situation where Miriam feels comfortable enough to share her feelings with him?

Methods of listening

As we already know, good communication also requires good listening skills. Listening is more than just hearing the sounds that someone is making; we need to listen actively.

Active listening involves:

- ❏ hearing the communicator's words
- ❏ thinking about what they mean (this involves feeling and understanding)
- ❏ thinking about what to say back.

Give individuals sufficient time to communicate

Ensuring service user rights and respect is an important part of good communication. It is important in any situation that communication should not be rushed. Just because you are busy and have deadlines to meet does not mean that either your service users or team members should be on the receiving end of poor communication skills from you!

It takes time and effort to engage in effective two-way interactions. A common mistake many care workers make, especially when they are under pressure to get through their workload, is to try to speed up conversations by finishing off the sentences for the service user. This is not acceptable practice as it is humiliating for the service user and can lead to misinterpretation and misunderstanding. As we have noted, it infringes their basic rights to be heard.

The individual should be at the centre of all you do. If this is truly the case then there is nothing more important than their voice. Avoid the temptation to rush communication by:

- ❏ setting time aside to communicate
- ❏ being organised with your workload
- ❏ recognising that getting it right first time every time saves time!

In situations where the individual is struggling to find suitable words, perhaps through the effects of a stroke, you will need to find suitable alternatives. This could be the time to use flash cards or word cards. Discuss with your line manager the most suitable alternatives for communicating, rather than trying to complete sentences or words yourself.

Concentrate, listen and respond appropriately

When communicating, it is important to concentrate fully. In busy workplaces there can be many distractions and it can be easy to become side-tracked, letting your eyes wander and indeed physically drifting away from the individual as you seek to assist someone else. The consequences of this can lead to a breakdown in relationships as well as the particular interaction

---

CARE VALUES

- Prepare for listening.
- Look and be interested.
- Hear the words being said.
- Read the body language being displayed.
- Think about the meaning.
- Checks on your interpretation and understanding of the meaning (this is usually by reflecting back).
- Ask appropriate, relevant questions.
- Ensure your body language is consistent and appropriate.
- Respond appropriately.
- Ask for help when you need to.
- Follow up any actions promised.

Fig 1.17 Flash cards can be helpful.

itself. The service user will almost certainly feel that the care worker is neither interested in them and their problems, nor actively listening to their views and wishes.

Demonstrating interest and concentration requires you to give the other individual your full attention. This is not always easy to achieve, but neither is it impossible. Ways of demonstrating attention can be achieved using both verbal and non-verbal techniques.

VERBAL TECHNIQUES	NON-VERBAL TECHNIQUES
• paraphrasing • questioning – use of open questions which require more than just a simple 'yes' or 'no' reply to encourage further communication and keep the conversation going • say things like 'Tell me more'	• maintain eye contact • smile • use gestures • use sounds that demonstrate sympathy or empathy • nod or shake head to show agreement or disapproval • short periods of silence to allow individuals to think or encourage the other party to talk

Responding appropriately to questions and concerns

We have already touched upon this aspect of communication elsewhere in this unit. However, it will do no harm to remind ourselves again of the importance of appropriate responses to questions and concerns.

To maintain credibility and further cement the user/worker relationship, it is essential to respond appropriately to the service user's concerns and questions. Responses should be prompt yet considered. Flippant, throwaway statements and inappropriate jokes all demonstrate disrespect and a lack of sincerity.

In situations where keyworkers require information, it is just as important to respond in a professional and competent manner. For example, responses should be:

❑ prompt

❑ accurate

❑ honest

❑ reliable.

Other keyworkers need to know they can trust any responses provided by you. The health and wellbeing of the individual is usually at stake in this kind of interaction.

Responding to family questions and concerns is often another of the duties of a care worker. These can be difficult to handle in some situations, such as:

❑ bereavement

❑ illness

❑ new care settings for their family member.

Family members may often be concerned for the wellbeing of their relative. In these situations the questions asked can be confusing both for them and for you. In some cases, anxiety leads to the demonstration of anger and impatience, often shown by shouting and refusing to listen. If this should happen, you must:

❑ remain calm

❑ be patient

❑ repeat information if necessary

❑ offer to fetch someone in a more senior position to yourself

❑ be willing to listen.

Fig 1.18 Stay calm when responding to difficult situations.

Seek additional advice and support

Listening to individuals' questions and concerns is essential if they are to feel valued and supported. However, it is not always straightforward for you to be able to provide the service they want or to answer the questions they raise. Sometimes it is beyond your remit, authority or knowledge base, and therefore you would not have the answers.

No one expects every care worker they come into contact with to have all the answers required. It is perfectly acceptable to admit that you do not know something, or that you need to ask the opinion of a more senior member of staff. What would *not be acceptable* would be pretending that you know the answers to questions that are beyond your remit.

To maintain and even enhance the relationship between yourself, your service users and other members of the health and social care team, it is important to be honest and inform them that someone else with more experience, understanding or authority needs to be involved from this point onwards.

Care workers who are not open, honest and truthful with service users and team members lose their trust, respect and confidence. The care worker who is not competent to deal with, support or advise their service user must always seek support from someone more senior. However, it is important to keep the service user informed and up-to-date throughout the process, so that they do not feel as though they have lost contact with you.

Communicate with individuals

To help you meet the requirements for this section of the unit you will need to know and understand about:

❑   Supporting individuals to use their preferred means of communication

Fig 1.19 Know when to ask for help and know that it is okay to do so.

- ❑ How to communicate at an appropriate pace, manner and level
- ❑ Enabling individuals to communicate
- ❑ Ways of adapting your communication
- ❑ Confirming understanding
- ❑ Taking action to address misunderstanding
- ❑ Respecting rights to confidentiality

Supporting individuals to use their preferred means of communication

It is essential to the caring process to ensure that individuals are able to communicate their needs and wishes effectively. If there are communication difficulties for the individual (or others), this may become a very difficult task for all involved. It is in this kind of situation that you may need to take an active role in promoting the exchange of information and good communication.

Individuals who use a different communication language from the one used by the service provider may need the services of an interpreter. Different languages could include modern foreign languages such as Spanish, French, Polish, as well as British Sign Language (BSL). It is best to use professional interpreters, as they are trained to be able to remain impartial during the discussions. This is vitally important during serious discussions such as case conferences, reviews, receiving test results and agreeing treatments or care packages.

REFLECT

Why is an impartial interpreter an important part of care reviews?

The use of family members or children may be an easy option for interpretation at first glance, because they are readily available. However, it is not always recommended, as they are often not impartial and may hold strong views as to what they feel is important for their family member. This could mean that they may not interpret the information in a neutral way, as they may not be able to hold back their own emotions or feel able to express their relative's emotions fully. It is also possible that using children or family relatives may lead to confusion, as they may not understand the information being given and will not accurately convey the meaning back to the service user. This often happens with complicated medical information.

CASE STUDY

Mrs Amin is visiting the antenatal clinic. Her sister Soreena cannot be with her today as she is working. Mrs Amin has taken Zain, her 12-year-old son, with her to the clinic, but is worried as she knows the midwife will want to examine her, and she cannot understand unless Zain interprets for her.

- How could this situation be handled better to the benefit of Mrs Amin and the midwife involved?
- Which other issues does the use of children as interpreters raise for both service user and provider?

Professional interpreters can be contacted through local social services departments, local NHS Trusts and advocacy services. Creating a list of suitable interpreters to keep in the workplace could save time in the future for you, your service users and the organisation.

If your workplace regularly has service users with specific communication and language difficulties, you may need to consider recruiting staff that have specific skills such as British Sign Language, Makaton or the required foreign language, so that there are interpreters available most of the time on most shifts. You could of course consider learning a new language yourself to help improve communication between yourself and your service users if necessary. Once again, this could link into Chapter 3, and you will find more information about local education providers in that section.

We have already mentioned flash cards, containing words and/or pictures elsewhere. These can help to provide a basic level of communication between you and your service users, to enable them to identify their basic needs or any other support they may require.

☑ ACTION

You have a new service user who is almost unable to speak. She has very little spoken language, the words she can say are slurred, and it takes her a long time to say them. Subsequently, she is frustrated and often cannot express her needs in time for them to be met, with embarrassing consequences.

List some key words and pictures that could be used to make a set of flash cards that she could use to quickly convey her needs.

Communicate at an appropriate pace, manner and level

Pace of communication

The way care workers talk and communicate with others is very important. If someone talks very quickly, the information and content may be lost. The service user may not have heard it, may have misheard and misinterpreted it, or just not understood it. Talking too slowly can lead to misunderstanding, as the care worker may inadvertently place emphasis on the wrong words and in so doing, change the meaning of the sentence.

Manner of communication

The way in which we speak to one another is also extremely important. In exactly the same way as we can pass on negative messages through non-verbal communication, so we can pass on negative messages through our manner of speech. Have you ever heard someone say that another person sounds 'arrogant' or 'posh', or some other description that refers to the way language is spoken? This is what we mean by 'manner'. It is possible to demonstrate disrespect for an individual or team member through the way we say something, and we should therefore be very aware of the messages being signalled through our use of the voice.

Level of communication

The actual choice of words and language we use can also form a barrier to effective communication. For example, jargon often creates an invisible barrier because the service user may not understand the terminology, especially when the language is referring to medical terms. It is possible that even individuals from neighbouring districts may use area-specific words with very different local meanings, that can lead to confusion.

REFLECT

Look at the following sentences and note that the changing emphasis on different words changes the meaning:

- **Do** you like knitting? (is knitting something you like to do?)
- Do **you** like knitting? (you like knitting rather than someone else)
- Do you **like** knitting? (do you actually enjoy this activity?)
- Do you like **knitting**? (you like knitting rather than sewing etc?)

REFLECT

The term 'passing water': what does it mean to you? What might it mean to someone else?

Fig 1.20 This individual is passing water!

Choice of words depends on the age, developmental stage and academic level of the individual or their representatives. Using long, complicated words may confuse or even undermine the esteem of the individuals with devastating results. It can be embarrassing to have to ask for an explanation of difficult terms and concepts, so it is important not to put your service users and their families into this situation. Just because you know the meaning of certain words and terms does not mean that everyone else does!

Communicating in such a way that uses appropriate words, at the correct pace and with the correct emphasis requires a lot of skill and practice. To show an understanding of service users' needs and preferences, care workers need to convey warmth, sincerity and understanding.

Enable individuals to communicate

As stated previously, active support may involve the use of third parties to act as an interpreter or advocate. Advocates provide impartial representation of service users' views, opinions and wishes on their behalf. They tend to represent those who are unable to express themselves due to disability, illness, language barriers or learning difficulties and disabilities. They can even represent individuals who are too shy or frightened to speak. It is important that you encourage and empower all service users to speak up for themselves in order to promote their rights.

Fig 1.21 Enabling effective communication is a key part of the carer's role.

Service users who have hearing difficulties need good environmental conditions to maximise their chances of hearing what is being said to them. They also need to be encouraged to use their hearing aids. You should always ensure that such devices are clean and in good working order with plenty of battery life.

Good practice

When communicating with a service user who has hearing difficulties, you should:

- sit facing or at a slight angle, and not too far away from them

- speak clearly and at an even pace

- not shout – this distorts the sound vibrations as well as the face

- not cover the mouth or face with your hands – this prevents lip-reading

- check hearing aids are switched on, at correct level and clean

- cut down on background noise and distractions

- ensure good lighting levels so face and lips are visible

- use gestures and simple sign language to convey or confirm message

- show pictures and flash cards, or write messages if service user can read

- not rush but allow plenty of time for all participants to express themselves.

Service users who have visual difficulties may struggle to read body language, especially facial expressions. This has the potential to lead to misinterpretation and misunderstanding of messages being given and received. Having poor sight can often mean that they struggle to read written messages and information. In cases such as these, you may need to read written information to them, and then clarify and check that they have fully understood the content. Alternatively, you may need to assist them to access written communication in larger lettering, or in some cases, Braille.

Most service users who have visual difficulties wear spectacles or use magnifiers to enlarge the print. To make such aids effective, you should ensure that all equipment, especially the lenses on glasses, are clean. It is also essential that your service users have their eyes tested and retested on a regular basis, as eyesight can deteriorate rapidly.

It is possible that service users who have learning difficulties or disabilities will need to be encouraged to express themselves and their needs and wants. They should be given the necessary time to speak out – remember, no rushing communication. You may also need to make adjustments to your own level and pace of language when paraphrasing, taking particular care not to use complicated language or jargon which could confuse or lower their self-esteem.

Focus communication on the individual

The focus of any communication needs to be centred on all the individuals taking part. It is an essential element of your role to ensure that the individual is able to take an active part, and has the time to express their views, opinions and wishes. Often in the busy care environment, there are many tasks that need to be undertaken, and care workers feel under pressure to complete their duties; this can result in limited communication.

In some situations, you may find that other people are present when you need to have a discussion with your service user. It is possible that you will find some people are more vocal than others and can drown out the 'voice' of the service user. As far as possible, you should make sure that it is the service user whose voice is heard and acknowledged.

In residential care settings, other service users may try to monopolise your time or interrupt when you are trying to discuss something with your service user. These situations need to be handled sensitively.

CASE STUDY

Irene wants to tell Elsie (her keyworker) about her plans for going home next week. She is really excited and looking forward to having Candy back with her. Candy is her little dog, and Irene has really missed her. Just as she is telling Elsie about her plans for a neighbour to walk Candy, Bill comes into the room and calls Elsie, asking her to come over to him. Irene tells Bill that she is just talking to Elsie and he will have to wait. Bill starts shouting, and tells Elsie that he is just as important as Irene.

- How could Elsie handle this situation without upsetting Irene or Bill?

Family members may feel that their information and the issues they have to discuss should take precedence over the family member who is receiving care. However, being ill does not make someone lose their senses; they are still capable of having choices, needs and wants, and it is important to respect that. Once again, handling families in sensitive situations can call upon all your skills and knowledge. Just remember that it is the individual who should be the focus of your communication, along with some input from others. It should never be the other way round.

There is a danger in some situations where carers become too close to the individual, and feel that they are better at making choices and communicating on their behalf. This should be something to avoid. While it often happens with the individual's best interests at heart, the focus on communication has to be with the individual. Only they can make choices that are right for them. Independence and autonomy should be at the centre of all our communications with our service users.

Adapting your communication

It is important that you constantly monitor the communication exchange that is taking place with your service users, noting any signs that may indicate that their needs are changing. For example, they may be developing difficulty in understanding the messages being conveyed. The signs you could look for include:

- ❑ lack of eye contact and looking around
- ❑ reduced concentration
- ❑ interrupting during conversations
- ❑ fidgeting or moving away
- ❑ misunderstanding
- ❑ failing to paraphrase
- ❑ inappropriate questioning or replies.

It is important to monitor the interaction constantly and then adapt communication so that the individual can fully participate. This might require you to:

- ❑ slow down
- ❑ take time to recap, reflect and summarise before moving forward
- ❑ ask questions to check understanding
- ❑ change location so there are less distractions, better lighting, etc
- ❑ check that aids and equipment are working properly
- ❑ avoid using jargon
- ❑ avoid using long or complex sentences
- ❑ use word cards or images to reinforce the meaning of the message
- ❑ use gestures and facial expression to reinforce the message
- ❑ involve other relevant people, eg interpreters, advocates, family
- ❑ find someone with more knowledge and understanding to take over or answer questions that are beyond your ability or remit.

Confirm understanding

It is important to remember that people may interpret messages in different ways. Therefore, when communicating it is important to check regularly on the receiver's understanding. Checking on understanding involves hearing what the other person has said and asking relevant questions to clarify the points being made. This requires the care worker to listen actively.

REMEMBER ☺

Active or good listening involves thinking about what is being said as well as checking on understanding as the conversation continues. This process of thinking and checking is known as reflection.

Good listening and reflecting is very hard work and requires plenty of concentration. Instead of being passive (just hearing an individual speak), an effective communicator has to use the information being received to build up an understanding of the service user – their needs, wishes, views, opinions and even their personality.

A technique that encourages an individual to talk and also shows that a person is actively listening, involves the use of questioning to check that the information being received is accurately interpreted. However, you will need to take care when using questions, to avoid making the service user feel uncomfortable and as if they are being interrogated.

There are five main types of question which you can use to check your understanding. They are:

1. **Closed questions** – these can be answered in just one or two words, and are useful for the rapid collection of factual information and beginning conversations or new topics; eg 'what is your name? do you want tea or coffee?'

2. **Open questions** – these encourage longer responses and require more detail to be given. They are often useful when collecting information about emotions. Open questions usually begin with: how? what? when? why? where? For example, 'why don't you want to come down for breakfast this morning?'

3. **Probing questions** – these questions develop the response to an open question; they probe further and deeper and are used to gather more detail and information on a subject. For example:

   (open) Why don't you want to come down for breakfast this morning?

   (response) *I'm tired and I've not really slept because I'm worried about my husband Tom; he's not very well.*

   (reflection and probe) He's been unwell! What's been the matter with Tom?

4. **Prompting questions** – these questions are used to keep a conversation going and gather more information about the topic. For example:

   (response) *I'm having a bad day today. My joints aren't good.*

   (prompt) So your joints are painful today?

5. **Leading questions** – these are used to assist someone to give the expected answer and are particularly useful if the individual is shy and lacking in confidence; 'you have walked a fair distance, perhaps you're tired and would like a rest?'

Keeping a discussion going using questioning techniques is known as 'funnelling':

Step 1 – at the start of a conversation you might use closed questions to extract some information quickly.

Step 2 – then you are likely to use open questions to allow the other individual to give more detailed, expanded responses. This should encourage the expressions of thoughts and feelings.

Step 3 – you might use another closed question to clarify the points made, or change direction or topic.

Step 4 – some probes, prompts and more open questions can be used to extract more detail and information.

Step 5 – closed questions will be used again to clarify key points, check understanding or extract new information quickly.

The whole process continues and so the conversation continues. Throughout, you will need to check that you have understood the message being communicated, whilst also checking that the service user has understood what you have said.

Taking appropriate action to address any misunderstandings

Misunderstandings may occur when communicating with your service user, your work team and or other relevant individuals. It is important that breakdowns in communication are identified immediately and not left or ignored. The caring process can be affected if there are misunderstandings and service users left without the support they need.

It is important to identify what misunderstandings have taken place as soon as possible. This might require all parties involved to sit down and discuss their thoughts, views and opinions about the subject matter. Reflecting on what each person has said can help to identify what the misunderstanding is, and then dialogue can resume to move the issue forwards to resolution. This is a clear example of a situation where notes and records of what should have happened are invaluable, and reinforce the earlier message of taking notes about communications wherever possible. In some cases, misunderstandings can be so severe that investigations into the circumstances have to take place. This is usually formal and can lead to staff losing their jobs.

When exploring misunderstandings that have taken place, you should implement the following:

❑ Give the individual time to explain their views.

❑ Value all opinions and contributions.

❑ Find out what happened from everyone involved.

❑ Use notes and records.

❑ Be willing to share information.

❑ Try not to blame.

❑ Be open and honest.

❑ Be willing to make changes to working practices.

If the misunderstanding cannot be resolved between a care worker and the individual, a third party may need to be brought in to act as an intermediary between all parties. It may even be necessary for other staff to take over from the care worker, or act as an advocate for the service user until the situation is resolved.

Respect the individual's and key people's rights to confidentiality

Confidentiality and respect is essential if the trust and rapport between you and your service user is to be maintained and developed further. Individuals must feel that they can trust you and your organisation not to gossip, or to lose or spread any information exchanged.

Clearly there will be many opportunities for an individual to pass on information that they consider is confidential. This may go beyond their medical condition or their need for care. It could involve information being shared with you about family members, wills, inheritances, or just feelings and opinions about other staff members. You should not share this information with anyone unless it is likely to affect the safety of the individual or anyone else. Even then, you should only talk to your line manager.

Further detail about confidentiality is contained later in this unit and you might like to turn to this section now, page 37.

Recording what you have done

Information gained about how an individual communicates, any difficulties they or you may have experienced and any adaptations used, must be recorded in their notes. This will help to ensure that effective communication channels remain open, even if you are unable to attend to the needs of the individual yourself.

When recording the information, you must be mindful of the requirements of confidentiality. This means that care must be taken to work within the boundaries of the confidentiality policies and procedures of your workplace, ensuring that all the information recorded is relevant and appropriate and has been agreed by your service user.

REFLECT

Appropriate people include:

- the individual
- their guardians or legal representatives
- their keyworker
- person in charge
- GP
- social worker
- previous care provider.

Fig 1.22 *Make sure you know and understand your workplace confidentiality policy.*

Accessing and updating records and reports

To help you meet the requirements for this section of the unit you will need to know and understand about:

❏ Seeking permission from appropriate people to access records

❏ Sharing confidential information

❏ Organisational policies, procedures and practices

❏ Reporting accurate and sufficient information

❏ Ensuring the security of access to records and reports

Seek permission from appropriate people to access records

Relationships between individuals and their health and social care workers are built not only on good communication but also on time and trust. Individuals must feel confident that the information they divulge will be kept private, and passed on to others only on a need-to-know basis. This means that you should seek permission from appropriate people (listed) before you access or share information relating to your service user to other people.

The information required by health and social care workers may be provided in verbal, written or electronic forms. Sometimes this information may not be held within the organisation but by a third party. There are extensive laws and organisational policies and procedures to protect information held about people.

You should never seek to access information held about one of your service users without good reason. This is why you need permission to search the records. Before you are allowed to do so, you will always be asked why you want the information and what you are going to do with it. In many organisations, there is an appointed person who is the only one allowed to access confidential records. This person is sometimes known as the 'Caldicott Guardian', and they will find the information you need for you (see page 38).

Sharing confidential information

Due to the team approach for providing care services, information given by an individual to their carer at any one moment in time will often need to be passed on to other members of the care team, and even to interested parties from other agencies, eg a practice nurse, GP, social worker, advocate.

No care worker should guarantee that the information they have been given by the service user will not be passed on to others. There is often a need to share the information with colleagues at the same level, eg carers on the next shift, the shift supervisor, the officer in charge or the manager.

Therefore, in order for you to protect relationships and maintain trust, it is essential that service users are made aware that information held about them may need to be shared with others and that they will be kept informed at all stages about this.

Organisations usually have policies and procedures which outline confidentiality arrangements. Good practice dictates that these are explained to service users on admission to the service, and service users provided with their own versions in an induction handbook or service manual.

Legal requirements

There are laws to protect individuals from the misuse of information relating to them and their personal situations. As a care worker, you should have a good understanding of the legalities surrounding the storage and passing on of confidential information.

> ### Legislation, policy and procedures
>
> The *Common Law Duty of Confidence* states that any personal information given or received in confidence for a specific purpose must not be passed on without the consent of the provider of that information.
>
> The *Data Protection Act 1998* is the major piece of legislation that protects the information held about individuals. The Act covers all data held about

any individual and includes credit and financial information, some paper-based records, computer-held records and medical as well as health and social care records.

The Act has eight principles; the information must:

1 be kept secure

2 not be kept for any longer than necessary

3 be fairly and lawfully processed

4 be accurate

5 be adequate, relevant and not excessive

6 be processed for limited purposes

7 be processed in line with people's rights

8 not be transferred to other countries without adequate protection.

Under the Act, employees can be held responsible for breaches in security, provided that it can be proved that they acted wilfully or neglectfully. Other legislation and codes of practice which make reference to the access and security of information include:

• Freedom of Information Act 2000

• Human Rights Act 2000

• Care Standards Act 2000

• Caldicott Committee Report published in 1997 (this made recommendations aimed at improving the way that the NHS handled and protected confidential patient information, especially the protocols for sharing information between NHS organisations, staff training and appointing a 'Caldicott Guardian' in each organisation as the named person responsible for confidentiality of information)

• The Code of Practice for Openness in the NHS published in 1995 (this required NHS trusts and authorities to state the services available, their targets, standards and results, proposals and planned changes to services, management and their responsibilities, complaints procedures, how to contact the chief commissioner and how individuals can access their personal health records)

• Children Act 1989

• Access to Medical Reports Act 1988

• Access to Personal Files Act 1987.

☑ ACTION

Choose two of the Acts listed above that might relate to your service user groups. Research the Acts and make notes of your findings.

Organisational policies, procedures and practices

Health and social care organisations have policies and procedures for dealing with the collection, recording, storage and passing on of information held about their service users. During each shift, a great deal of information is passed on to colleagues to enable staff to perform their duties and provide appropriate services. Although there are organisational policies and procedures in place to maintain confidentiality arrangements, it is the health and social workers themselves who have the responsibility for implementing them.

Following the introduction of the Care Standards Act 2000, the Department of Health (DoH) have published a series of guides for providers of care. All make reference to the protection of information and record-keeping.

Legislation, policy and procedures

The following extract is taken from the 'Care Homes for Older People – National Minimum Standards' published in 2002. It is available on the DoH website (see address below).

Record-keeping

OUTCOME – Service users' rights and best interests are safeguarded by the home's record-keeping policies and procedures.

STANDARD 37

37.1 Records required by regulation for the protection of service users and for the effective and efficient running of the business are maintained, up-to-date and accurate.

37.2 Service users have access to their records and information about them held by the home, as well as opportunities to help maintain their personal records.

37.3 Individual records and home records are secure, up-to-date and in good order; and are constructed, maintained and used in accordance with the Data Protection Act 1998 and other statutory requirements.

(http//www.doh.gov.uk/ncsc)

FIND OUT

Obtain a copy of your organisation's policy on *Confidentiality/Data Protection.* Make notes about:

- the storage of records
- the purpose of records
- who has access to information
- checks on validity
- permission to read records held about you
- complaints procedure if unhappy with the security of information
- breaching confidentiality.

On 1 October 2001, four Social Care Councils were set up, one for each country of the UK. The Councils have the duty to develop, maintain and uphold agreed codes of practice as part of their contribution to raising the standards within all social care services. There are codes both for employers and for social care workers, which are complementary and have mirroring responsibilities.

Regardless of the care setting, records relating to the job and to each service user are made, stored and referred to when necessary. Many care workers have complained that it feels like a

Legislation, policy and procedures

Extracts below come from the 'General Social Care Council Code of Practice for Social Care Workers and Code of Practice for Employers of Social Care Workers' published in September 2002 and available on the DoH website. The importance of communication, relationships, record-keeping and confidentiality can be found under each standard; the text in brackets explains how the standard can be linked to this unit.

1 *As a social care worker, you must protect the rights and promote the interests of service users and carers. (Rght to freedom of speech, to have a say in their care, to communicate views and wishes and to be treated fairly and equally)*

2 *As a social care worker, you must strive to establish and maintain the trust and confidence of service users and carers. (Keeping information safe and secure, informing service users and seeking permission)*

3 *As a social care worker, you must promote the independence of service users while protecting them as far as possible from danger and harm. (Protecting service users from harm, from exploitation and abuse, breaching confidentiality if they are in danger)*

4 *As a social care worker, you must respect the rights of service users while seeking to ensure that their behaviour does not harm themselves or other people. (Protecting by communicating concerns, eg breaching confidentiality)*

5 *As a social care worker, you must uphold public trust and confidence in social care services. (Protect the personal information and records held)*

6 *As a social care worker, you must be accountable for the quality of your work and take responsibility for maintaining and improving your knowledge and skills. (Maintain clear, accurate records and seek assistance and advice from others if unsure how to proceed)*

(http//www.gscc.org.uk)

chore to have to complete so many documents about the job, and that it feels like more time is spent record-keeping than actually providing hands-on care.

Knowing why records need to be made and stored can help to make the process more purposeful. Records need to be made for a variety of reasons:

❑ to pass on information about the individual to the next shift

❑ to pass on information to other members of the multi-disciplinary team who will meet some of the different care needs of the individual

❑ to provide an accurate record of the care procedures, actions and changes that have occurred

❑ to provide an accurate legal record that may be used in a court of law, by a regulatory body or professional committee

❑ to provide statistical information that can be used to plan resources

❑ to provide information that can inform change to policies and procedures.

However, it is important to remember that the information is of no use if it cannot be understood! Records need to be:

❑ accurate

❑ relevant

❑ factual.

Often, care workers find it difficult to know what to write and how to write it, yet each care worker is responsible for what they write or say.

Most organisations now provide training for care workers on how to complete records, as they are such an important aspect of the work carried out.

Written records

These need to be:

- factual, consistent and accurate
- written immediately after the event (or as soon as possible afterwards)
- logically and consecutively ordered
- written clearly and legibly
- signed, timed and dated at each entry by the writer themselves (some organisations require a senior line manager to countersign too).

They should:

- have alterations that can be clearly seen, no correction fluid used and alterations and additions be again clearly signed, timed and dated
- avoid the used of jargon and abbreviations
- avoid the use of hearsay, speculation and subjectivity
- be written in black ink
- be written in terms that service users and staff can understand
- provide a clear record of the care given, any decisions made, any changes made or any concerns and subsequent actions taken.

☑ ACTION

Make a list of all the records relating to your service users and your job. Are they well-written and accurate? How would you feel if they were to be used in a court of law? Confident or not?

☑ ACTION

Read the following daily record made by a care worker, and in the table write down the phrases that are:

- factual and objective
- opinion, personal views and hearsay.

'Mrs Carlotti smelled terrible today. I have repeatedly reminded her of the importance of personal hygiene, that she must clean her teeth, wash and change her clothes, but again she has not taken any notice. Another resident told me that Mrs Carlotti has said to her that she cannot be bothered anymore. On asking Mrs Carlotti directly, she eventually communicated that she was always tired and found it hard to wash herself.

This was discussed with a colleague, and it was felt that Mrs Carlotti was just wanting someone to do it for her, and that she regularly tried to get out of being independent.

Later, Mrs Carlotti appeared upset and was crying. On approaching her, she became verbally abusive towards me and began speaking gibberish (Italian). She said some nasty things to me, even when I offered to help her and listen to her.'

FACTUAL, OBJECTIVE CONTENT	OPINION, PERSONAL VIEW AND HEARSAY

Recording or passing on information about the individual's needs and preferences

During care interactions, it is vitally important for you to promote your service user's right to express their views and opinions about their care needs and their preferences. This should also include the preferred ways in which your service user communicates, such as their preferred language, use of hearing aid, spectacles, magnifier, communication cards etc.

REFLECT

What kind of information have you been asked to pass on by your service users? How did you do this? Was the outcome successful in the service user's view?

Being able to assist your service users with their communication is vital if information is to be shared between service users and other care workers as well as yourself. Not all service users can or perhaps want to communicate their wishes easily.

If positive relationships are to develop between service users and care workers, the information discussed needs to be passed on, both in written and verbal forms, so that all members of the care team can meet the service user's needs and preferences. With new service users, this usually takes place formally at initial care planning sessions and care planning case conferences/reviews, and then much more informally on a day-to-day basis as care workers complete the daily records for each individual in their care.

Over time, if you actively take part with communication building, you should be able to understand your service user as they express their wishes. By using reflecting and paraphrasing techniques, you should be able to check your own and your service users understanding, so that you can pass the information gained on to the other members of the care team.

It is also important to make sure that you pass on any concerns that the service user may express. They may wish to make a complaint, and may need some assistance and support to exercise their right to do this.

Reporting accurate and sufficient information

Keeping records up-to-date about the care of each service user is vital if misunderstandings, accidents and mistakes are to be avoided. Failing to report and record a change in your service user's condition, as well as failing to write accurately, legibly and relevantly, could lead to confusion and have serious consequences, possibly even resulting in the death of a service user.

Keeping others informed of difficulties you may have had in carrying out care routines through your recording of information, is essential for the smooth running of the workplace and for the provision of care for each service user. This means that you must

☑ ACTION

Think about the consequences to the service user in the following situations for failing to record vital information accurately. Then fill in the consequences side of the chart.

SITUATION	CONSEQUENCE RELATING TO THE SERVICE USER
Service user complains of being in pain. Painkillers are prescribed on his medication chart and are administered but member of staff fails to record this. An hour later, service user complains to someone else that he is in pain.	
Service user has been displaying unusual behaviour. She appears distant and withdrawn. At handover between the evening staff and night staff, this is not recorded in her records, nor is it verbally passed on. The individual has a history of self-harm.	
A service user approaches a member of the care team and begins to disclose information about another member of staff. He complains that this woman appears to be short-tempered, impatient and handles him roughly. He goes on to say that he feels that she does not like him because he is from Pakistan. The carer reassures him that this person is a good carer, would not behave like this and that he must be feeling a little 'sensitive' today. The carer lets the matter pass without informing anyone else.	

have access to the relevant recording systems for each individual. If for any reason you cannot access records to update them, you must inform your line manager immediately.

It is clear that if service user records are not available, there will have been a breach of legal requirements, as each workplace and each individual worker employed there, including you, has a legal obligation to protect all the records and information being held.

If records are missing then information cannot be recorded. This could lead to serious errors, especially in relation to certain types of care, the administration of medication and for individuals who are in danger due to their psychological or physical health status.

POINTS TO NOTE

Records may not be available or may be missing for a variety of reasons:

- accidentally filed in wrong place
- failure to file away – left lying around in office
- records sent to another external organisation
- records not transferred into the workplace on admission
- someone else is using or updating the records and has not informed everyone
- computer access is denied
- computer records have been deleted
- computer has crashed or broken
- service user has misplaced records in the home.

If records are not available, action is needed immediately to investigate where they have gone. The fact that they are not available to others within the organisation must be reported so that everyone can look out for them. The person with the ultimate responsibility for security of information will need to be informed, and if after thorough initial investigation they cannot be located, the individual to whom they relate and/or their guardian will need to be informed, as this is a very serious matter and they may wish to pursue the matter further with their legal representative.

Support individuals to understand why you have reported

Information given by service users to their care workers must be kept safe and secure but there are times when you cannot guarantee this. One of the most difficult situations for a care worker occurs when a service user asks them 'not to tell anyone else about . . .' This is a difficult situation because you have to face the dilemma of wanting to respect a service user's confidence or risk breaking their trust.

A good way of handling any situation like this is for you to explain that you cannot guarantee that you will keep the information about to be disclosed confidential. Tell this to the individual first, so that they still have the choice to decide whether or not they are going to tell you. You should also make certain that they know you will not gossip and will only pass on the information to relevant others.

If the information that they give indicates that the service user is a risk to themselves or to some other person, or that they have information that implies that someone else is a danger to others, you are bound by a duty of care to protect those individuals from harm by disclosing the information.

REFLECT

Think of situations when service users may have asked you not to tell anyone else about something. What did you do? How did you feel?

CARE VALUES

Reasons why information may need to be disclosed include:

- protection of others, eg abuse (physical, sexual, psychological, financial)
- being in the best interests of an individual, eg safety, missing person, etc
- police investigation into a serious crime/incident
- court order or use at a tribunal
- health – individual's personal health or in the interests of public health
- multi-disciplinary team use, eg social workers, foster carers, etc.

Fig 1.23 Every individual has the right to access information held about them in official records.

Besides informing individuals that there may be times when the information they give may have to be shared, it is important to reassure them that the information held and recorded about them will be held securely, and that access would only be on a need-to-know basis. The key point to remember is that only the specific information required for a specific purpose will be passed on to others, not every record! All individuals have the right to know what information is being held, in what form and for what purpose; they also have the right to see the information held about themselves if they so wish.

Legislation, policy and procedures

The Freedom of Information Act 2000 fully came into force on 1 January 2005 and has further extended the rights of individuals to access information held about them in official records, such as medical and education records. To access the information, individuals must seek written permission and will only be able to access information about themselves. Information relating to others in their records will not be available.

Once permission is sought, individuals may access the records and files held about themselves. It is very important to consider what information is recorded, how it is recorded and its content! Derogatory comments and subjectivity may be deemed as slanderous and could result in litigation.

It is important that each service user is informed at admission and subsequently reminded perhaps in a service user policy guide, how they can access information held about themselves if they so wish.

It is also important to consider the ability of the individual to understand the information written about them; eg a person with learning difficulties may not be able to read and/or understand the information as written. In this case you or another member of staff may need to advocate or interpret and relay the information in terms which the individual understands.

You should remember that access to information can lead to difficult questions being raised that the individual will require to be answered. This may not be within your remit or ability and training, and so may require you to record the questions formally and pass them on for someone in an appropriate position to reply.

It is very important that this issue is borne in mind when records and reports are made. Having a policy of openness can help to eliminate some problems. It can enhance relationships and foster service user rights, but it can also make your role more demanding and complicated.

In some workplaces, with certain service user groups it may be appropriate for care workers and service users to sit together and openly discuss what is going to be included in the daily record of their care plan. In other organisations this may not be appropriate, but nevertheless, service users have the right to know what information is being recorded and each organisation should make clear the policy and procedure for them to apply to see the records being held that relate to themselves.

☑ ACTION

Find out about your own workplace procedures for applying to see personal records and files, are there specific timescales and specific people named?

Ensure the security of access to records and reports

In order to maintain the trust between service user and the organisation, any information held about them needs to be kept safe and secure. This means that information should only be used and accessed by appropriate people, for its intended purpose and only on a need-to-know basis. This includes verbal, written and electronic information.

REMEMBER ☺

The eight principles of the Data Protection Act 1998

All records, files, notes, charts, diary entries and care plans need to be stored and locked away where they are safe and secure. Within the workplace this can be monitored, but it is harder if files and records need to leave the workplace, eg for case conferences, hospital appointments, etc. This also includes files stored electronically, eg computer records.

In order to be able to find records quickly and efficiently, they need to be stored in filing systems that logically categorise the information, making it easy to find. This can be done for paper-based records; manually, in a filing cabinet or electronically on a computerised system, eg on a database.

Manual filing systems often place records in paper folders or ring-binders. These records should be fastened securely in the folder to prevent documents falling out; they should also be filed in date order and preferably be numbered.

These files should then be indexed either numerically or alphabetically depending on the number of records.

Fig 1.24 Service user information is often 'password' protected.

In hospitals or large workplaces where there are thousands of service user records, it is not practical to use an alphabetical system because there may be hundreds of people with the same surname, eg Smith. Therefore each service user is given a unique identification number. It is also important that this number corresponds and can be cross-matched to the person's forename, surname and date of birth in order to avoid confusion!

In many organisations, more and more records are being held on central computer systems. The advantage is that vast amounts of information can be stored and accessed easily and quickly from different parts of the organisation. The disadvantage is that they can be expensive to set up, staff will need special training to use the system, and many people may be able to access the records. This could mean that information may be changed or deleted accidentally or on purpose.

Organisations with computerised records need to have very clear policies and procedures in place to protect the information and maintain service user and staff confidentiality, if they are to work within the eight principles of the Data Protection Act 1998.

In all organisations, access to computer records should be protected by passwords. In larger organisations, the passwords may have different levels of authority attached to them so that some staff can only access one or two types of information and other more senior staff can have the clearance to access more. Information can also be protected from being deleted and staff can only add to records. Some records may be classed as 'read only' and so information can neither be added nor removed.

Care needs to be taken when using and answering the telephone, that information is not divulged which would breach confidentiality. It can be quite difficult to say to someone that you cannot give them the information they want or need, because you have no guarantee that they are who they say they are. It is very easy to drop your guard when on the telephone and discuss information in more detail than is appropriate.

POINTS TO NOTE

- Remember, permission must be sought before information is given out! If in doubt – do not give it out.
- Do not forget that you can ask for advice from more senior, experienced colleagues and managers.

☑ **ACTION**

Check your knowledge and practice.
Fill in the table below.

RECORDS/INFORMATION	HOW CONFIDENTIALITY IS MAINTAINED AND KEPT SAFE AND SECURE
During telephone conversations in which service user's personal details will need to be discussed	
Daily care plan and service user records about the care received	
All records relating to a service user that is no longer with the organisation, eg moved on, or deceased	
Sending information over the Internet to a service user's relative who is requesting personal information about a recent test result	
Sending a fax message about a service user to another care provider, eg GP, district nurse or social worker	
A member of the press asks for information about a service user who is about to hit the headlines	

Summary

In this chapter we have examined the importance of good communication skills for both our service users and the people we work with. By applying the skills and knowledge you have gained through your studies and your working practice, you should be able to demonstrate:

❏   respect for individuals through the communication methods you choose

❏   ways of identifying service users' needs by applying listening skills

❏   respect for culture and diversity through the use of appropriate verbal and non verbal language

❏   encouragement and support for individuals who find communication difficult

❏   good use of resources with service users to support your communication with them

❏   good practice through the appropriate use of organisational policies and legislation

❏   confidentiality through communication and the storage of information

❏   good written skills in the recording of service user and organisational information.

2

UNIT HSC22

Support the health and safety of yourself and individuals

> ### → Introduction
>
> This unit is about providing a healthy and safe working environment for yourself, your service users, and other people with whom you may come into contact in the normal course of your work activities. These can include relatives and visitors to your workplace, other professionals who provide a service to your service users, and contractors who may be required to enter your place of work to repair, replace or service work equipment. Maintaining safety sounds easy, and making safe the place in which you work is a simple concept. However, when you think about it, what does this mean? What is it that we need to be safe from? The answer is, a wide range of things, such as other people, equipment, substances, slips, trips, falls, fire or any harm that may come to us and our service users from carrying out work-related tasks.
>
> In this unit you will learn:
>
> ❑ how to carry out health and safety checks before you begin work activities
>
> ❑ how to ensure that your actions support health and safety in the workplace
>
> ❑ how to take action to deal with emergencies.

★ KEY WORDS

ACCIDENT	An unexplained or unplanned event that may lead to the injury, loss or damage to people, property or equipment.
EMERGENCIES	A dangerous occurrence, threatening danger to individuals and/or others.
ENVIRONMENT	The area in which you carry out your work activities.
LEGISLATION	The law and how it relates to health and safety.
HAZARD	The potential to cause harm.
RISK	The probability of a hazard occurring.
RISK ASSESSMENT	Assessing risk so that it can be reduced to the lowest level possible.

When thinking about health and safety in the workplace, it can be helpful to divide the information into two sections. For example:

1 Employers have responsibilities to:

- ❑ provide a safe place of work
- ❑ provide and maintain safe equipment
- ❑ provide adequate information, instruction, training and supervision
- ❑ update systems and procedures.

2 Employees have responsibilities to:

- ❑ adhere to safe procedures and practices
- ❑ avoid misusing anything provided in the interests of health and safety
- ❑ ensure their own health and safety welfare as well as that of all others
- ❑ inform their employer of any unsafe conditions, or gaps in the systems or procedures when in use.

Carry out health and safety checks before you begin work activities

To help you meet the requirements for this section of the unit you will need to know and understand about:

- ❑ Health and Safety at Work Act 1974
- ❑ risk assessments relating to work activities
- ❑ how to maintain health and safety while also protecting the rights of your service users
- ❑ recording procedures relating to health and safety.

Health and safety issues

When you start work for an organisation, your employer has a duty to make you aware of the health and safety issues within the work environment. Each workplace is different and so you will need to familiarise yourself with:

- ❑ the layout of the building
- ❑ the individuals living or staying there
- ❑ equipment
- ❑ other staff.

To help you do this, your staff induction will include policies and procedures, and opportunities to meet staff and individuals. However, it is impossible to retain all the information given to you. Therefore you will need to be able to have access to the policies and procedures of the establishment, to be able to review and update your knowledge on a regular basis. These policies will include:

❑ Control of Substances Hazardous to Health Regulations 1988 (COSHH)

❑ Reporting of Injuries, Diseases and Dangerous Occurrences Regulations 1985 (RIDDOR)

❑ infection control

❑ moving and handling.

Prior to commencing any work activity, you will need to know whether the activity has been risk assessed (see chapter 6). If a risk assessment is in place, you have a responsibility to be aware of it and to follow the guidance provided. Risk assessments will be in place for:

❑ work environments including sitting-rooms, dining rooms, toilets, bathrooms, corridors, bedrooms, kitchens and any grounds outside the building

❑ moving and handling of individuals

❑ operating work equipment.

Asking for help

Before commencing any work activity, you must ensure that you have been shown or have had training in how to complete the task. Carrying out activities that you are not trained for increases the risk of an accident happening. After checking the risk assessment, complete the task if competent (if unsure, you must ask for assistance from a more experienced member of staff or the manager). Under the Health and Safety at Work Act 1974, you have a responsibility towards yourself to maintain health and safety at all times. This means informing others that you need instruction or training to complete any tasks asked of you. This can be difficult at busy times, eg when carers are helping residents to get up in the morning, or if you are working on your own in the individual's own home.

Peer pressure or time pressure sometimes makes us do things which we know to be wrong. This must be avoided for everyone's sake. Think things through first. By admitting that you need help, you are acting as an advocate for your service user and ensuring that they are being cared for in a healthy and safe environment. Remember that the individual is at the centre of all we do.

CASE STUDY

You are working alongside an experienced member of staff, assisting individuals to bed. On checking the risk assessment for an individual, it states that a hoist must be used and two members of staff must be present. You find that your colleague has already put that individual into bed on their own.

- What action would you take and why?

CASE STUDY

Think about what would happen if you were working in an individual's own home. The risk assessment is the same as for the case study above. The visit is coordinated to ensure that two carers arrive at the same time. However, after waiting for 15 minutes, you ring your office to be told that the other carer has gone home, and they ask you to manage on your own.

- What would you do in this case and why?

Clearly the decisions you make will affect both the individual and yourself. It is important to remember that the health and safety of all concerned comes first!

When commencing work activities, after ensuring that you have checked the risk assessment, you need to make sure that the area you are working in is free from hazards. There are many environmental and indeed social hazards which can cause injury to people. These hazards are increased with factors such as age, illness, physical or mental disability.

Environmental factors

- ❑ furniture which causes obstruction to service users/others/fire doors
- ❑ wet or slippery floors
- ❑ worn carpets, rugs or other floor coverings
- ❑ electrical flexes either worn or left trailing across the floor to cause tripping hazards
- ❑ too much furniture for the size of room
- ❑ poor lighting inside or outside of the building
- ❑ weather conditions.

Equipment and materials

- ❑ worn or faulty electrical or gas appliances
- ❑ faulty brakes on wheelchairs or beds

❑ faulty or worn lifting equipment

❑ faulty or damaged mobility aids

❑ cleaning fluids incorrectly labelled or placed in unsuitable containers

❑ faulty waste disposal equipment.

People

❑ moving and handling procedures

❑ visitors

❑ intruders

❑ violent or abusive behaviour.

Your responsibility to maintain a safe environment means more than being aware of potential hazards; you must ensure that you take steps to remove where possible any hazards that might pose a health and safety risk to yourself and others. You can do this through two methods, direct action and indirect action.

Direct action

Deal with the hazard yourself by:

❑ removing trailing flexes and storing them safely

❑ making sure floors are dry and signposts put out warning of any danger

❑ removing obstacles to firedoors or any item causing obstruction

❑ removing any cleaning substances not correctly labelled

❑ removing and labelling any faulty equipment

❑ following your organisation's procedure for raising the fire alarm

❑ challenging people who enter your workplace, asking for identification and asking them to sign the visitors book.

Indirect action

Inform your manager of any faults or defects to equipment. This then places responsibility on the management team to ensure that equipment complies with health and safety requirements. Potential problems include:

❑ worn floor coverings

❑ obstructions too heavy to move

❏ people behaving suspiciously on or around the building

❏ faulty locks.

CASE STUDY ✍

You are making beds in your establishment and you notice that one of the bedroom doors which is normally locked, has been left open. On investigation you find that it has a faulty lock – it sticks and is hard to open. You also know that the individual whose room it is keeps valuables in their room, and tends to be anxious about this. You report the situation to your manager, who tells you that they will arrange for a maintenance person to fix it.

- Which health and safety issues does this situation raise?

- What options and measures are available to you while waiting for the repair to be carried out?

CASE STUDY ✍

You are working in the community and are attending an individual who lives alone. You struggle to gain entry because the front-door lock is sticking.

- What issues does this situation raise?

- What measures would you take to rectify it?

REMEMBER ☺

Everyone has a responsibility under the health and safety legislation to maintain a safe environment. Never assume that someone else will have dealt with an issue; if you see something that needs to be reported, then do so and record your action in the staff communication book.

REFLECT

Moving and handling of individuals is the main cause of injury to people working within the care sector.

- What factors are in place in your work setting to reduce the risk of injury to yourself and your service users?

Moving and handling

The moving and handling of service users is covered elsewhere in this book (chapter 6). It would be helpful to read this now to refresh your memory. However, there are health and safety implications relating to moving and handling for individuals and care workers that we will touch upon here.

The Manual Handling Operations Regulations 1992 require employers to reduce the risk of injury by manual handling tasks 'so far as is reasonably practical'. All places of work must have policies and procedures relating to lifting practices. Carers need to be aware of the changes within care organisations, as we are moving away from task-orientated work procedures to

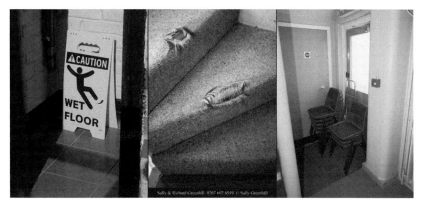

Fig 2.1 Be alert to health and safety hazards such as these.

person-centred ones. This means that time should be taken to allow individuals to be safely moved, using the right equipment. It is possible that some carers still think it is quicker and easier to lift someone manually than use a hoist. If they do this, they are breaking the law.

Although there should not be any occasions where you have to take a person's full weight, there could be an emergency situation where this may happen. This should be an exception rather than a rule!

When carrying out workplace activities, you should take into consideration the needs, wishes, preferences and choices of your service users while also maintaining the safety of yourself and others. To do this, you need to consult with your service users and other key people who may be involved, on the best way to proceed. Although you have a duty of care towards your service users, this must not put you or any others at risk of injury. When you are completing a risk assessment, involve everyone and seek a solution if conflict arises. If changes need to be made to the environment, always ask permission first and ensure that you return items to their usual place.

CASE STUDY

Megan, the domestic assistant at Mytown House, is called away to mop up a spillage. Instead of putting away the hoover she is using, she leaves it leaning against the wall in the corridor by the residents' bedrooms. When she returns, she finds Mrs Smith, who is very frail with poor eyesight, lying on the floor. She has tripped over a piece of the flex which was looped across the floor. Megan calls for a member of the care staff, who realises that Mrs Smith has hurt herself and goes to fetch the manager. The manager assesses the situation, reassures Mrs Smith and then leaves a carer with her while she rings for the paramedics. Two paramedics arrive and feel Mrs Smith needs to go to hospital. The manager arranges extra cover to allow one carer to escort Mrs Smith to hospital. The manager then rings Mrs Smith's relatives at their place of work. They inform the care manager that they will meet their mother at the hospital.

Mrs Smith is seen in Accident and Emergency by the triage nurse and then by the doctor who feels that an x-ray is required. By this time, Mrs Smith is distressed, in pain and wants to go home. After the x-ray, she is seen by the doctor again who informs her that she has fractured her femur and will need to stay in hospital and have an operation. Back at the residential home the manager spends time completing reports, filling in accident forms and carrying out an accident investigation. Mrs Smith meanwhile goes to theatre and has her operation. In attendance there is an orthopaedic specialist, a senior house officer, a scrub nurse, two theatre nurses and an anaesthetist. Two hospital porters take her to theatre, and after her operation she has a nurse to look after her in recovery.

After two weeks' stay in hospital, Mrs Smith returns to the residential home. She now needs the assistance of a carer, whereas before she had been able to manage by herself. After completing her investigation, the manager has spent time with Megan, discussing health and safety policies and procedures. Megan has also been informed that any more breaches of health and safety will lead to a disciplinary hearing, which could eventually lead to the loss of her job.

If only Megan had put the hoover away – what a lot of time she would have saved.

- Discuss with another person what might have happened if Mrs Smith's relatives had filed a complaint about the incident.

CARE VALUES

To you, your place of work is simply that; but for the people you are caring for, it is their home. Whether in their own home or a residential setting, people surround themselves with things which will be of value to them. You have to balance the need for health and safety with the rights of people to arrange their furniture and belongings as they wish.

CARE VALUES

Both you and the person you care for have the right to be looked after in a healthy and safe way, but remember that your service user has the right to choose how they want to live.

Learning the procedures

When you commence employment in any organisation, you should find health and safety procedures already in place. During the induction period, you should be informed of your responsibilities in relation to the procedures. For example, you will have responsibility for:

- ❑ checking water temperatures before bathing someone
- ❑ reporting any hazard which you think presents a risk
- ❑ reporting unfit equipment.

If you work in the community however, there are differences. Your employer will still need to have policies and procedures and carry out a risk assessment to put control measures in place; eg two carers to assist someone to rise from bed. What your employer cannot do is remove environmental hazards such as worn carpets, trailing flexes or old equipment. They can only make suggestions to the person whose home it is of the possible risks and what they might be able to do about it.

CASE STUDY

It is Wednesday morning, hairdresser day at Green Meadows Intermediate Care Home. The care team want to make this a special activity for individuals. As the hairdresser is working, you assist by escorting the individuals to the salon. You notice that the wire on the hairdryer is frayed, and tell the hairdresser.

- Consider what action you would take.
- What responsibilities do you have in this situation?

CASE STUDY

You are working in the community and notice a frayed wire on the hoover, exposing the cable inside.

- What would you do in this case?
- Compare your responsibilities in this situation with those at Green Meadows.

When you are carrying out workplace activities and problems arise, you have to try to resolve them. However, it is important that you are aware that over time, risk assessments can change and will require updating. If you are experiencing the same problem each time you perform a task, alternative action should be sought.

👍 POINTS TO NOTE

All work places must display a health and safety poster that will inform the reader of the person responsible for health and safety issues.

REMEMBER ☺

All health and safety issues which arise in your place of work must be reported to the responsible person, and the appropriate documents completed.

Ensure your actions support health and safety in the workplace

To help you meet the requirements for this section you will need to know and understand about:

- ❏ infection control measures
- ❏ Control of Substances Hazardous to Health Regulations (COSHH) 1988
- ❏ how to maintain security.

Working with others

It is important to recognise that you need to work with others in order to minimise potential health and safety risks in the place where you are working. These could be:

- ❏ team members
- ❏ service users

FIND OUT

Locate the health and safety poster in your workplace. Make a note of the responsible person. Then walk around your place of work and make a list of anything that you think is a risk to health and safety. Discuss them with the health and safety manager to find out the control measures that are already in place or need to be put in place.

- visitors
- managers
- health and safety representatives.

It is important that you are aware of your colleagues' attitudes toward health and safety issues. It can be very difficult if you are the only person following policies and procedures. If you spot other people breaking the law, you can help to support good practice by:

- always following policy and procedures yourself – set a good example
- explaining why you are following policy and practice – help to 'educate' others
- pointing out to people where the information is held – help to develop other people's knowledge of the workplace
- asking your manager to raise issues in a staff meeting – build a team approach to health and safety.

Minimising risk

When talking about minimising risk in the workplace and checking for hazards, we are often looking for the obvious. For example:

- trailing wires
- worn carpets or furniture
- obstructions.

However, we must also consider the things we cannot see, such as bacteria. If bacteria are present (and they always will be), we need to take precautions to reduce their presence to safe levels, to minimise any harm they may cause.

CASE STUDY

It is Sunday evening and you are not on duty until Monday afternoon. You are feeling ill and during the night you suffer from sickness and diarrhoea.

- What would your organisation's policy be on reporting sickness?
- When should you return to work following such illness?
- What should you do if your symptoms persist?

Protective clothing

Protective clothing is worn by care workers to protect both themselves and their service users while performing 'dirty' tasks, to help reduce the risk of cross-infection. Protective clothing includes:

These should be worn whenever there is a risk of passing illness and disease from one person to another. It is important to remember that not only do gloves protect you from infection, but just as importantly they protect your service users from the risk of cross-infection. However, wearing gloves does not remove the need to wash your hands.

Uniforms should be laundered separately from other clothing, at the highest possible temperature for the fabric. This will minimise possible infection from harmful bacteria harbouring in the material of your uniform. Where possible, you should change your clothing on entering the workplace and before leaving to go home.

Hand washing

As you probably know, following a good hand-washing technique is the most effective way of reducing the spread of infection. It is easy to learn and can reduce the spread of infection. You must always wash your hands following:

❑ a visit to the toilet

❑ coughing and sneezing

❑ contact with body fluids

❑ cleaning

❑ moving from one individual to another.

Good hand washing removes the transient micro-organisms that are picked up during normal work activities.

There are three types of hand washing:

1 routine

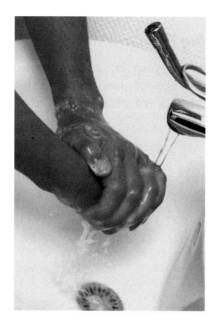

Fig 2.2 Always wash your hands thoroughly.

REMEMBER 🙂

Bars of soap are not recommended for use in communal settings. Liquid soap is the preferred option, as bars of soap can harbour harmful bacteria.

2 disinfection

3 surgical.

A routine hand wash using soap should be used:

❑ before starting work and after completing work activities

❑ after making beds

❑ after removing gloves

❑ after any work activity which involves direct service user contact

❑ before and after giving medication

❑ before preparing or handling food

❑ after handling waste materials

❑ after using the toilet.

A disinfection hand wash using antiseptic soap should be used:

❑ before invasive procedures

❑ before carrying out aseptic procedures

❑   after handling equipment contaminated with bodily fluids

❑   before and after handling wounds, catheters, or
    intravenous (iv) lines.

There is also an alternative method often used for disinfecting hands. This is an alcohol hand rub and should be used:

❑   on hands not visibly soiled

❑   when there is no access to water for hand washing

❑   before and after attending to service users or patients.

Remember, it is recommended that alcohol should only be used a maximum of three times before having to wash hands with soap and water.

CASE STUDY ✍

You arrive at work, and as usual it is a busy morning. You take the report from the night staff and then go to assist your service users with rising. This involves washing, dressing, going to the toilet, cleaning teeth and making beds. When everyone is up, it is time to help serve breakfast. After breakfast you do the laundry, clean the commodes and tidy bedrooms. Now it is time for your break.

  • Make notes of when you should wash your hands.

  • Which hand wash should you use, and why?

Working with the risk of abuse

When carrying out workplace activities, you need to be aware that there is always an element of risk involved when working with other people. There is a higher risk of personal abuse occurring to health care workers than others who work in more traditional office settings. People who work in the community are at risk from a range of sources; for example:

❑   abuse by people

❑   bites or wounds from domestic animals

❑   homes which are dirty

❑   homes in a poor state of repair.

If you are working on your own, follow some basic rules to protect yourself and reduce the risk of harm:

❑   Always follow your work schedule, and only make
    changes in agreement with your employer. This ensures
    that your employer is aware of where you are at all times.

❑   Always let someone know when to expect you home or
    back to base.

CARE VALUES

Reducing infection can only have a positive effect in your workplace: healthy individuals often have a feeling of wellbeing; staffing levels are more easily maintained; relatives are generally pleased with the standard of hygiene and subsequent care that their loved ones receive. The organisation benefits from a good reputation!

- ❑ Carry a personal alarm and use it if you need to.
- ❑ Carry a torch for dark nights or unlit areas.
- ❑ If confronted, try to calm situations by talking quietly.
- ❑ Leave if people are being aggressive, and ring for advice from your manager.
- ❑ Call or shout for help if needed.
- ❑ Ask for animals to be removed from the work environment if possible.

REMEMBER

By ensuring that someone knows where you are at all times, you are protecting yourself from the risk of harm.

CASE STUDY

You are working in the community and attending an individual for the first time. You have been told that the individual has dementia and suffers from short-term memory loss. When you arrive, the front door is open and there is a broken pane of glass. The home is full of refuse and rotting food, and the service user is shouting and screaming at you. In fact, they are accusing you of being a thief and stealing their bag.

- What action would you take in this situation?

FIND OUT

Does your organisation have a policy for lone workers? If not, what do you think such a policy should contain? Make notes of some of the risks of working alone, and what you can do to minimise those risks.

Health, safety and security risks

When carrying out workplace activities, you need to be aware of the health, safety and security risks which you may come across, and take appropriate action to reduce them. Included here is a table to help you identify hazards that could occur in your working environment.

REMEMBER

If you become used to checking as you are going about your normal duties, you will be able to identify hazards easily, and respond by putting control measures in place quickly and efficiently.

HAZARDS	CHECK
Floors	Are they dry?
	If wet, is there a warning sign?
	Have they been polished?
	Is it uneven, or are there steps involved?
Carpets and rugs	Are they worn, stretched or have curled ends?
	Are they likely to move?
Doorways	Are they clear?
	Are they fitted with suitable doors, locks and closing mechanisms?
Corridors	Are there any obstructions?
	Are they well lit?
Fire doors	Do they close properly?
	Are they propped open?
Store rooms	Are they locked?
	Are the contents well laid out and securely stored?
Wheelchairs	Are the footrests in place?
	Do the brakes work?
	Are they suitable for the service users?
Beds, chairs	Are they high enough for you and your service user?
Equipment	Are plugs and flexes intact?
	Have they been PAT (Portable Appliance Test) checked?
Lifting equipment	Has it been serviced?
	Are slings worn?
	Do you know how to use it?
	Have you been trained?
Mobility aids	Are they worn or damaged?
Cleaning fluids	Are they labelled and stored correctly?
	Do you know where and when they can be used?
Containers	Are they intact?
	Are they labelled and stored appropriately?
Visitors	Have they signed in?
	Have they got any identification to show you?
External to your building	Are the grounds even?
	Is there enough lighting?
	Is there any salt or sand in case of snow or icy conditions?
	Does the door open onto a busy main road?

Open door policy

Most establishments have an open door policy. It is the individual's home and unless there are restrictions due to registration, then people will be able to come and go as they please. If you see someone you do not know, ask them who they are! No one who has a right to be there, will mind being asked for identification (ID). Keeping your service users safe is of paramount importance.

It is always helpful to make sure that there is a pen available next to your visitor's book. One of your roles could be to check to see that your visitor's book is being used as it should be. Make sure you ask everyone to sign in and out as they leave the building.

Undertaking potentially hazardous activities

When you are undertaking potentially hazardous activities, you need to follow these guidelines:

- ❑ Moving and handling – always ensure that you use the correct equipment as identified in the risk assessment for that specific person.

- ❑ Workplace activities – always make sure your uniform is clean, and gloves and aprons are worn at appropriate times. Some organisations colour code their aprons; one colour for personal care tasks and another for wearing at mealtimes.

- ❑ Using and storing equipment and materials – all organisations should have a COSHH policy. This informs you of the chemicals you are allowed to use, any risk that they may carry and how to use and store them.

- ❑ All equipment should be tested for safety and stored in locked cupboards if appropriate.

- ❑ Dealing with spillages and disposal of waste – in the event of spillages of blood, vomit or bodily fluids, it is important that the spillage is contained as much as possible in paper towels. These should then be treated as clinical waste.

Any waste which may contain blood or bodily fluids or which may be contaminated with large numbers of bacteria is called clinical waste. This includes:

- ❑ used gloves
- ❑ aprons
- ❑ incontinence pads
- ❑ urine bags

❑ disposable nappies

❑ wound dressings.

Clinical waste should be placed in a yellow bag and kept in a locked container until it is removed and incinerated. Clinical waste has a high risk of cross-infection, and great care should be used to ensure it is handled properly.

FIND OUT

Identify the different kinds of waste you have in your establishment. Find out who removes it, when and how.

Take action to deal with emergencies

To help you meet the requirements for this section of the unit you will need to know and understand about:

❑ what to do in case of fire

❑ how to maintain security

❑ how to deal with a serious or minor accident

❑ basic first aid.

Your workplace should have procedures to follow in the case of an emergency.

Fire safety procedure

Your organisation should have a fire procedure that all staff must be aware of and follow if the fire alarm bell sounds. If fire is suspected:

1 Raise the alarm.

2 Make the back-up call to the fire brigade by ringing 999.

3 Meet at the fire panel to give or receive instruction.

4 Follow your organisation's evacuation procedure to ensure everyone is safe.

5 Go to the external fire assembly point and await the fire brigade.

6 Do not re-enter the building.

One of the first things you should do when starting work in a new establishment is to familiarise yourself with the layout of the building.

❑ Find out where all the fire exits are and where the fire extinguishers and fire blankets are situated.

❑ Check that fire doors close properly and make sure that none are propped open.

Fig 2.3 Find out the different uses for each fire extinguisher.

Fire extinguishers

There are four different kinds of fire extinguishers. In the past they were colour-coded but now all new fire extinguishers are red. Each one has its purpose written on it and a patch of colour relating to its appropriate use.

REMEMBER ☺

- ❑ If the alarm sounds, treat it seriously.
- ❑ Do not silence the alarm until the fire brigade have attended.
- ❑ With frail elderly individuals, try to move them beyond two fire doors.
- ❑ Never prop fire doors open.
- ❑ Stay calm.
- ❑ Do not run or let others run, as it creates panic.
- ❑ Direct those who can move themselves and help those that cannot.
- ❑ Use wheelchairs to move people more quickly.

Safety and security

Everyone in a care environment has the right to feel secure. They need to be secure from the risk of:

❑ intruders

❑ theft

❑ abuse.

One way to reduce the risk of intruders is to always challenge anyone who enters your building, and ask for identification. Some larger organisations may issue all staff with photo ID cards and insist they are worn at all times. This easily identifies people outside of the organisation.

Dependant individuals in care environments are more at risk of intruders; staff need to be very vigilant to protect them. However if your service users live in their own homes, you will need to impress on them the importance of asking people for their identification, and of keeping their doors locked. Using the password scheme from the utilities can be helpful, as can warden schemes which operate in some areas.

> **FIND OUT**
>
> More about the password scheme and how it could help you or your service users to maintain security.

REMEMBER

❑ If you find or suspect an intruder on the premises, do not challenge them but raise the alarm.

❑ Always show your ID to individuals if you are working in their homes.

❑ Inform the police or local warden schemes if you are concerned about anyone who is vulnerable and living alone.

Responding to accidents

When having to respond to a serious or minor accident, your employer will have procedures in place which you must follow. When someone has an accident, you will need to call the appropriate person to deal with it. Regulations state that there must be a qualified first-aider on duty at all times. This is usually the person you will call upon in the event of an accident. If accidents or injuries occur at work, either for you or a service user, you will have to fill in a record of the accident. Your employer will have their own method and forms for reporting accidents. Accident reporting is a legal requirement under RIDDOR 1985 and the Commission for Social Care Inspection.

You have a responsibility to report any accident that you are involved in. This includes accidents that you have witnessed. You should report the matter to your manager or the person in charge. The manager will then be required to make an assessment as to whether any medical treatment is needed. If this is the case, it should be arranged without delay. When an accident occurs to a person you are caring for, you need to ask them if they wish you to contact anyone such as friends or family. However, if they cannot make an informed choice due to the accident suffered or physical or mental disability, you should inform the next of kin straight away.

Below is an example of an accident form which should be filled in for all accidents.

Example form to be filled in

NAME	ADDRESS
Date of Birth	GP name and address
Sex M/F	
Date	Location
Time	
Witness	Address
Details of accident	First Aid required yes/no
	If yes give details
RIDDOR Informed	Risk Assessment Completed
Yes/no	Yes/no
Further action required	
Signature	Date

As well as completing an accident form, your manager will also complete an accident investigation. This explores any underlying reasons as to why the accident happened. From the result of this investigation, a risk assessment should be completed and an action plan put in place to try to prevent a re-occurrence.

When a health emergency arises there are certain steps that you must follow:

❑   Call for assistance as soon as possible.

❑   Clear the environment. Take other people away from the area and leave it clear. If possible, ask someone to reassure any individuals who have witnessed the incident.

❑   Offer help to the competent person dealing with the casualty.

The kind of assistance required from you may depend on the place where you work and the circumstances involved.

❑ For people working in residential care, there should always be someone else around to support you and deal with the emergency. This may not be professional help but they will access professional assistance on behalf of the individual and will give you instruction on how you can assist them.

❑ If you are working in a hospital where there are always medical experts on hand, it is unlikely that you will have to deal with the casualty yourself. Your role may be to call for help.

❑ When working on your own in the community, it is vital that you call for assistance as soon as you can. You will be asked a series of questions by the person taking the phone call, and they will give you advice and instructions to follow while waiting for the paramedics.

Taking action

In this next section we will look at some of the injuries or conditions you may come across and the initial action you may have to take. Common injuries and conditions that you could become involved with include:

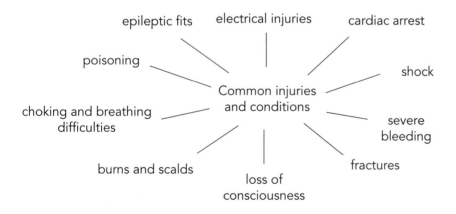

Cardiac arrest

A cardiac arrest happens when the heart stops beating. It can stop for many reasons but the most common is when someone has had a heart attack.

Symptoms

❑ not breathing

❑ no pulse is present.

Aims
To preserve life.

How

- ❑ Assess the situation.

- ❑ If the person is unconscious but breathing, place in recovery position.

- ❑ If they are not breathing, assume it is a heart attack and commence resuscitation if you are competent to do so and have had first aid training. If you have not had training, summon help immediately.

- ❑ Keep up resuscitation until help arrives.

Shock

Shock can contribute to the failure of circulation. This results in an inadequate supply of blood to vital organs caused by a drop in blood pressure. Shock can result from most cases of injury and can prove fatal.

Types of shock

- ❑ physical: loss of fluid volume (bleeding, burns, diarrhoea)

- ❑ mental: nerve stimulation (pain, fear, bad news)

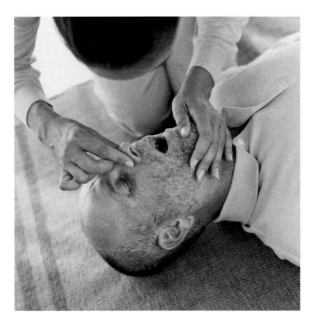

Fig 2.4 You never know when resuscitation skills may be required.

- ❑ electrical: high voltage, low voltage

- ❑ anaphylactic: allergic reaction, often to drugs or chemicals.

Symptoms

- ❑ very pale skin

- ❑ skin cold and clammy

- ❑ rapid and weak pulse

- ❑ feeling thirsty

- ❑ feeling weak or faint

- ❑ feeling anxious or restless

- ❑ nausea

- ❑ unconsciousness.

Aim

To restore oxygen to vital organs.

How

- ❑ Treat the cause.

- ❑ Lay the individual down and raise their legs.

- ❑ Loosen any tight clothing.

- ❑ Make the casualty as comfortable as possible.

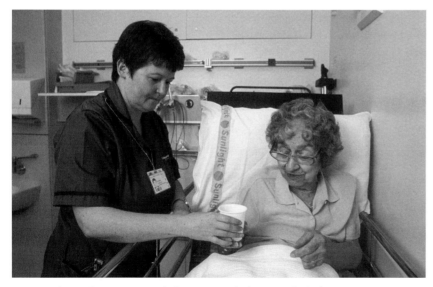

Fig 2.5 Always obtain permission before giving a drink to an individual in an emergency situation.

- ❏ Moisten lips but DO NOT give drinks.

- ❏ Protect from the cold.

- ❏ Monitor the situation and seek assistance.

Severe Bleeding

May result in shock if large amounts of blood are lost.

Aim

To stop the bleeding.

How

- ❏ Put on disposable gloves if available.

- ❏ If a major bleed, seek help immediately.

- ❏ Expose the wounds and check for any object embedded in the wound. DO NOT remove the object; simply apply pressure to the sides of the wounds.

- ❏ Apply direct pressure with your fingers or palm over a sterile dressing if possible. You can ask the casualty to apply the pressure themselves, but do not waste time in looking for a dressing; you will need to apply direct pressure over the wound for ten minutes to allow the blood to clot.

- ❏ Lay the casualty down and raise the affected part if possible.

- ❏ Secure the dressing with a bandage.

- ❏ If further bleeding occurs, apply a second bandage over the first.

- ❏ If bleeding still occurs then ring for the paramedics.

Nosebleed

- ❏ Lean forward, pinch soft part of nose, ask the casualty to breathe through their mouth.

- ❏ After ten minutes release pressure.

- ❏ If the bleeding has not stopped, continue two further periods of ten minutes.

- ❏ If still bleeding after 30 minutes, hospital treatment is required.

You will need to be aware of infection risks when dealing with casualties who are bleeding. If you have a cut or graze care should be taken, although you should have applied dressings as

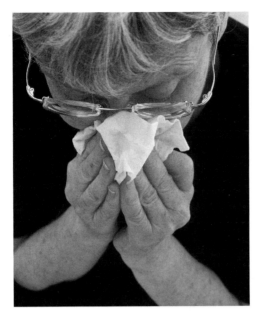

Fig 2.6 Check after 10 minutes to see if the nosebleed has stopped.

soon as they were required; wear gloves if possible and wash your hands as soon as you can. If the casualty is bleeding around the mouth and resuscitation is required, use a mask. Blood-born viruses such as HIV or hepatitis can be passed on if the blood of an infected person comes into contact with broken skin.

Fractures

A fracture is another word for a broken bone. Fractures can be caused by:

❏ direct force, eg a kick or a blow

❏ indirect force, when the bone breaks some distance from the area where the force is applied.

Types of fractures

❏ Closed – there is no break in the surface of the skin.

❏ Open – the skin is broken above the fracture, or broken ends of the bone are protruding through the skin.

❏ Complicated – these are breaks with an associated injury to organs, major blood vessels or dislocation of a joint.

Signs and symptoms

❏ swelling around the affected area

❏ irregularity or unnatural shape

- ❑ deformity, leg shortening, unnatural angle
- ❑ pain around the site of the injury
- ❑ unnatural movement
- ❑ shock.

Aims

To prevent further damage to the injured part.

How

- ❑ Steady and support the limb; help the casualty to feel comfortable.
- ❑ Immobilise the limb with padding or cushions.
- ❑ Take the casualty to hospital or call an ambulance.
- ❑ DO NOT allow the casualty to have anything to eat or drink.

Loss of consciousness

People can lose consciousness for many reasons; it may be as simple as fainting, or it could be as a result of serious injury or illness.

Signs and symptoms

A lack of response to outside stimuli.

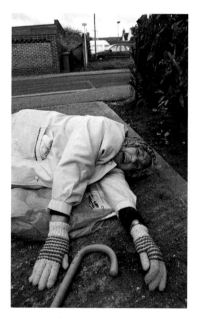

Fig 2.7 Where possible, you need to find out what has happened in order to take appropriate action.

Fig 2.8 Keep the airway open.

Aims

- ❑ to keep the airway open
- ❑ to preserve life.

How

- ❑ Keep the airway open, lay the casualty down, lift the chin and tilt the head backwards.
- ❑ Look for a medical reason which may be indicated on a necklace or bracelet which would tell you the likely cause of the unconsciousness.
- ❑ Put the casualty in the recovery position.

Burns and Scalds

There are several different types of burns:

- ❑ dry burns caused by flames, hot metal or friction
- ❑ scalds caused by hot water, fat or steam
- ❑ cold burns caused by cold metals, freezing agents or liquid oxygen
- ❑ electrical burns caused by electric current or lightening
- ❑ chemical burns caused by acids or alkalis
- ❑ radiation burns caused by the sun or x-rays.

Signs and symptoms

❑ Superficial burns involve only the outer layers of the skin, and result in general redness, swelling and tenderness. This type of burn usually heals well.

❑ Partial thickness burns involve the formation of blisters which may be intact or broken. The surrounding area will be red, and these burns may become infected.

❑ Deep burns involve all layers of skin. The skin may appear pale, waxy and sometimes charred, because the nerve endings are damaged. Deep burns always require medical attention.

Aims

❑ to prevent infection

❑ to preserve life.

How

❑ Treat all burns under cold running water for 10 minutes, or 20 minutes for chemical burns.

❑ Remove any rings or jewellery if possible in case of a swelling reaction.

❑ Cover with a sterile dressing.

Burns that require the individual to go to hospital

❑ all deep burns

❑ all burns that extend around an arm or leg

❑ all partial thickness burns larger than one per cent of the body (size of the palm of the hand)

❑ all superficial burns larger than five per cent of the body (size of five palm areas)

❑ if you are unsure of the severity or extent of the burn

Remember:

❑ DO NOT remove anything which is stuck to the affected area.

❑ DO NOT use any ointment or cream.

❑ DO NOT cover facial burns; instead, keep pouring water on the area until help arrives.

REMEMBER 😊

When a person has suffered any kind of injury, they will be distressed and sometimes in a great deal of pain. You will need to talk to them and offer reassurance until help arrives.

Choking

This is caused by an obstruction to the airway.

Aim

To remove the obstruction and restore normal breathing.

How

- ❑ If the casualty is able to cough, encourage them to cough to remove the obstruction.

- ❑ If the casualty is not coughing but is distressed, silent, gasping or pointing to the throat, give five back blows with the heel of the hand between the shoulder blades.

- ❑ If unsuccessful, adminster the Heimlich manoeuvre: give up to five abdominal thrusts – stand behind the casualty, arms round to the front, form a fist and pull sharply upwards and backwards.

- ❑ If successful, send to hospital to be checked.

Fig 2.9 Knowing how to treat someone who is choking is a useful tool for a carer.

> **REFLECT**
>
> Would you know how to apply the Heimlich manoeuvre properly? If not, find out more now!

❏ If unsuccessful, continue alternate five back blows and five abdominal thrusts until the obstruction is removed and help arrives.

REMEMBER

All casualties who have had a choking episode caused by an obstruction need to be examined by a medical practioner often, or usually, in Accident and Emergency (A&E).

Poisoning

People can be poisoned by many substances, drugs, alcohol, plants and gases. Poisons can be:

❏ inhaled

❏ ingested

❏ absorbed

❏ injected.

Any chemical passing into the body in sufficient amounts could be fatal to the individual.

Aims

❏ to remove the casualty from danger without endangering yourself

❏ to arrange urgent removal to hospital.

How

❏ If possible, remove the casualty from the danger.

❏ Ring for the paramedics.

❏ If unconscious, place in the recovery position.

❏ Try to find out what the poison is.

❏ DO NOT try to make the casualty vomit.

Epileptic seizure

Epilepsy is a medical condition that causes brain disturbances, which can result in unconsciousness and involuntary movement of muscles. This occurrence is often known as having a fit or seizure. When an individual is having a seizure, they will not be aware of what is happening to them. It is possible that they may harm themselves when falling.

Aim

To make sure that the casualty is safe and does not harm themselves during the seizure.

How

- ❑ Try to make the environment safe by removing obstacles which could hurt the casualty.
- ❑ Loosen any tight clothing.
- ❑ Monitor the individual.
- ❑ When the seizure is over, place them in the recovery position.
- ❑ When the casualty awakes, reassure and support them.
- ❑ If the seizure lasts longer than five minutes, send for medical help.

REMEMBER ☺

Some people may know when they are going to have a seizure and will be able to give you warning.

Electrical Injuries

People are electrocuted when an electric current passes through their body.

Symptoms

- ❑ Burns may result from where the electric current has left the body.
- ❑ Cardiac arrest is a possible result of the electrical current passing through the body.

Aims

- ❑ to remove the casualty from the source of the electricity if safe to do so
- ❑ to preserve life.

How

If the injury is caused by high voltage current, eg overhead power cables or rail lines:

- ❑ Ring for the paramedics immediately.

- ❑ Do not go within 18 metres of the casualty until the electric supply is switched off.

- ❑ Place in recovery position while waiting for help.

Injury caused by low voltage current, eg household appliances:

- ❑ Switch off the source of the electricity.

- ❑ Do not touch the casualty while they are still in contact with the current as you will receive a shock yourself.

- ❑ Use a wooden pole to remove the casualty from the source of the charge.

- ❑ When the service user is removed from the source of the current, put them in the recovery position while waiting for help to arrive.

REMEMBER 😊

Do not use anything made of metal or anything wet to remove the casualty from the source of the current.

The guidance given here for basic first aid is very limited. You must undertake recognised first aid training as soon as you can. Once you have gained certification you should update your training on a regular basis.

If you are not qualified to give first aid assistance – always seek help and assistance in an emergency.

REMEMBER 😊

You may also be upset by what has happened or what you have witnessed. There are many emotions which you could experience, and you may feel the need to discuss these with your manager. It sometimes helps to 'take time out', such as having a drink and a rest following an incident.

After any accident or incident, remember that you need to record accurately what has happened. Your organisation will have their own recording procedure for you to follow.

Summary

In this chapter we have looked at ways of promoting safe practices at work. It is important that you:

- ❏ understand the importance of following organisational policy and procedures relating to health, safety and security
- ❏ respect individuals' wishes, needs and choices when carrying out work-related activities
- ❏ identify health and safety issues in the workplace and how to report them
- ❏ understand your own limitations and seek assistance when needed
- ❏ identify and work with others to minimise risk in the workplace
- ❏ ensure that your own health and hygiene does not pose a threat to other people
- ❏ understand the appropriate action to take in health emergencies
- ❏ how to summon assistance appropriate to the emergency
- ❏ support other people affected by the emergency.

3

Develop your knowledge and practice

→Introduction

An essential activity within the health and social care professions is the continuous professional development that care workers are expected to undertake. It is essential that as new technologies, methods of care and medicines are developed, the staff involved in the frontline delivery of these should be up-to-date and knowledgeable. It is through continuous professional development that we learn to become better carers.

For this unit, you must demonstrate that you take part in continuous professional development through evaluating your own work and using new and improved skills and knowledge in that work.

In this unit you will learn:

❑   how to evaluate your work

❑   how to use new and improved skills and knowledge in your work.

★ KEY WORDS

ACTIVE SUPPORT	Support that encourages individuals to do as much for themselves as possible to maintain their independence and physical ability, and encourages people with disabilities to maximise their own potential and independence.
INDIVIDUALS	The actual people requiring health and care services. Where individuals use advocates and interpreters to enable them to express their views, wishes or feelings and to speak on their behalf, the term 'individual' within this standard covers the individual and their advocate or interpreter.
KEY PEOPLE	These are the people who are essential to an individual's health and social wellbeing and make a difference to their life.
OTHERS	These are the people both inside and outside of your workplace who have a role in helping you to carry out the tasks and knowledge required for you to fulfil your own job role.
RIGHTS	These are the rights that people have. Read Chapter 4 for a full explanation of the way in which they are central to all the work that you carry out.
SERVICE USER	An individual who receives care and support from your organisation.

How to evaluate your work

To help you meet the requirements for this section of the unit you will need to know and understand about:

❑ Why you should evaluate your own work

❑ What evaluation is

❑ The forms of evaluation

❑ Ways to evaluate your own work

Why evaluate your own work?

People who work in the health and caring professions are expected to keep themselves and their daily practices up-to-date, in line with the guidance provided through best practice and evidence-based practice. However, we know that it is impossible to do this successfully if we have no idea about how accurate and appropriate our current caring practices are. If we were to ask one hundred social carers why they evaluate their work, it is very likely that we would be told:

❑ to improve our practice

❑ to plan for future developments

❑ to identify what we can and cannot do

❑ to find our strengths and weaknesses

❑ to learn from our experiences.

Each of these reasons for evaluation are valid and important, but we can also add the requirement from a health and caring system to ensure that we all contribute to the caring process through high quality, efficient and rational services. It is becoming more

Fig 3.1 Evaluation – why bother?

and more important to use evidence-based practice in all that we do in order to serve our service users' best interests.

Another aspect of the rationale for carrying out evaluation is to help (at an organisational level) to secure funding from those statutory or independent agencies who purchase the caring service they need for their service users.

In this unit however, we are concentrating on evaluation which is used to improve practice at an individual level.

What is evaluation?

Before we continue any further we need to be clear about the meaning of the term 'evaluation'.

'Evaluation' means to review or assess something; perhaps a task that we have been asked to carry out to find out how well we did it (or not, as the case may be!) or how suitable an action may have been. For example: if we wanted to know that the information we had provided to a service user about bus timetables was suitable, we could ask her if she managed to catch the bus. If she did, we can assume the information was sound. If however she tells us that there were no buses all morning and she had to get a taxi, we can assume that the information was out of date and unsuitable for use with our service users.

Asking a service user about her experience is a form of evaluation. It is important to recognise that evaluation is part of a quality assurance process that helps managers and organisations to improve continuously their service to service users and funders. Quality assurance helps to:

Fig 3.2 Evaluation can help to monitor the service we provide to individuals.

Fig 3.3 Quality assurance keeps the service provided on 'the right track'.

❑ recognise good practice, which can be shared with others

❑ improve continually the service on offer

❑ identify staff development needs

❑ improve communication

❑ compare performance between different organisations

❑ inspire confidence in our service users

❑ identify and target resources.

Forms of evaluation

It is easy to write and talk about quality assurance and evaluation of performance, but how do we actually do it? One of the most important points to remember is that we all need to be involved in quality assurance and contribute to the process of evaluation, from the owners and managers of an organisation through to the service user.

There are three kinds of evaluation that you could use to assess how well you carry out your work activities. These are:

1 pre-action evaluation

2 ongoing evaluation

3 post-action evaluation.

Pre-action evaluation

This is when an intended action is examined to try to find out in advance what the implications would be of actually carrying out the activity. This is a good method of evaluation if you are unsure about the impact of a particular action, either upon a service user or a member of the care team.

CASE STUDY

Marjorie is 78 years old and lives at home very independently. However, she has just been diagnosed with shingles in her head, and her eyesight has been severely affected. Her relatives have been in touch with social services to obtain support for her. A meeting has been arranged to discuss the implications of placing Marjorie in an intermediate care setting for the next six weeks. Her daughter-in-law is worried that Marjorie may become dependent on carers, so the team have discussed ways of maintaining her independence while in intermediate care.

- What action might you take to make sure that Marjorie maintained her independence?

- Which methods might you use to check that her independence was actually being maintained?

Ongoing evaluation

In this case, evaluation is carried out throughout the whole task or action. In order to do this, you have to have a plan of action with milestones (different steps or stages of action to take, or things to achieve) for working towards your goals and targets. The idea is to evaluate how well you are completing each stage of the action plan, or to identify any barriers that may be stopping you from achieving your goals and targets and taking the appropriate action to overcome them. The benefit of this form of evaluation is that it allows you to make changes at the time, to ensure successful outcomes.

Post-action evaluation

In this form, evaluation is carried out at the end of the task or activity by collecting evidence of performance and reviewing the outcomes. The main difficulty with this method is that there is no time to put things right at the time; you can only change future working practices and learn from the experience.

You have probably realised by now that all three methods can be used separately or together to obtain the best possible evaluation results. There is no point in assessing your performance if you are not going to obtain reliable and trustworthy results.

REFLECT

Which method of evaluation would you want to use to check out how well you carry out your work?
What might be the benefits of using all three forms of evaluation together?

Ways of evaluating your work activities

Once you have decided upon the kind of evaluation you want to use, you need to think about how you are going to carry out the task. In the main there are four ways in which you can assess or evaluate your work activities. They are:

1   self assessment

2   peer assessment

3   manager assessment

4   service user feedback.

Self assessment

In theory, *you* drive this method of assessing how well you carry out your work activities. You can choose the methods you use and the time you take to allocate to the task. However, in reality this is often not the case.

Many organisations have a set time when they review the practice and procedures that they use in order to care for older people, for example. Whatever date is chosen, organisations should be aiming to review their service on an annual basis, if not more often. This means that you should also be reviewing your performance on at least an annual basis.

Peer assessment

This form of evaluation is often used in the health and social care sector, and when used appropriately can prove to be both helpful and supportive. Peer assessment can be both:

❑   formal and

❑   informal.

Fig 3.4 Having your work assessed by others allows you to develop and grow in your role.

REFLECT

How often have you asked for feedback from a team member or been asked to give feedback? How did it feel to participate in this way?

Formal peer assessments are usually arranged in advance, and involve written feedback about your performance, by your peers (colleagues). The results obtained are then often used as part of staff appraisal by managers and supervisors with regard to carer's career development, pay rises, organisational restructures, etc.

Informal assessments on the other hand, can take place when one or more work colleagues are helping one another to learn new tasks. For example, when two people are working together to help an individual to wash and dress in the morning, one carer might ask their more experienced team worker to watch them carrying out a task and then tell them how well they have done. This would be classed as informal peer assessment.

Read Lucy's case study to find out more about peer assessment.

CASE STUDY

Lucy is following an NVQ Level 2 in health and social care, and needs to complete an assessment of her own practice. Unfortunately she has no idea of how to do this. So her manager has developed a task for her, to give her some insight into the kind of activities that she will need to undertake. Her first task is to complete the chart below while one of her team members is preparing and serving the evening meal in the residential care home where she works.

Lucy's development task

HYGIENE IN THE KITCHEN	EVIDENCE OF GOOD PRACTICE	EVIDENCE OF POOR PRACTICE
criteria for checking Cooked or raw meat Chopping boards Cook's hands	Taken from fridge and prepared on the correct preparation board	Did not wash them prior to food preparation No protective clothing worn
Cook's clothing Dishcloths Work surfaces	Not used Cleaned thoroughly before and after the food was prepared	

Once Lucy had completed the chart, she arranged to meet with her manager to discuss her findings.

It is clear that Lucy would have found the task almost impossible without the list of criteria that she used to measure the hygiene practices in her care home. Without them, she could have missed some seriously poor practice!

REFLECT

What could have been done to make sure that Lucy would not be in this situation?

REFLECT

What difficulties might Lucy have experienced when she met with her manager to discuss her findings?

REFLECT

What difficulties would Lucy have experienced in completing this task without the list of hygiene practices already being written into the grid by her manager?

It is likely that Lucy could have felt like she was 'telling tales' about another member of staff, and so may not be entirely truthful about her findings.

Ideally, when carrying out any peer assessment or evaluation of practice or knowledge, the person or persons involved should be informed that the activity is going to take place, and agreement should be reached about when and where it will happen. The person being observed should also have the opportunity to see the criteria against which they will be measured. This could help to jog the memory about some of the stages involved in the task being carried out.

Manager assessment

This should always be a formal activity, often resulting in written feedback about your work performance. Of course, there are always informal opportunities available as well, eg when a manager praises you for something that you have carried out to a high standard. However, these informal situations should never take the place of formal evaluation of your work.

The most common form of manager assessment occurs during staff appraisal. This should be carried out by a senior manager or by your supervisor or line manager at least once a year. The process would generally follow this format:

Fig 3.5 Appraisal is your opportunity to discuss your developmental needs.

❑   A date and time is set to meet with your manager.

❑   At the meeting, the issues to be discussed during appraisal are agreed.

❑   Another date is set for the actual appraisal to take place.

❑   During the appraisal, the issues agreed as discussion points are discussed, and written notes made.

❑   An action plan is developed for the next year that allows the person being appraised to develop further their professional skills and knowledge.

❑   A further date to meet and review the action plan is set.

CASE STUDY

Adam has just been informed by his line manager that his appraisal is due next month and she wants to see him tomorrow to agree the content. Adam is worried as this is his first appraisal. He tells his team worker about his fears.

'Don't be daft' says Aisha, 'Appraisal is a great opportunity; you can use the time to tell your manager about wanting more responsibility. All you have to do is to convince her that you are ready to lead a team of your own.'

During Adam's appraisal, his manager agreed that he could spend the next year completing an NVQ Level 3 in preparation for leading a team of his own.

- How are appraisals managed in your workplace?

- How often do you have an appraisal?

- How could you better prepare for an appraisal?

Service user assessment

In some ways, perhaps this type of assessment should have come first in the list as service user satisfaction is so important!

Obtaining feedback from a service user is not always easy. In some cases it can be almost impossible for the reasons listed here:

❑   The service user may be too ill to participate.

❑   She may have insufficient mental development for full participation.

❑   There may be communication barriers.

❑   She may not want to participate.

Despite some of the difficulties listed here, obtaining your service user's evaluation of the work you do is vitally important, as they should be at the centre of all you do.

Fig 3.6 Feedback from your service users is often a good measure of your performance.

CASE STUDY

Nancy has called on Mrs Hall in her own home. Her care plan says she is due to have a bath today.

Nancy walked straight into the house without knocking and startled Mrs Hall by walking straight into her bedroom. She greeted Mrs Hall by saying how little time she had, and couldn't she have had her dressing gown on ready for the bath to save her time? Mrs Hall felt rushed and pushed, and was sorry that Nancy had so little time to speak with her. If anything, it added to the embarrassment of needing help with her bathing routine.

- Discuss with another person the kind of feedback you think Mrs Hall would have given to Nancy if she had asked for it.

- What difficulties might Mrs Hall have experienced in giving the feedback?

In order to create the best possible evaluation process, we need to:

- ❏ respect the views of others

- ❏ be open and honest about our findings

- ❏ be committed to the process

- ❏ be willing to change our behaviour or attitude where necessary

- ❏ be willing to share feelings and information

- ❏ perhaps most importantly, have a mutual trust of each other.

Assess how well you carry out your work activities

In this unit, the standards are asking you to evaluate your work and to use the information that you collect to develop and use new and improved skills and knowledge in your work. It is important to recognise from the outset that everyone, no matter who, can always improve their working practices. If the day ever dawns when you would say that 'I cannot possibly get any better', that is probably the day when you should stop caring for others!

In order to assess your work activities, you need to have a good understanding of your job role. This understanding is the key to a successful evaluation of your own work.

CARE VALUES

People have a right to be cared for by staff that are trained to the highest possible standards in their job roles. Individuals have a right to expect their care workers to be knowledgeable and professional in all that they do, and to be constantly updating their practice.

REFLECT

How knowledgeable are you about best working practices? What professional development have you taken part in during the last 12 months? What professional development *must* you undertake each year?

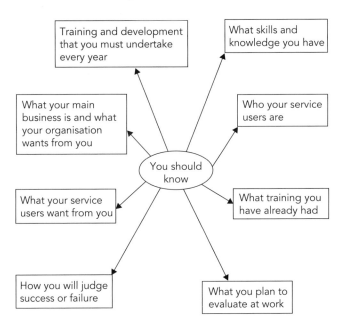

Fig 3.7

☑ ACTION

Obtain a copy of your job description and have a look at the roles and responsibilities that are outlined in it. Consider if it is still up-to-date, or have things changed? Does it still reflect the job you do?

Once you have examined your job description, you need to decide which aspects of your job role you want to evaluate. It is unlikely that you will be able to evaluate everything that you do as part of your job role, so it is important that you make the right choices. It would be helpful to agree with your line manager the key aspects of your role that need evaluating.

Fig 3.8 Use your job description to help you choose aspects of your work to evaluate.

It is possible that your discussions will have included most if not all of the following:

- ❏ your relationships with individuals
- ❏ your timekeeping
- ❏ organisational skills
- ❏ team work
- ❏ knowledge about the work you have to carry out
- ❏ your obligation to following service user rights guidance
- ❏ communication skills
- ❏ annual statutory training requirements
- ❏ compliance with health and safety regulations
- ❏ hygiene practices
- ❏ attitude to service users.

As you are planning to evaluate aspects of your work, you will most likely find yourself thinking about career development. This is a good thing to be planning and thinking about at this point. However, it is important to confine your planned developments and evaluations to the work you actually do and the kind of skills and knowledge that will enhance your existing job role. There is no point in planning to add skills and knowledge to your job role that are not appropriate or of no real use to you, your service users or the organisation you work for!

Identify how values, belief systems and experiences affect your work

When you are deciding which aspects of your work you want to evaluate, it is important to include an opportunity to examine your own beliefs and values, and the potential they have to affect your work with individuals. This can be an aspect of ourselves that we do not consider very often, as it is something we have developed from a very early age and is therefore an integral part of us.

A good starting point is to explore what we mean by 'values' and 'beliefs'. In general, we can say that **values** are made up of those things which an individual feels strongly about. They are influenced by the way we are socialised (brought up) and the things we have experienced throughout our lifetimes. In the caring professions, our values relating to those we care for are about respect, equality, empowerment, independence and autonomy. On a personal level however, we may hold other values; eg we may believe in family values, which puts a strong emphasis on the traditional family unit. We may hold values about alternative therapies, seeing them as positive or negative depending on our value system.

Beliefs are very similar to values and vary enormously from person to person. Our beliefs are formed through our religion, culture, social class, education and our peer groups. Beliefs can be totally wrong, but because they are often formed through our personal experiences, they can be hard to change.

CASE STUDY

Ernie has spent the last six years visiting a close friend in the residential care home for people with Alzheimer's disease. The time has now come for him to live in a care home, and he is terrified. He is convinced that he will be locked in and not allowed to go out on his own. He is very worried about his independence.

- How has Ernie's experience affected his beliefs about residential care?

- How could a social carer help him to overcome these beliefs?

Clearly the values and beliefs we hold have the potential to affect the work we carry out. The values and beliefs of others also have the potential to affect the service we provide. Clearly, these effects can be positive or negative towards service users and our work. While it is important to accept that often values and beliefs are hard to change, we can prevent them from interfering in the work we do.

CASE STUDY

Monica has been caring for Elaine for four years. Elaine has multiple sclerosis and suffers from pain in her arms and legs. She has just been telling Monica that she is going to spend £50 on visiting an alternative therapy practitioner to seek relief from the constant nagging ache. Monica knows Elaine does not have much money and thinks all alternative therapists are 'quacks'. Monica loses her temper with Elaine for being so foolish with her money.

Elaine is upset by Monica's reaction and cannot see how it concerns her anyway. She has decided to ask the care agency to send another carer in future.

- Discuss with another person how Monica's personal values and beliefs have affected her work with Elaine.

- What could Monica have done differently to maintain a good relationship with Elaine?

REFLECT

It may be a good idea to examine your own values and beliefs as part of your evaluation of your working practices. If so, how will you do it? Who might help you?

Our core care values contribute significantly to the avoidance of any situation where our own beliefs and values may affect the care we provide. However, it is important to recognise situations where our own values and beliefs could conflict with those of the rights of the individual; great care must be taken to ensure this does not happen.

Obtaining feedback

Once you have decided which aspects of your work you want to evaluate, you need to think about the types of evaluation that you are going to use. For example:

Fig 3.9 You will need to be honest with yourself when considering your beliefs and values.

❑ Will you use ongoing evaluation, or will you use post-action?

❑ Do you want to involve others in the collection of information about your knowledge and performance?

❑ If so, who should these people be and how can you achieve the best result from them?

REMEMBER 🙂

The performance criteria requires you to support individuals and key people to give you feedback. This means you need others to be involved in the evaluation of your working practices.

We have already discussed the fact that key people for feedback are likely to be:

❑ your manager

❑ your service users

❑ your peers

❑ and of course . . . yourself!

The question now is, how do you obtain the feedback you need? First of all remember the KIS principle: 'Keep it Simple!' When you are assessing how well you carry out your work activities, you need the process to be as straightforward and as simple as possible. For example:

❑ Be clear about the performance that you are trying to measure.

❑ Know the people who can contribute to your assessment.

❑ Be realistic in what you are trying to measure (evaluate).

❑ Be realistic about your expectations of others.

❑ Be sure the time is right for the evaluation to take place.

❑ Check that the action you want to measure is actually measurable!

❑ Do not use jargon unless you really have to.

In other words, you need to follow the SMART guidelines. This stands for:

❑ **S**pecific

❑ **M**easurable

❑ **A**chievable

❑ **R**eliable

❑ **T**imely.

It is helpful to ask yourself if each of the acronym words can be applied to your chosen subject for evaluation. If the answer is no to any of the words, you are likely to have difficulties in carrying out the evaluation.

Collecting the information you need – methods of assessment

We have already seen one method of collecting information with Lucy's case study. However, it is important to recognise that there are many other ways of evaluating your practice. For example:

❑ a skills and knowledge audit of yourself

❑ reflective accounts, including keeping a diary

❑ questionnaires, both written and verbal

❑ interviews with individuals or groups of people.

Each of these methods offers you the opportunity to involve a range of people in collecting the information about your work in different ways.

Fig 3.10 It will be helpful to use more than one method to collect performance information.

Collecting information

METHOD	WHO CAN HELP	WHAT CAN BE COLLECTED	ADVANTAGES	DISADVANTAGES
Skills and knowledge audit	Managers and supervisors can help you to develop the questions you need to check your skills and knowledge	Information about your skills and knowledge related to the job	<ul><li>quick</li><li>easy</li><li>involves yourself and others</li><li>can be done often</li></ul>	Takes time to develop the right questions
Reflective account	You keep a diary or write down the things that have hap-pened during a working day	Thoughts and feelings about how well you performed. You can include any changes that you would make the next time this situation happened	You can look back and see if anything has changed	You might not be completely honest with yourself
Questionnaires				
Interviews with service users				
Interviews with colleagues				

☑ ACTION

Use the grid to complete the last three rows. You may need to read a research book or use the internet to help you find out more about questionnaires and interviews.

CASE STUDY

John has developed a questionnaire for his team members to use. It is all about him and the kind of work he does. He is reading through the questions one last time before he asks them to fill it in for him.

	True	Not sure	False
Q1 I stay calm when faced with difficult situations			
Q2 I keep clear records of my work with individuals			
Q3 I am well organised			
Q4 I am a reliable member of the team			
Q5 I attend team meetings regularly			
Q6 I refer service user problems to the appropriate people in good time			
Q7 I am willing to ask for help when I need it			
Q8 I am always polite to individuals			
Q9 I demonstrate respect and value to my service users			
Q10 I always follow health and safety guidelines			
Please add any comments that you wish to make about my work or my membership of the team.			

- Working with another person, examine the questions which John is going to ask.
- How helpful do you think these questions will be in helping John to evaluate his work?
- How would you use answers to similar questions about your work?
- Who could complete a similar questionnaire for you?

Support individuals and key people to give you feedback

Asking people to give you feedback about your work may at first glance seem an easy task to complete. However, in reality giving feedback is very difficult and you may have to support the giver of feedback as they provide the information, especially if it is something you do not want to hear!

Have you ever been asked for your opinion about someone's appearance or an action they plan to take? You probably have, and you may have avoided giving a completely true answer to avoid hurting that person's feelings.

Fig 3.11 Receiving feedback about your work should not be allowed to create conflict.

The same principles apply in the workplace. Telling a work colleague that their work is below standard is hard for anyone and can lead to gossip and ill-feeling between teams. While we often cannot tell a colleague to their face that work is below standard, we find it fairly easy to moan and groan about the work of colleagues to others. This is not a satisfactory situation when working in teams.

As a result of these difficulties, you need to support your colleagues to provide you with accurate and honest feedback. This means you may have to persuade your colleagues that you are genuine in your request for accurate and honest feedback, to enable you to continue your professional development. Taking feedback is a skill in itself! It is easy when we are given praise to smile and give thanks for the feedback. However, this is much harder when the feedback is negative, although it is even more important to smile and say 'thank you'. This not only helps the receiver to feel better but also assists the giver of negative feedback to feel supported.

When the feedback is being provided, you will be expected to demonstrate your commitment to honest feedback by:

❑ being prepared to accept the information given

❑ avoiding defensiveness (making excuses)

❑ actively listening to what is being said

Fig 3.12 A professional approach would have helped to keep the communication channel open.

❑   asking what you could have done differently

❑   writing the information down

❑   asking for clarification where necessary

❑   not taking negative feedback as a personal insult.

In addition to taking and responding to feedback from colleagues, you will also have to receive feedback from your managers and service users. Once again, this should be taken calmly and with a professional attitude.

CASE STUDY

Maria has just been given feedback on her appearance at work. Her manager told her when she took up her post that excessive amounts of jewellery should not be worn at work, and that her hair should be kept clean and tidy. For the first two months Maria followed this guidance, but now she is wearing seven gold chains around her neck, long dangling earrings, a nose stud and a gold ring (or two) on every finger. Her hair looks greasy and is hanging around her shoulders and face. Her manager has told her that she looks unprofessional and unhygienic. She said, 'How could an individual put their trust in someone who looks like you!' Maria is furious! She has told her manager 'to mind her own business', and is now sitting in the kitchen having slammed every door she has passed through on her way there.

• Discuss with another person the way Maria has taken this feedback.

• Does she have justification for her behaviour, and if not, how could she have reacted differently?

• How could her manager have handled the situation differently?

Using questioning skills to give support and gain feedback

It is possible that in some situations, such as when working with service users, you may need to ask additional questions about your work to ensure that you have received comprehensive and useful feedback. In this case make sure you:

- ❑ use open and closed questions as appropriate
- ❑ avoid asking leading questions – 'Don't you think it would be better . . .'
- ❑ avoid asking questions with multiple parts to them (more than one answer is required)
- ❑ Avoid using conversation 'stoppers' (looking at your watch, yawning, rubbing your hands together and stretching).

It would be helpful at this point to revisit the unit of study on communication skills, as many of the issues raised in there are relevant to this unit in terms of accepting and gaining feedback on your work activities.

Time for feedback

It is important when giving or receiving feedback that you consider the timing of the information. There is no point in asking for feedback when you do not have the time to stay and listen, or the giver of the feedback is in a hurry to go somewhere else. This would only result in a poor level of feedback and the application of poor listening skills. Therefore you should:

- ❑ plan a suitable time to receive the feedback
- ❑ ensure privacy for the meeting
- ❑ find a warm, comfortable place for the discussion
- ❑ have pen and paper to hand
- ❑ make sure you have plenty of time
- ❑ ask not to be disturbed
- ❑ be as open-minded as you can.

Using the feedback you have been given

Once you have received feedback about your work, it is important that you take the appropriate action resulting from the feedback. This tends to be fairly straightforward when the feedback is given as part of an appraisal. This is due to the fact that an action plan (or development plan) is usually agreed at the end of the appraisal that tells you what action is required and when it should be taken.

However, there may be occasions when the feedback you have collected is outside of the appraisal process. This does not mean that you cannot use the information to develop new and improved skills. Identifying the gaps in your performance and knowledge through feedback is the starting point for your personal and professional development.

In order to help you plan for your development, it may be possible to divide the information you have been given into separate types. For example:

1 your **knowledge** levels about a particular aspect of your job

2 the **skills** you have developed or need to learn in carrying out the tasks required of you

3 your **attitude** towards individuals, team members and managers

4 your **appearance** and **role** as an ambassador for your organisation.

Classifying your feedback into different types should help you decide what action needs to be taken next. For example, a lack of knowledge about a particular issue or subject can be easily

Fig 3.13 Updating your knowledge can be done 'on-line'.

remedied, providing you are willing to ask for help or search for the answers yourself. You can:

❑ ask a senior member of staff for the information

❑ search the internet

❑ obtain books and professional journals

❑ attend college or other studies

❑ follow a distance-learning programme

❑ attend inhouse staff development.

On the other hand, if you required more practice in using hoists or other moving and handling equipment, you could ask to be sent on a moving and handling course, or you could be given inhouse training with a qualified trainer.

If your feedback concerned issues around your values, behaviour, appearance or attitude towards individuals and others, you could obtain a copy of the code of conduct for your organisation and make yourself familiar with the contents. It is interesting (and indeed useful) to note that there are codes of conduct for many professions, including:

❑ health visitors

❑ nurses

❑ social workers

❑ physiotherapists.

You could search the internet to make comparisons between the different professions, searching for similar content among them. The information you obtain would also prove very helpful to you in your caring role, as it would identify some of the practices that you should be following.

It is important that you use the feedback given to you to identify the training and development you need, to improve your working practices and develop new skills and knowledge about your work.

Producing your own training and development action plan

While you can easily find ways of updating your skills and knowledge, without careful planning the activties could become haphazard and inconsistent. Therefore, as part of your continuing development you would probably find it helpful to plan your training and development needs in a structured and systematic way (planning is a useful skill to develop).

Developing your own action plan is fairly straightforward and the results obtained can be worth the time spent on its development. Your plan will need to contain:

❏ the criteria (actions you will carry out)

❏ timescale (when you will carry out the actions)

❏ people involved (all the staff and others who may need to help)

❏ the actions you need to take (how you will accomplish the tasks)

CASE STUDY

Soraya has just made a list of the things she needs to do in order to improve her practice when carrying out daily hygiene routines with her service users. Her supervisor has told her that she needs to:

• encourage more independence from Mrs Tallon

• give Mr Carlisle more choice in the clothes he wears

• encourage Miss Noblett to join in recreational activities sensitively.

Soraya has written each of these three points into a grid that looks like this:

ACTION	HOW	WHEN	WHERE	OUTCOME	HELP REQUIRED
Independence for Mrs Tallon	Pass her clothing to her in the morning and assist her to dress rather than doing it for her. Make sure she has her walking frame to hand in the morning, rather than using the wheelchair.	Morning and night.	Individual's bedroom, bathroom.	Mrs Tallon will be more mobile and independent.	Guidance from the physiotherapist about how much walking Mrs Tallon should do in a day.
Choice for Mr Carlisle					
Recreation for Miss Noblett					

• Practice completing an action plan by filling in the boxes for Mr Carlisle and Miss Noblett.

• Consider how an action plan such as this could support your own training and development needs.

- ❏ outcomes (what the expected results might be)
- ❏ evaluation (how you will measure the success of your actions).

Use new and improved skills and knowledge in your work

To help you meet the requirements for this section of the unit you will need to know and understand about:

- ❏ Ways of developing new and improved skills and knowledge
- ❏ Using new and improved skills and knowledge
- ❏ The evaluation and review cycle

Developing new and improved skills and knowledge in your work

Once you have produced your action plan and identified any gaps in either your performance or your knowledge, you can begin the process of acquiring the new skills and knowledge required. It is likely that you will use some of the sources of help and learning methods already touched upon, but to do this effectively you need to know what services are available to you and then how to access them. Your training and development needs can be met via a range of different methods. We have already noted:

- ❏ the internet
- ❏ inhouse staff development
- ❏ learning from other experienced staff.

However, we can also add a whole range of organisations and methods that you could use to access training, eg:

- ❏ Colleges of Further Education
- ❏ the Open University
- ❏ private training agencies
- ❏ distance-learning organisations
- ❏ Learn Direct.

Other methods you can use to develop your professional practice include:

- ❏ work-shadowing
- ❏ attending conferences and workshops

CARE VALUES

An important aspect of your caring role is to ensure that you understand and can apply legal and organisational requirements on equality, diversity, discrimination and rights when working with others. If you do not understand any aspect of these care values – now is the time to take action!

Fig 3.14 Reading, whether from books or journals, is a good way of updating your knowledge and understanding.

❑ action-learning sets (groups of people gather together to debate and solve an issue)

❑ membership of professional bodies and organisations

❑ reading, eg professional journals, magazines, books, conference papers, reports and case studies.

However, it is important to realise that if you are going to use the internet to access reading material, you will need to exercise some caution as not all material is reliable and valid.

👍 POINTS TO NOTE

Good reading habits:

• Set time limits to the reading.

• Prioritise your reading – do not try to read everything.

• Avoid being on mailing lists unless they are valuable.

• Maintain a good posture – do not slouch.

• Avoid reading when you know you will be distracted.

• Make notes of key points you want to remember.

• Copy useful information to colleagues and team members.

Good writing and recording habits:

• short and simple documents

• short sentences

• straightforward words

• short paragraphs

• bullet points for key items.

Do not forget to discuss your programme of learning with your supervisor or line manager to make sure that the course is both relevant and suitable for you.

Once you have learned new ways of working, it is important to begin using the new skills and knowledge immediately. If you do not start putting the new techniques into practice, you may forget what you have learned or lose confidence in your ability to operate in new ways.

A good way to retain new information is to review the new information or skill:

❑   at the end of the first day's learning

❑   after one week

❑   at the end of one month

❑   after six months.

At this point, the information and learning will be committed to your long-term memory, as long as you keep using the new techniques and knowledge gained.

As you begin to apply your new ways of working, you should arrange to meet with your line manager or team leader to review the usefulness (and accuracy) of your new skills. This should be a supportive process for both you and the organisation. For example:

❑   You can talk through any concerns.

❑   You can check that you are carrying out the tasks correctly.

❑   Your manager can help you review the impact which any changes may have on your service users.

❑   You can take time to review the changes, to make sure the outcomes are what you both expected.

❑   You can check on the usefulness of the changes to all involved, ie you, your team, the individuals and the organisation as a whole.

❑   You can also give your manager the chance to review the changes to see if they are still happy with them, or whether further changes should be implemented.

It is also important to check that your new learning meets with the legal requirements of health and safety and the Care Standards Act 2000. You can do this by discussing your new routines and actions with your line manager and asking them to approve your planned actions.

REMEMBER

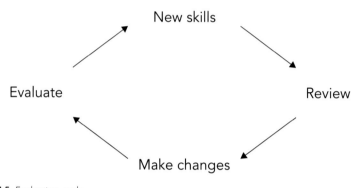

You should never implement changes to working practices without first discussing them with your manager.

When you start the process of reviewing the new skills and knowledge you have acquired, you are then straight back into the review and evaluation cycle but with a 'higher' starting point.

New skills

Evaluate

Review

Make changes

Fig 3.15 Evaluation cycle.

You can see from this circle that the process of developing your knowledge and practice never stops! It is the learning of new skills and the increasing of your knowledge that underpins quality care for our service users and the whole of your career development.

Summary

In this chapter we have explored the importance of continuous professional development. This is the only way that health and social care staff can progress to become senior staff, or move into other branches of the caring services such as nursing. However, we should never forget that our service users are at the centre of all we do, and that they will benefit hugely from our professional development through:

❏ better health and social care provision

❏ the use of up-to-date equipment and technology

❏ the application of knowledge-based care

❏ the knowledge that they can trust us to provide the best possible service.

Important skills for developing knowledge and practice include:

❏ being open to change

❏ actively seeking out feedback on performance

❏ taking action on the feedback provided

❏ continuously developing new skills and knowledge

❏ developing the skills to reflect upon and learn from experience.

4

Ensure your own actions support the care, protection and wellbeing of individuals

→ Introduction

Working with individuals involves having an understanding of their rights to a safe, secure and healthy environment. This chapter will help you to understand your role in protecting vulnerable individuals and providing an environment which contributes to this.

To succeed in this unit, you must demonstrate that you value and treat people equally and with respect and dignity; that you encourage and respect their choices and preferences; and that you will protect them from danger, harm and abuse.

You will learn:

❑ how to relate to and support individuals in a way they choose

❑ how to treat individuals with respect and dignity

❑ how to assist in the protection of individuals.

★ KEY WORDS

APPROPRIATE PEOPLE	Those people to whom you need to report, according to legal and organisational requirements.
ABUSE	Causing physical, emotional and/or sexual harm to an individual or failing/neglecting to protect them from harm.
ACTIVE SUPPORT	Support that encourages individuals to do as much for themselves as possible to maintain their independence and physical ability, and encourages people with disabilities to maximise their own potential and independence.
AUTONOMY	Having free will and the right to self-governance.
CHOICE	Opportunity to make life choices with assistance as appropriate.
CONFIDENTIALITY	Passing on service user information on a need-to-know basis.
CULTURE	A set of values, norms, beliefs and behaviours that distinguish a group of people.
DANGER	The possibility that harm may occur.
DIGNITY	Treating all people with respect, recognising each individual's unique characteristics.

DISCRIMINATION	When an individual or group are treated (often unfairly) differently because of their religion, colour, disability, gender etc.
DIVERSITY	Respecting all people and valuing differences.
EMPOWERMENT	Where an individual is given the power to control their own lives as much as possible.
EQUALITY	Providing the same opportunities, access to services and income to all people.
INDEPENDENCE	Right to act and think without reference to another person.
INDIVIDUALS	The actual people requiring health and care services. Where individuals use advocates and interpreters to enable them to express their views, wishes or feelings and to speak on their behalf, the term 'individual' within this standard covers the individual and their advocate or interpreter.
KEY PEOPLE	These are the people who are essential to an individual's health and social wellbeing, and make a difference to their life.
PRIVACY	Rights of individuals to be left alone or undisturbed and free from interference in their affairs.
SERVICE USER	An individual who receives care and support from your organisation.

CARE VALUES

People have a right to be cared for in a way that meets their needs and takes account of their choices. Care workers therefore have a responsibility to promote the independence and autonomy of those in their care.

The term 'autonomy' means being free from control, able to make your own decisions and choices about the way you live your life.

Wherever possible, individuals should be enabled to take control over their own care and feel empowered to do things for themselves. When people feel they have control over their own life, their self-esteem increases.

Relate to and support individuals in a way they choose

To help you meet the requirements for this section of the unit you will need to know and understand how to:

❑   find out about individual needs, wishes and preferences

❑   develop appropriate relationships with individuals

❑   support individuals to fulfil their potential

❑   respect individual choices

❑   resolve any conflicts and seek extra support

❑   observe and report any changes which could affect an individual's care needs

Traditionally, health care professionals such as doctors, nurses, carers and social workers, have taken all the decisions for those in their care, as they were seen as the 'expert'. However, this is no longer the accepted view, and individuals themselves are now considered to be best placed to identify their own needs and make decisions on how those needs should be met.

Find out about the individual's needs, wishes and preferences

Whenever possible, you should offer choices to those people in your care. This includes the level and type of care needed, where the care should be, when and by whom it is to be carried out. This means asking those people that you are caring for about their needs, wishes and preferences, so that you can take these into account when you plan and provide care. Making a record of these choices is important so that all members of the care team are aware of the service users' wishes.

Examples of the different ways in which you can offer choice to your service users:

SUBJECT	TYPES OF CHOICES
Food	When do you want to eat? Where do you want to eat? (tray, own room, dining table) What do you want to eat? (choice of menu) How much help do you need? (assistance, special utensils) Who do you want to sit with?
Personal hygiene	When do you want to wash? (morning, afternoon or evening) Do you want a wash, bath or shower? How hot do you want the water? Which toiletries do you prefer? Do you need any help? (how much help?)

The range and extent of choice will clearly vary, depending on the situation and people involved. For example, an individual with a physical disability may want to have a bath unaided, but is prevented from doing so by their condition. Even though there may be certain restrictions on choice, the basic principle stays the same. Individuals must be involved in all aspects of decision-making about their care, and not have that care imposed upon them.

Develop appropriate relationships with individuals

In order to ensure that your actions empower those in your care and promote independence and autonomy, it is essential that you develop appropriate, effective and respectful relationships with your service users. A good working relationship requires respect and the use of good communication skills. More information about communication is available in Chapter 1.

REFLECT

How much choice do you have in your own life about what you do and when you do it?
How would you feel if that choice were taken away or restricted in some way?

REFLECT

Using the table as a guide, think about the range of choices offered to individuals in terms of how they socialise or spend their free time.
What kind of questions might you want to ask to ensure they are offered choice?

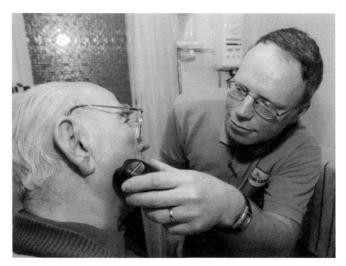

Fig 4.1 Use every opportunity to talk to your service users.

CASE STUDY

A service user is asking his care worker for advice about a problem he is having with his overprotective son and daughter-in-law who want him to go and stay with them for Christmas. He clearly doesn't want to go and so the care worker says 'If I were you I would not go'. Why is it important for care workers not to give direct advice?

REFLECT

Think about a good relationship you have with an individual. What is it that makes the relationship good?
Think about another relationship with an individual that you have found more difficult. How does this relationship compare with the first one? Why is this relationship not as good? What could you do/have done differently to improve this relationship?

It is important that you consider the effect your moods and behaviours may have on your service users. If you are happy and positive, they are more likely to relax with you and tell you their needs. If you are always rushing around and tend to be impatient and abrupt, it is likely that they will withdraw from you. This will probably result in their needs and wishes not being fully met, leaving them feeling disempowered.

Good working relationships require you to work together with your service users and not to impose your views and values on them. This can be quite difficult when individuals ask you for advice. However, it is important when someone asks, 'If you were me, what would you do?', that you do not give direct advice about what they should or should not do. Concentrate on giving clear, impartial and relevant information and support them in the decision they make.

There are many obstacles to developing and sustaining good relationships, including:

❑ language barriers

❑ prejudice – forming a wrong impression about someone based on a set of assumptions about them

❑ conflcting or differing beliefs and values

❑ poor communication skills

❑ environmental factors – eg in an environment which is noisy and chaotic, it may be difficult to develop or maintain good relationships.

POINTS TO NOTE

Remember, care should be seen as a partnership between the care worker and the service user.

Support individuals to state their preferences

In all aspects of care, it is essential that care workers assist their service users to feel part of the process. A way of doing this is by involving the individual in the planning and execution of their care, and making sure they know that their needs, wishes and preferences are being taken into consideration and respected. As care workers, you need to remember that individuals have a right to be consulted and involved in all aspects of their care, and even to refuse that care if they so wish.

There are various ways of supporting individuals to be actively involved in their care. You need to make sure that:

1 individuals understand the need for their care or treatment. Helping them see the advantages and benefits of the care is important. Remember, if they do not understand the purpose of care or treatment, they are more likely to refuse

2 the individual is not worried about any aspects of their care or treatment – for example, if they have previously had a fall while having a bath, they are likely to be frightened about this happening again, and therefore be reluctant to take another bath

3 the service user knows what is happening, or going to happen, to them during the whole process of the treatment or care – it can be very frightening to have something done to you that you do not fully understand. You should constantly check that they are fully aware of everything that is happening to them so that they feel in control and central to the process.

CASE STUDY

It has been a busy morning and Judith, a relatively new member of staff, is feeling under pressure to complete everything she needs to do by lunchtime. She rushes into Mrs Jones' room to get her out of bed and take her for a bath, but in her haste, forgets to inform Mrs Jones about what is happening.

- How might Mrs Jones feel?
- What could Judith have done differently to involve Mrs Jones in her care?
- How could the person in charge provide more support for Judith?

👍 POINTS TO NOTE

You should:

- give individuals as much choice as possible in their care or treatment
- take into account their opinions, needs and wants at all times
- involve them in the planning and implementing of any care or treatment required.

Remember, if individuals do not feel part of the decision-making process, they are unlikely to 'own' their care routines, and may just go along with everything to keep 'you happy'. Clearly they will not receive the full benefits intended from the care. For individuals to benefit fully, they need to be actively committed, which means involving them as much as possible.

Informed consent

Informed consent is intended to protect people from abuse so that their rights are not violated. Obtaining a service user's consent is essential when providing most forms of medical treatment, for example before an operation when a consent form requires a signature. Consent in a care setting can often be informal but it is still good practice to ask your service user for their permission. For example, before getting someone out of bed in the morning, if you say, 'Shall I help you to get up now?' you are seeking their consent. Waiting for a response such as, 'Yes, please,' suggests that the person has given their consent and agreed to your help.

Providing information

People can only make sound decisions about their care and treatment if they have been provided with sufficient information to do so.

It is important that you find out what your service users want and need, so that you can provide the information which is appropriate in helping them achieve their own goals. Sometimes individuals may not be aware of what is actually available to them. In these cases it is your responsibility to inform people of the availability of services in your area.

The types of information individuals may require include:

❑ how to arrange a home help or meals on wheels

❑ information about a particular illness

❑ the social activities that are available

❑ information about pensions and benefits.

FIND OUT

Each workplace has a policy required by law for obtaining consent. Find the relevant policy in your workplace? And make yourself familiar with it

CARE VALUES

Individuals have a right to access information about themselves. Giving information is an important part of empowering individuals and increasing their independence and ability to make choices. Information can be given verbally, such as informing the service user about a particular entertainment event, or written, for example, within a leaflet about social activities in the area.

It is unlikely that you will have all the information that individuals need to know. However, you can be aware of sources of information to pass onto the service user for their (or others) action. The source of information will depend on the type of information that is required.

Citizen's Advice
Bureau

the care
manager

Sources of
information

library

GP

social services
departments

Sally & Richard Greenhill 0207 607 8549 © Sally Greenhill

Fig 4.2 Advice on a range of issues is available to you and your service users – know your local services.

👍 **POINTS TO NOTE**

Information needs to be:

- clear and easy to understand
- relevant to the needs and requirements of individuals
- accurate and up-to-date.

☑ ACTION

Two older women (sisters) have just arrived at your residential home, feeling nervous and intimidated by their new environment.

- Design useful information which will help to reassure and empower these new service users; eg plans of the building and grounds, charts explaining who people are and what they do, or details of daily routines such as mealtimes and social activities.

FIND OUT

... about the types of information available for the service users in your workplace.
Do you think this information empowers the service users?
If so, how?
What other information would help to empower them and increase their independence?

Support individuals to fulfil their potential

Limited choice and advocacy

We have seen that in order to be able to exercise choice and free will, people need to have information about the services that are available to them. However, individuals also need to be in a position to understand that information in order to form and express their views and opinions. Some individuals may not be able to make their own decisions or exercise individual choice due to a wide variety of reasons. These could include:

- ❑ older people who are confused or suffering from dementia
- ❑ children who lack understanding because of their immaturity
- ❑ people with learning difficulties who do not understand
- ❑ people with physical or sensory disabilities, eg those who are blind, in a wheelchair etc.
- ❑ those with a long-term limiting illness such as chronic arthritis or a stroke
- ❑ minority ethnic groups who may not understand the language used
- ❑ Individuals who have a low self esteem or are shy or even in fear.

In situations such as these it may be necessary to have an advocate to represent the service user. An advocate is someone who tries to understand the needs and wishes of the individual and then speaks or argues on their behalf.

Advocates may be:

- ❑ A professional – for example, lawyers representing an individual in court or through other legal systems and processes

❑   Professionals – people employed and paid to act as an advocate

❑   Volunteers – who may have had some training to act as an independent advocate on behalf of the individual

❑   Family members – acting on behalf of their relative

Advocacy is important because it is concerned with helping to secure peoples' rights, empowering them, encouraging full participation and promoting access to care and treatment. It is important that the interests of individuals are protected and promoted, as many people may be vulnerable and incapable of protecting their own interests. You can assist this process by providing information in a way that the service user can understand and by helping the individual to feel confident with their own decision making skills.

Care workers can act as advocates for individuals, but it is important to be aware that conflicts may arise between the role of advocate and that of employee or service provider. Situations where this might apply could be:

❑   If a service user wished to complain about their care

❑   Where there is conflict between the rights of the service user and those of the carer

It is also difficult for care workers to represent an individual whom they do not know in detail. It may well be that a relative or family friend could take on the role of advocate more successfully in these situations

Other types of advocacy include:

1 **Self advocacy** – where individuals are helped to argue their own case. This requires the individual involved to have a high level of understanding, communication skills and determination.

2 **Group advocacy** – Individuals with similar needs join together to argue for their needs as a group. The group situation provides each individual with mutual support. Self help groups such as Alzheimer's support groups are an example of this kind of advocacy.

Skills for effective advocacy:

❑   Work towards a pre-arranged agreement – establish the goals the service user wants to achieve.

❑   Do not directly advise or instruct the person. Avoid phrases such as, "I think you should . . .", or "If it was me, I would . . ."

> **REFLECT**
>
> Can you remember from your own experience, occasions where an individual would have benefited from the help of an advocate?
> If this service was available for them, how effective was it?
> If an advocate was not available, what was the effect on the individual?

> **REFLECT**
>
> If you were unable to communicate your own beliefs and feelings, what sort of person would you want to act as your advocate? And why?

❑ Maintain professional boundaries at all times in your relationships with individuals.

❑ Ensure decisions focus exclusively on the needs of the individual.

❑ Listen to the service user's perspectives and views.

❑ Be informed – ensure that you know as much as possible about the rights and needs of those you are representing.

❑ Take care to minimise any conflicts of interest, and if necessary find someone else to represent the individual involved.

Important issues for an advocate to consider:

❑ ways of increasing the individuals participation in decision making over time

❑ avoiding actions that result in restrictions on the individual's freedom

❑ the views of relatives about the individual's wishes

❑ the individual's past and present wishes.

CASE STUDY ✍

Jim is a 62-year-old resident suffering from early onset of dementia.

• List the different areas of his everyday life where he might benefit from an advocate.

👍 POINTS TO NOTE

• Advocacy means representing the interests of people who cannot speak for themselves because of illness, disability or other disadvantage.

• An advocate is someone who speaks on behalf of another and has the faith, confidence and trust of the person whom they are representing.

REFLECT

Think about a time when you spoke on behalf of someone else. What were the reasons for this? Do you feel that you adequately represented that person's opinions and wishes? If not, why not?

Respect individuals' choices and desire to care for themselves

Respect for individuals' autonomy means that you should respect the choices they make about their own lives. One way of demonstrating this is to discuss with them any proposed care or treatment, so that they can decide for themselves whether to accept or refuse it. The information you give to service users should help them to decide what is in their own best interests.

For those working in health and social care, the best way of making sure your service users' choices are respected and that information is passed on, is to write it down. When an individual enters residential care, an admission form is completed, containing general information such as name, date of birth, medical information and next of kin, it includes information about likes, dislikes and religious preferences.

Care plans are also developed at this time, and the individual is encouraged to become involved so that they can contribute to their plan of care. This involves recording personal choices such as diet, level of care needed, etc.

CASE STUDY

Mrs Williams has just moved into the residential home where you work.

- What paperwork would you as a care worker complete to make sure her rights and choices are considered?

When service users are denied choice, disempowerment may be the results. This occurs when individuals are expected to fit in with the organisation, rather than fitting the service to the individual's requirements. For example, expecting a patient in a nursing home to have a bath at a time convenient for the staff, rather than when they want to have one. Your responsibility as a care worker is to ensure that your service user maintains their independence and their right to choose.

It is sometimes difficult and frustrating to watch an individual struggling to carry out a task when you know that you could do it quickly and easily. However, you need to stand back and allow them to complete the task themselves, unless they ask for your help. Assisting the service user to eat a meal by providing the correct utensils and sitting with them as encouragement, may take much longer than feeding them yourself, but it is important for them to be allowed to be independent.

At all times, individuals should be encouraged to make choices about their own care, even if that means they may refuse certain treatment or care.

Legislation and policy

People have the right to be cared for in a way that meets their needs and takes into account their individual choices. This emphasis on the rights of individuals to be involved in their care and be consulted about the care they receive, is reflected in the many types, of legislation, codes of practice and charters. These emphasise the importance of joint partnerships between providers of care (nurses, care workers) and service users.

Types of legislation that promote individual choice include:

- Children Act 1989
- NHS and Community Care Act 1990
- Carers and Disabled Children Act 2000
- Human Rights Act 1998
- Care Standards Act 2000.

Care workers are duty bound to work under the requirements of various charters and codes of practice that relate to their area of work. Each care organisation has formal policies that relate to service user rights.

The care charter 'Better Care, Higher Standards' published by the Department of Health in 1999 sets out the values expected of services providing care. These are:

- to treat people with courtesy and honesty, and to respect their dignity

- to work in partnership with people to provide the services they need

- to involve people in decisions and give them sufficient information to make informed choices

- to help people to have a voice through advocacy and other representative organisations

- to treat people fairly on the basis of any risks to them and their needs

- not to discriminate against people on the basis of age, abilities, ethnic background, race, religion or belief, culture, gender and sexual orientation

- to ensure that people feel able to complain about the standard of services provided and that they should not be afraid to do so.

Recognising an individual's right to choose is clearly outlined in the Nursing and Midwifery Code of professional conduct:

- Recognise and respect the role of service users as partners in their care – identify their preferences regarding care, and respect this within the limits of professional practice, legislation and resources.

- You are accountable for ensuring that you promote and protect the interests and dignity of service users, irrespective of gender, age, race, ability, sexuality, economic status, lifestyle, culture and religion.

- You must maintain appropriate boundaries in relationships.

- Promote the interests of service users – help them to gain access to health and social care, information and support relevant to their need.

Resolve conflicts

Restrictions on choice

There are occasions when individuals may have restrictions placed upon them which limit their choices. An example of this could be when someone who has a disability or illness preventing them from participating in an activity because of health and safety reasons. Where there are such restrictions in place they must be explained to the individual in a way that they can understand.

Sometimes individuals can become frustrated or angry when they are prevented from doing something they want to. This may result in them refusing to cooperate with you. The way in which you approach this situation is very important. If you react in a way that is irritable or demonstrates impatience, your service user is likely to respond by being more obstructive. If you try to stay calm and relaxed, they are more likely to trust you and respond positively.

When trying to resolve conflict:

❑ have individuals think of their own solution to the problem

❑ discuss the risks involved in a non-threatening and objective manner

❑ stay calm and relaxed

❑ acitvely listen to the points being expressed

❑ offer clear explanations but avoid arguing

❑ try to solve the problem with sensitivity, taking care not to embarrass the individual

FIND OUT

Each place of work should have a charter of service users rights displayed. This states the importance of promoting choice, self-esteem and a sense of belonging, together with rights such as privacy and the importance of individuals being involved in decision-making. Find out what the charter of rights in your workplace states.

REFLECT

What restrictions are placed on your behaviour in the following places:
• a restaurant
• a hospital out-patient waiting room
• a library
• your workplace
How do you feel about these restrictions? Now think about restrictions placed on your service users. What might they feel about these?

CASE STUDY

You are helping to serve lunch in your workplace, and the choice of puddings available is rather limited, either chocolate gateau or fresh fruit salad. Mrs Thomas, an individual who has diabetes, refuses the fresh fruit salad and chooses the gateau instead.

• How would you deal with this situation?

• What should you do if Mrs Thomas continues to insist on making this choice?

Conflict with other people

Sometimes the rights of one person may conflict with those of another person; eg one service user insists on watching a

REFLECT

Think about the reasons why you should call for assistance when dealing with potential conflicts.

particular television programme, which the other service users do not want to watch. How you handle this situation is very important. You will need to deal with it in a sensitive manner and may need to make a compromise with the service users to ensure that each person is able to maintain a degree of choice. It may be necessary when dealing with conflicting behaviour to seek help from your supervisor or a more experienced member of staff.

CASE STUDY

Mr Evans, a new service user, arrived last week in the residential home where you work. He smokes 40 cigarettes per day and insists on smoking in a non-smoking area of the sitting-room.

- How would you explain to Mr Evans that he cannot smoke in this area?
- How could you ensure that Mr Evans' right to smoke is respected?

CASE STUDY

Mrs Parkinson suffers from dementia and often wanders around at night in a confused state. She does not seem distressed, but her behaviour upsets other residents, especially when she wanders into their rooms.

- As a care worker, how would you deal with this situation and promote freedom of choice for all involved?
- Whose rights are more important and why?

Observe and report changes to core needs

In order to support individuals in a way they choose, you need to be aware of any changes that could affect their care needs, and therefore their level of independence and ability to make their own choices.

A central part of planning care is the assessment process, where an individual's care needs are assessed and a care plan is designed to meet those needs.

Careful and regular monitoring of how the individual is responding to the level and type of care given is very important, as this may highlight any changes in their condition, such as their general state of health, level of mobility or mental state. The individual themselves may tell you that they are concerned with their health status or the level of care they are receiving. You must listen to the information and respond accordingly. Encouraging your service user to be involved in monitoring their own care is an important role for you.

What action do you take?

Careful monitoring of individuals' needs is to help both the other members of the care team and the individuals themselves to assess how well the care plan is working. It is therefore important that you, along with other members of the team, report any changes you observe and feedback those changes to the appropriate people. This involves good team-working skills (covered in Chapter 5) and good literacy skills as records should be clear, accessible and up-to-date.

Treat people with respect and dignity

To help you meet the requirements for this section of the unit you will need to know and understand how to:

- ❑ treat and value each person as an individual
- ❑ respect the dignity and privacy of individuals
- ❑ respect each person's diversity, culture and values
- ❑ avoid discrimination and take appropriate action when behaviours and practice discriminate against individuals
- ❑ encourage individuals to comment on their care

Treat and value each person as an individual

To provide high-quality care for individuals, you need to be able to value each person as unique. This means not making assumptions about their characteristics and needs but learning to appreciate them as individuals with their own distinct personality and life experiences. This not only benefits your service users, but can also be very rewarding and enriching for you as a care worker.

The anonymous writer of this poem could not speak, but communicated her feelings and experiences of being cared for.

Mattie's Poem

What do you see, nurses, what do you see,
what are you thinking when you're looking at me?
A crabby old woman, not very wise,
uncertain of habit, with faraway eyes.

Who dribbles her food and makes no reply
when you say in a loud voice, 'I do wish you'd try?'
Who seems not to notice the things that you do,
and forever is losing a stocking or shoe.

Who, resisting or not, lets you do as you will
with bathing and feeding, the long day to fill.
Is that what you're thinking? Is that what you see?
Then open your eyes, nurse; you're not looking at me.

I'll tell you who I am as I sit here so still,
as I use at your bidding, as I eat at your will.
I'm a small child of ten with a father and mother,
brothers and sisters, who love one another.

A young girl of sixteen, with wings on her feet,
dreaming that soon now a lover she'll meet.
A bride soon at twenty — my heart gives a leap,
remembering the vows that I promised to keep.

At twenty-five now, I have young of my own
who need me to guide and a secure happy home.
A woman of thirty, my young now grown fast,
bound to each other with ties that should last.

At forty my young sons have grown and are gone,
but my man's beside me to see I don't mourn.
At fifty once more babies play round my knee,
again we know children, my loved one and me.

Dark days are upon me, my husband is dead;
I look at the future, I shudder with dread . . .
For my young are all rearing young of their own,
and I think of the years and the love that I've known.

I'm now an old woman and nature is cruel;
'tis jest to make old age look like a fool.
The body, it crumbles, grace and vigour depart,
there is now a stone where I once had a heart.

But inside this old carcass a young girl still dwells,
and now and again my battered heart swells.
I remember the joys, I remember the pain,
and I'm loving and living life over again.

I think of the years; all too few, gone too fast,
and accept the stark fact that nothing can last.
So open your eyes, nurses, open and see,
not a crabby old woman; look closer — see ME!!

(anon, printed in Vida Carver and Penny Liddiard (eds) *An Ageing Population*,
Hodder & Stoughton and Open University, 1978)

REFLECT

- How was the woman in the poem treated?
- What effect did this have on her?
- What are the needs of older people?

Respect the dignity and privacy of individuals

Everyone wants to be treated with respect and feel they are valued by those around them. This is especially true for those in care situations, where individuals may be vulnerable or feel isolated from family or friends. Clearly it is important that care workers make every effort to ensure that the way they work shows respect and value for those in their care.

Here are some of the ways in which you can demonstrate respect for the dignity and privacy of those in your care:

- ❑ Before you enter someone's room, always knock on the door.

- ❑ If necessary introduce yourself when you enter someone's home or room.

- ❑ Find out how the individual wants to be addressed – some older people do not like to be called by their first name.

- ❑ Do not express negative attitudes towards individuals, especially if you find that person difficult to care for.

- ❑ Always maintain privacy especially during dressing, washing or going to the toilet.

- ❑ Ensure that people are given choice and control over their life.

CARE VALUES

Treating people with respect and dignity builds good relationships. People may need help with very personal tasks such as dressing, washing, or using the toilet. Here, you must remember that it is not just *what* you do, but the *way* that you do it that is important. In order to show respect, you need to be able to understand people's feelings and wishes, and treat them in a way which demonstrate consideration and value.

👍 POINTS TO NOTE

A good standard to work from is to think about how you would like to be treated, and to treat others in the same way.

CASE STUDY 🖎

Flora, an 82-year-old service user, has fallen over in the middle of the sitting-room in front of other residents.

- How might she be feeling?

- What can you do to help maintain her dignity and privacy while you assist her?

CASE STUDY 🖎

You are working with June, a fellow carer, and are about to help Frank (a rather aggressive and uncooperative individual) to rise from bed. June tells you that she does not like Frank and wishes that she did not have to help him. She marches into Frank's room and throws back the covers. Frank looks a bit shocked and starts to protest. Before he can say anything, his bedclothes are stripped off and some clothes are selected from his wardrobe and he is being clothed. By this point Frank has become very agitated. In an offhand manner, June pulls Frank to his feet and takes him to the dining room for breakfast.

- In which ways did June show disrespect to Frank?

- Why did she treat Frank in this way?

- What could she have done differently in order to show respect for Frank?

- What action should you have taken?

Respect the individual's diversity, culture and values

We live in a diverse society made up of many groups of people from different backgrounds and cultures. We are all different from one another. It would be a very dull world if we were all the same! Care work especially should involve celebrating the fact that we are different and have different beliefs and opinions. It is therefore important that we do not expect people to be all the same (stereotyping), so that they fit into roles and behaviours that we expect of them.

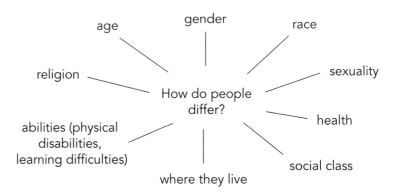

People also differ in their values, beliefs and personalities. Each one of us has a variety of experiences that has helped shape who we are today. These include our past experiences throughout childhood and early adulthood, the social group we belong to, our political or religious beliefs and our level of self-confidence.

Valuing diversity

Valuing diversity is a central principle of care work and a key part of the care value base. The care value base outlines how carers should treat those in their care, in order to help them develop to their full potential.

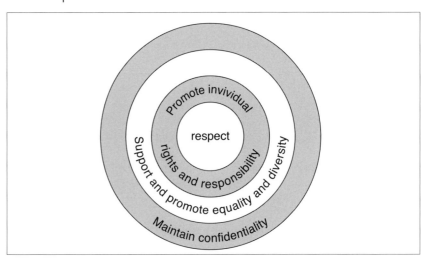

Fig 4.3 Respect is the cornerstone of the care value base.

Why is valuing diversity so important?

- ❑ It is essential for non-discriminatory practice.
- ❑ It helps create good relationships with individuals.
- ❑ It helps to understand other people's lives.
- ❑ Relating to others who are different enriches your own life.
- ❑ Treating other people equally is central to good care.

☑ ACTION

Look at the following activities. How could you adapt them so that they value diversity amongst different groups of people, eg different cultures, ages, physical abilities etc?

- playing bingo
- singing Christmas carols
- old-time dancing
- wine and cheese party for an individual's birthday.

CASE STUDY ✍

You are on duty when a new service user, arrives. She was born in India and follows the Hindu fatith. List the ways in which she might be affected by coming to live in your workplace. Think especially about the following areas:

- food and drink
- surroundings
- staff
- religious observances.

Shared needs

We have looked at some of the many differences between individuals. However, all human beings have basic needs that they have in common. As we have already noted in Chapter 1, Abraham Maslow (1908–70) believed that there are different levels of need, and that the needs at each level have to be met before you can develop beyond that level:

- ❑ physical needs such as food, water, air, freedom from pain
- ❑ emotional/safety needs such as protection and shelter

> **REFLECT**
>
> Consider your role at each level of need. How do you support service users to meet each need?

❏ belonging/affection needs such as feeling accepted, loved and building good relationships

❏ self-esteem needs such as having self-confidence and feeling valued and respected

❏ personal growth such as realising your full potential, being able to develop your abilities and talents which then results in a high level of satisfaction and contentment. Maslow called this stage 'self-actualisation'.

See page 8 for a diagram of Maslow's hierarchy of needs.

Focus on the individual's beliefs and preferences

In order to treat all people with respect, you need to understand that other individuals may think and behave differently from you. Recognising that people have different beliefs and preferences involves observing their behaviour and getting to know them as individuals by spending time talking to them.

Sometimes this can be difficult, especially if we feel our own beliefs and values are being challenged. We may not always be aware of our own opinions or beliefs until someone or something challenges them. Just because we see things in a certain way does not mean that everyone else will feel the same. As care workers, you need to be able to recognise differences in other people, and respect their diversity. We should never treat people unfairly or less favourably because of their values and beliefs.

Do not discriminate against any individual

It is essential that the way in which you work does not discriminate against anyone. People should be treated equally, and their right to be different respected. In order to do this, it is important to understand why discrimination occurs.

Prejudice

Prejudice comes from the verb, to pre-judge. This means forming an impression about someone based on a set of ideas you already have about them, often formed before you even know the individual concerned. These first impressions will often influence the way we behave to that person. When we judge someone else, we usually think we are better than them in some way. This belief is based on our own set of standards and expectations. For example, if someone thinks that one person they know looks scruffy and dirty and is lazy and not to be trusted, they may develop a prejudice against all people who look scruffy and dirty.

Fig 4.4 It is important to challenge your own beliefs and stereotypes.

Stereotyping and labelling

Stereotyping is based on prejudice and occurs when you believe that all people from a certain group have the same characteristics. This means that individual differences are not acknowledged or appreciated. These beliefs are often incorrect, negative and harmful. Often stereotypes start with the words 'all men are . . .', or 'all older people are . . .'. Labelling happens when you apply a stereotype to an individual person.

Stereotypes are often created and reinforced by the media.

The next time you are tempted to make a judgement about a service user based on a stereotype . . . STOP! Try to look beyond your preconceived ideas about them and see them as an individual in their own right.

Discrimination

Discrimination is the outward result of prejudice. It means treating people unfairly because of their differences and your prejudices against them. Discrimination often occurs because of differences in race, gender, class, age, religion, sexual orientation or disability.

Discrimination can be direct (open) or indirect (hidden, or not as obvious). Examples of direct discrimination include:

- ❏ bullying or offensive behaviour towards the victim
- ❏ abusive language, sexist or racist jokes.

> **REFLECT**
>
> Look at the pictures and consider the following questions:
> - What are your first impressions of these people?
> - Which stereotypes are your impressions based on?
> - How do you think you formed these stereotypes?
> - What do you think are the possible effects of stereotyping on these people?

135

Fig 4.5 Be aware – body language alone can easily demonstrate prejudice and disapproval.

Examples of indirect discrimination include:

❑   avoiding an individual from a different race or ethnic group to yourself

❑   having leaflets and posters only in English when there are service users from other countries who do not speak the language

❑   showing discrimination by your tone of voice or body language.

CASE STUDY

Look at the following situations and decide which are direct or indirect forms of discrimination

• a gang of white teenagers attacking a black teenager in the street

• not having a vegetarian option on the menu

• a woman being denied promotion because she is pregnant

• lack of a disabled toilet in a library

• a colleague treating someone differently when they find out they are homosexual.

Effects of discrimination

All types of discrimination are harmful and people can be affected in many different ways. Short-term effects on individuals may include anger, loss of self-esteem, depression, isolation, feeling stressed or unable to cope. Long-term effects could include loss of motivation, reduced individual rights, restricted opportunities, limited access to services and mental illness caused by stress.

CASE STUDY

Discuss the impact of discriminatory practice on the lives of the following individuals:

    1 An older service user who is constantly patronised because he is deaf.

    2 A black care assistant who receives persistent racial remarks from a colleague.

Provide an equal and inclusive service

As a care worker, it is your legal responsibility to make sure that the service you provide is delivered equally (the same standard and level of care for all) and inclusively (to all people, without excluding anyone).

Sometimes you may be caring for service users for whom English is a second language. In non-discriminatory practice, it is important that you make every effort to ensure that all written or spoken information is available in the individual's appropriate language. This may mean using interpreters or having written information translated so that the service user can understand and respond accordingly.

Provide active support to encourage participation

An essential part of valuing and respecting individuals is to actively support those in your care to participate in activities as much as they want or are able to. This means making every effort to ensure that activities are open to all people irrespective of their culture, age, religion or background.

Challenging discrimination

It is important to be aware of the types of behaviour that may result in discrimination, so that you can take appropriate action where necessary. Firstly, it is important that you identify and challenge your own beliefs and prejudices that could lead to discrimination. This involves thinking about why you hold a particular opinion or value and changing it if necessary.

You should be aware of your responsibility to challenge discriminatory behaviour in others. This can be difficult and is likely to require confidence especially if the source of discrimination is a colleague or manager.

Seek extra support and advice

If you are finding it difficult to act in a way that supports equality and diversity, you may need help and support from others. It is essential that you deal with any difficulties quickly and

CARE VALUES
Ways of working which promote equality include being aware of any potential problems such as prejudices and stereotypes, and dealing with these before they can result in discrimination. Addressing issues individually and as an organisation requires having an awareness of the rights of individuals and knowledge of the relevant laws, codes of practice and charters which promote and support those rights. Individuals have a legal right not to be discriminated against, and services should be designed with this in mind.

REFLECT
What would have to change in terms of the types of information available and how you carry out your job, if you had a non-english speaking service user in your care

FIND OUT
. . . what anti-discriminatory policies there are in your workplace.

137

☑ ACTION

One of the ways of ensuring that you do not discriminate against individuals because of their culture is to educate yourself about their way of life and beliefs. Find out more about the Hindu way of life and ways in which you could provide a culturally acceptable service.

CARE VALUES

Challenging discrimination in yourself:

- Challenge and acknowledge your own beliefs and prejudices.
- Educate yourself about how people may differ.
- Be careful about the type of language you use, eg not referring to people as epileptics, but instead as people who suffer from epilepsy.
- Remember-people first.

Challenging discrimination in others:
This can be difficult because it often means challenging others about their attitudes and behaviour. This is particularly difficult where colleagues are concerned, and it requires you to have examined and dealt with your own beliefs and values first. However, ignoring this form of behaviour can have serious consequences for those who are suffering from discrimination, and you have a responsibility to act in a way that promotes equality and respect.

- Be clear about what behaviour is causing discrimination.
- Be assertive, not aggressive.
- Be respectful when you try to help them see what effect their action has.
- Where necessary, seek support from other colleagues or senior staff.

Legislation and policy

All care organisations must be aware of their legal obligations under the various Acts of Parliament for dealing with any act of discrimination. These acts include:

- Equal Pay Act 1970
- Sex Discrimination Act 1975
- Race Relations Act 1976 (and Race Relations (Amendment) Act 2000)
- Disability Discrimination Act 1995
- Human Rights Act 1998
- Sex Discrimination (Gender Reassignment) Regulations 1999
- Employment Equality (Sexual Orientation) Regulations 2003
- Employment Equality (Religion or Belief) Regulations 2003.

professionally; doing nothing is not an option. It is important that you seek help from your manager as they will be able to offer you extra support and if appropriate in-service training. You may also find it helpful to talk to more experienced colleagues about the way they challenge discrimination in the workplace.

Legislation and practice

Individuals have the right to complain and to know and understand the correct procedure to follow if they have any comments about their care. All organisations have a complaints procedure, which usually involves talking to those involved to try to resolve the matter, filling in a complaint form, reporting to senior management and sometimes external agencies such as social service departments.

Individuals may need to seek more formal help from statutory bodies such as:

- the Commission for Racial Equality
- the Disability Rights Commission
- the Equal Opportunities Commission.

COMMISSION FOR RACIAL EQUALITY

Fig 4.6 Protecting the rights of all.

FIND OUT

. . . about people who follow the Muslim religion.

- How does their religion influence the way they live?

- Does their religion place any restrictions upon them?

- How might their religion have an effect on their beliefs and values?

- How could you address these issues in the workplace?

Encourage individuals to comment on their care

There may be occasions when a service user wants to complain about some aspect of their care. Carers and care organisations need to be helpful and supportive in this process. Firstly, it is important to make sure that individuals know their rights under the various laws and policies designed to protect them. Secondly, they should be provided with information about how to complain and thirdly, which procedures and organisations are there to support them through a complaints procedure.

Assist in the protection of individuals

To help you meet the requirements for this section of the unit you will need to know and understand how to:

- ❑ assess potential risk of abuse

- ❑ protect individuals from actual or likely abuse

- ❑ disclose information about actual or likely abuse

- ❑ develop trust and communication with individuals and key people

- ❑ observe the signs and symptoms of abuse

- ❑ avoid putting yourself and others at unnecessary risk

- ❑ alert appropriate people when you discover or suspect individuals are in danger

FIND OUT

. . . about current information regarding discrimination issues by contacting the Disability Rights Commission through their website – www.disability.gov.uk

The word 'abuse' covers a variety of different behaviours ranging from neglect to actual violence. Abuse can be institutional (the way in which an organisation works) or individual (through a particular behaviour). It can take place in the home or in a care setting, and can consist of only one act or many repeated acts. It may be the professional care worker who carries out the abuse, or a service user, relative, friend or colleague. Irrespective of who carries out the abuse, no one should be treated in a way that causes distress or harm.

Assess the potential risk of abuse to the individual

One of the ways of assessing the likelihood of abuse taking place is to be aware of the situations where abuse has the potential to

REFLECT

Are there occasions when you have found it difficult to treat individuals equally? What were the reasons for this? What could you do to obtain help, advice and support?

occur. This means having your eyes and ears open to observe what is happening around you. If you are aware of the potential causes and signals of abuse, you will be more likely to predict potentially dangerous situations, and therefore respond promptly.

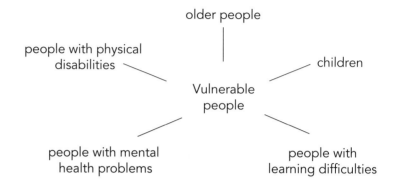

Causes of abusive behaviour

There are many reasons why people abuse others. One reason is to exert power and control over a vulnerable individual.

❑ Power and authority – where people believe they have the right to manipulate and take advantage of others.

❑ Stress – through tiredness, exhaustion, low morale, too much work, lack of time (often through staff shortages).

❑ Previous experiences – where those who have been abused treat others in the same way; often called the 'abuse cycle'.

❑ Organisational systems – where the general belief within an organisation is that vulnerable people need to be controlled. This can lead to abuse and reflects a lack of understanding about treating all individuals with respect and dignity.

❑ Lack of knowledge – being unaware of our own actions and their impact on others.

Assessing the risk

As a care worker, it is your responsibility to be aware of any likelihood of danger, harm or abuse occurring to those in your care. You also need to be aware of your own behaviour and that of other people in order to reduce the possibility of abuse taking

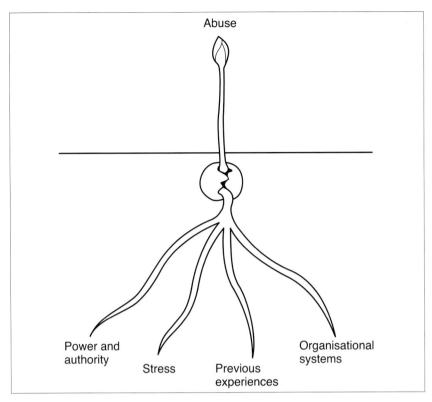

Fig 4.7 Recognising the 'root' causes of abuse can help to prevent it becoming established in your workplace.

place. It is part of your role to look out for any warning signs that may endanger yourself or others. One way of doing this is by being aware of possible warning signs that abuse could take place. Signals to look for:

❑ evidence or suggestions of aggression

❑ poor body language or eye contact

❑ the use of language – language can be a very powerful weapon

❑ racist remarks or jokes

❑ reinforcement of negative stereotypes

Another way of assessing risks of danger, harm or abuse, is to carry out a risk assessment. A risk assessment should identify potential dangers and suggest ways of reducing those risks. Risk assessments are carried out as part of a team, and final decisions are usually made by the team manager who has access to all of the facts. It is important to remember that care workers have a duty of care to make sure that the interests and wellbeing of service uses are at the forefront of any assessment or decision-making.

REFLECT

A valuable skill for all care workers is being able to predict situations where there is a risk of abuse. Sometimes the way an individual acts can indicate that something is happening to them. Make a list of what might you see or hear that could warn you of an abusive or potentially abusive situation.

Difference of opinion regarding abuse

Occasionally there may be differences of opinion about the extent or seriousness of abuse taking place. Individuals involved may deny that anything is wrong, even where there is evidence to the contrary.

There are many reasons why views may differ. Sometimes a service user will be resigned to the situation, and accept their treatment as normal because they regard it as a part of being old and vulnerable. Individuals may be afraid of reporting abuse because of the possible consequences. Whatever the reason, you need to be aware that even if abuse is taking place, those involved may not react in a way that you expect them to. You will need to deal with the situation in a calm and supportive manner and to reassure the individual of your support, while respecting their opinions and decisions. However you must accept that you have a responsibility to protect those in your care and forward your concerns to your line manager.

Individuals' abilities to cope with actual or likely abuse

People react differently to the risk of danger or harm; some do not want help or support, others may not be able to acknowledge the situation or make their concerns known to others. This could be because they lack communication skills, or are confused and frail. It is therefore important that you make a careful assessment of the individual's ability to understand what is happening to them and support them to make their own decisions about the necessary action. If you feel that the service user is unable to recognise the situation they are in and there is an immediate risk, you should report the incident and get help as soon as possible.

POINTS TO NOTE

Questions to ask yourself when assessing an individual's ability to cope with danger, harm and abuse:

- Are they aware of what is happening around them?
- Are they able to make any concerns known?
- Are they able to acknowledge or recognise potential risks?

Protect individuals from actual or likely abuse

It is important for those working in care to protect both themselves and those in their care from dangerous, harmful or abusive situations. There are many ways of guarding against such occasions. Everyone applying to work either with children or vulnerable adults will be subject to a criminal records' check in order to obtain a disclosure certificate. Regular training and supervision will also be provided to help you deal with potential situations in your workplace and to help you recognise your duties and the professional guidelines available.

It is important in situations of potential abuse to try and predict any occurences before they actually take place. This is easier if you know and understand those in your care. When faced with unacceptable behaviour from team members or service users:

- ❏ try to estimate as quickly as possible how serious the problem is, and how you plan to deal with it

- ❏ seek assistance if you are alone

- ❏ stay calm both in your behaviour and tone of voice – speak slowly and clearly, maintain eye contact

- ❏ find a quiet room for discussions, to avoid distressing others

- ❏ avoid arguing – be assertive but not aggressive

- ❏ treat the person involved with respect and empathy.

Abuse is more likely to take place when staff are under pressure and experiencing increased stress. Often this is because of staff shortages, working for long periods alone, lack of knowledge and skills or low morale within the team. It is important to be aware of these warning signs so that if necessary you or your colleagues can seek help and support.

REFLECT

Why might individuals be reluctant to report abuse?

FIND OUT

What the warning signs linked to abusive situations might be.

CASE STUDY

Mr Smith (a service user in your care) has a hospital appointment for a check-up. You take him to the hospital and are asked to wait. Mr Smith is showing signs of becoming more upset and agitated at having to wait. He starts to shout and act in an aggressive manner. Everyone in the waiting room looks distressed and uncomfortable at the outburst, and begin to complain to the receptionist.

Think about the following questions:

- Why might this situation have the potential to lead to an abusive episode?

- Why do you think Mr Smith became aggressive?

- What could you have done to prevent this from happening?

- How could you deal with this situation in an assertive manner?

- How might the environment have an influence on abusive behaviour?

CARE VALUES

Care workers have a responsibility to protect individuals from potentially harmful situations. It is therefore vital that you are aware of the possible signs and symptoms of danger, harm and abuse.

Observe signs or symptoms of abuse

Types of abuse

There are five main types of abuse:

TYPE OF ABUSE	EXAMPLE OF BEHAVIOUR
Physical	Hitting, burning, pushing, restraining, slapping, hair pulling
Psychological	Shouting, swearing, ignoring, humiliating, teasing, threatening
Sexual	Unwanted sexual attention, rape, assault, sexual interference
Financial	Withholding or controlling money, unauthorised use of individual's property (money, valuables, pension book)
Neglect	Deprived of food, warmth, clothing, comfort, cleanliness, medication or social activity

Individuals can suffer from one or more forms of abuse.

Fig 4.8 Abuse can occur at all levels and between a variety of individuals.

Effects of abuse

Abuse often takes place in secret, and therefore may not always be obvious. However, there are several signs which you can look

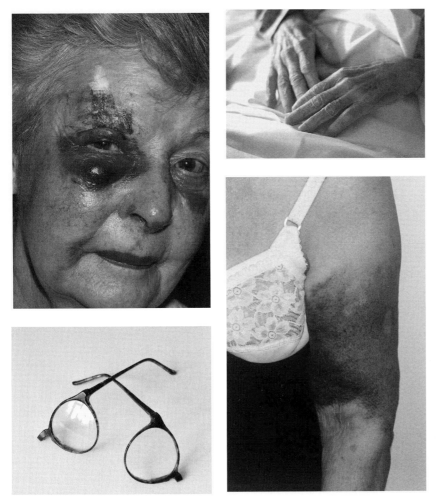

Fig 4.9 Evidence of abuse is not always this clear.

☑ ACTION

Before reading any further, make a list of all the signs you can think of that might lead you to think an abusive situation is occuring with one of your service users.

Then ask an experienced colleague for their list.

Compare your findings. Are there any differences? If so what are they? and why might they have come about?

---

out for, which may indicate that someone is being abused. Often individuals will appear anxious or depressed, and have low self-esteem which causes them to be withdrawn. There could also be evidence of disturbed sleep patterns. As a care worker, there are several signs and symptoms that you should be aware of.

Possible warning signs of physical abuse:

- ❏ bruises, cuts, lacerations, puncture wounds, black eyes, burns, bone fractures
- ❏ poor skin condition or hygiene
- ❏ loss of weight
- ❏ physical signs of being restrained, marks around wrist or neck
- ❏ person telling you they have been hit, kicked or mistreated.

Possible warning signs of psychological abuse:

- ❏ withdrawn and uncommunicative, hesitation to talk honestly
- ❏ emotional, upset, fearful or agitated
- ❏ sudden unexplained change in behaviour
- ❏ confusion or disorientation
- ❏ person telling you they are being verbally or emotionally abused.

Possible warning signs of sexual abuse:

- ❏ bruises around breasts or genital area
- ❏ anal or vaginal bleeding

Fig 4.10 Talking about abuse can be difficult and emotionally charged for all involved.

Fig 4.11 What might lead you to think this individual is suffering from some type of abuse?

❑ reluctance to undress, bathe or change clothes

❑ recurrent urinary tract infections

❑ individual telling you they have been sexually abused or raped.

Possible warning signs of financial abuse (often in older people):

❑ sudden changes to wills or bank accounts

❑ the withdrawal of large amounts of money by another person

❑ bills frequently unpaid, especially when someone else has responsibility for paying them

❑ unexpected appearance of relatives previously disinterested

❑ different signatures on cheques, or the addition of other names for an older person's bank account.

Possible warning signs of neglect:

❑ poor personal hygiene, unclean or inadequate clothing

❑ skin problems such as rashes, sores or lice

❑ malnourished or dehydrated

❑ dirty living conditions, often with a smell of urine or faeces

❑ withdrawal, excessive amounts of time spent alone

> **REFLECT**
>
> Many of the 'warning signs' may not be linked to abusive situations. How can you be sure? What action should you take?

👍 POINTS TO NOTE

Suspected situations of abuse can be identified through:

- self-disclosure by the individual
- care worker recognising signs and symptoms
- reported concern from a third party (friend, relative, other professional care worker)
- care worker reporting stress and problems with coping.

REFLECT

Procedures for dealing with abuse

Each place of work will have set procedures for dealing with danger or abuse in the workplace. As a care worker, it is your duty to make yourself aware of these procedures and what your specific role is in dealing with danger and harm.

Disclose information about actual and likely abuse

In situations where you have to intervene in order to deal with observed or reported abuse, you need to keep the service user involved at all times. You should respond in a way that causes the least possible disruption to the individual.

You may be asked not to tell anyone about what has occurred. 'Never promise not to tell' – withholding information, which may result in harm to others, is beyond your professional responsibility. It is your duty to break confidentiality wherever there is a risk to others. Following any observation or disclosure, be clear that you will report the incident, but only to those who need to know. This is the only way to protect those involved.

CASE STUDY ✍

You are on duty when a service user's relative strides into the dayroom and starts to shout at you and act in a very aggressive manner.

- How would you deal with this situation?
- Why is it so important to deal appropriately with behaviour such as this?

CASE STUDY ✍

You notice one morning that Bethan has bruises on both her arms. Initially she is reluctant to tell you what has happened, but later she calls you over to tell you that another member of staff caused the bruises and has been quite aggressive with her. She clearly does not want to let anyone else hear and tells you not to say anything.

- How should you respond to Bethan and why?
- Why might Bethan be reluctant for you to report the abuse?

Develop trust and communication with individuals and key people

Trust is an important part of any relationship between carers and service users, especially when individuals are vulnerable and dependent. Often people who are experiencing abuse are reluctant to provide details. They may feel upset or guilty for disclosing the information, and may worry about the effect it could have on them or others. There is also the possibility that they could have been threatened 'to stay quiet' by the abuser. The following points may help you to respond to disclosure in a way that maintains and promotes trust:

- ❑ Listen carefully to the disclosure or information been given.
- ❑ Make sure you explain the legal requirement to report any evidence of abuse, but that information will be treated in confidence, with only those who *need* to know being informed.
- ❑ Do not react negatively (verbally or non-verbally) to what is being said.
- ❑ Know your limits – do not become too involved; refer to a senior colleague if you are getting 'out of your depth'.
- ❑ Do not ask leading questions.
- ❑ Make sure that your discussion is carried out privately.

Avoid putting yourself and others at unnecessary risk

As a care worker, it is important to think about how you can deal with people in a way that avoids putting yourself and others at risk, and reduces potential conflict. Sometimes the way we deal with individuals can provoke a negative reaction in them, which can result in aggression or violence. You need to find ways of working, particularly where there is the risk of conflict, that will calm the situation.

Alert appropriate people and organisations to abuse

You must act quickly if you think or know that abuse is taking place and individuals are in danger. You have a legal responsibility to report any suspicions or evidence you may have that abuse is taking (or taken) place.

It is important to take seriously the person who is reporting abuse. Listen carefully to what they are saying, and demonstrate empathy. It may not be easy to listen to such reports, due to the content and nature of the information. However, it is essential that you do not react out of your own emotions but respond in a calm, professional and supportive manner.

> **REFLECT**
>
> Think about an occasion where you had to deal with an actual or potential risk of danger, harm or abuse. How well do you think you dealt with it? Is there anything you would have done differently? Why?

> **REFLECT**
>
> What actions of yours could trigger negative reactions from others?

> **REFLECT**
>
> How would you feel if you were asked to work an extra shift because a colleague phoned in sick? How would you ensure that you did not let your feelings influence how you treated your service users?

149

CASE STUDY

In the residential nursing home where you work, a colleague has told you that he has been loaned a large sum of money by one of the service users. Although she is able to write her name herself, she suffers from early onset dementia.

- What type of abuse is being experienced?

- What professional issues does this raise?

- How should you deal with this information?

You must report the information to the person in charge as soon as possible, and submit a written report.

Confidentiality

As a care worker, you are likely to access a great deal of personal and medical information about your service users. It is important that you maintain the confidence of those in your care by ensuring confidentiality at all times.

CASE STUDY

Mabel tells you that she is being physically abused by another service user. She wants action to be taken and asks for your help.

- What would you advise Mabel to do?

- Do you think Mabel has the right to confidentiality? Why/why not?

- How would you deal with this situation?

The reasons why you should maintain confidentiality include the following:

- ❏ There is a legal requirement to do so.

- ❏ It helps develop trust and respect with your service users.

- ❏ You may lose your job if you breach confidentiality.

- ❏ It helps to maintain safety – sharing personal information about an individual makes them more vulnerable to abuse.

In the main, you should obtain consent from individuals before sharing any information with others. However, as discussed elsewhere in the book, there are occasions when you may have to disclose personal information and break confidentiality.

FIND OUT

. . . about the types of information that must be kept confidential. Make a list and think about how you would ensure confidentiality in each case.

Legislation and policy

A recent report by the Caldicott Committee recognised that there may be occasions where service user information needs to disclosed in the best interests of the individual, and highlights principles to help identify those situations:

- Information shared should be on a strict need-to-know basis in the best interests of the service user.

- Do not confuse confidentiality with secrecy.

- Informed consent should be obtained, although there may be occasions where this is not the priority.

- It is inappropriate to give assurance of absolute confidentiality in situations of abuse, particularly when there are vulnerable individuals involved.

CASE STUDY

You have noticed that Kwane, a new member of staff, has become quiet and withdrawn, and you ask him what the matter is. He tells you about a conversation he had with a service user who told him that he did not want to live any longer, and had asked his wife to bring some tablets in for him to take.

- What should you advise Kwane?

- What are the arguments against keeping this information secret?

CASE STUDY

You overhear two members of staff discussing a service user on a staff night out. Their conversation went something like this:

Ed: How much longer do we have to look after Harold?

Fran: Why?

Ed: Because I've had enough of him calling for us every two minutes. I've lost count of the number of times I've had to clean him up when he hasn't managed to get to the toilet on time.

Fran: I know. Do you know, he told me the other day that it really upsets and embarrasses him when he has an accident.

Ed: Well, if I was him I would be ashamed of myself too. It's about time he did something about it.

- In what way are these colleagues breaking confidentiality?

- What potential may there be for an abusive situation to develop?

Record and report abuse

You must report any incident of either actual or suspected abuse, or evidence of any risk of danger as soon as possible to your manager. You may also need to make a written report of the incident as this may be required to investigate the incident at a later date. Information must be recorded clearly and accurately and as soon after the event as possible. Your memory for the actual details will lessen over time. Make sure you know the correct procedures to follow in your place of work. Good communication and team work are essential in situations involving abouse.

👍 POINTS TO NOTE

When responding to a reported disclosure or actual risk of abuse:

- Make a record of your evidence, making sure it is accurate, factual and recent – do not jump to conclusions.
- Stick to the facts and do not use emotive language.
- Inform senior staff of your concerns.

Legislation related to suspected or alleged abuse

LEGISLATION	CONTENT
Mental Health Act 1983	Protection for those unable to manage their financial affairs because of a mental health disorder or learning disability
Children Act 1989	Legal right for children to be protected from abuse
Health and Safety at Work Act 1974	Protection in the workplace from violence and danger. Risk assessments are carried out
Care Standards Act 2000	Protection for vulnerable service users from abuse. Individuals considered unsuitable to work with vulnerable adults to be placed on a register

Legislation and policy

The only legislation that relates specifically to abuse is for the protection of children from abuse. However, there are many laws related to all areas of care work, which make provision for the protection of vulnerable individuals. Within the workplace there are also different policies and guidelines which provide a framework for protection. You need to make sure you are aware of the policies and procedures in your own workplace.

Legislation and confidentiality

The Data Protection Act 1998 and Access to Health Records Act 1990 make it a legal requirement to keep recorded information confidential. All places of work must have policies and procedures relating to the confidentiality of information.

Types of confidential information that are covered by the Data Protection Act 1998:

- spoken
- written
- on computer.

The Act also establishes an individual's right:

- to confidentiality – unauthorised people should not have access to information about them
- to refuse to provide information
- to know what information is being kept about them and have access to the information
- that information about them should be up-to-date and accurate, and not stored for longer than required.

CASE STUDY

Read the following possible situations. What action would you take and why?

1 A friend of someone you work with telephones you and asks for their address.

2 A newspaper rings and asks for details about one of your service users.

3 A colleague asks what medication one of the service users is taking when they come on duty.

4 A relative comes into the office while the manager is talking to the doctor about one of the service users.

Fig 4.12 Remember your notes can be read by other people. If the information is confidential – protect it.

Summary

In this chapter we have looked at some key areas which will help you to ensure that your own actions support the care, protection and wellbeing of individuals. You should always:

- ❑ respect the choices made by individuals
- ❑ empower individuals to take control over their own life and make their own decisions
- ❑ treat and value people equally
- ❑ respect their dignity and privacy
- ❑ acknowledge and respect the differences between people
- ❑ ensure that you do not discriminate against people because they are different
- ❑ protect individuals from the risk of danger, harm or abuse
- ❑ be aware of the warning signs and symptoms that abuse may be taking place
- ❑ ensure that you deal appropriately with situations of danger, harm and abuse, reporting and recording any incidents appropriately.

UNIT HSC241

Contribute to the effectiveness of teams

> **→Introduction**
>
> For this unit, you need to show that you are able to participate effectively as a team member. Most work in care involves working as part of a team, whether in a residential home, hospital, in the community or elsewhere. Wherever you work, good team-working skills are vital to providing effective and high-quality care for your service users. This involves being able to build good relationships with other people, and developing personally and professionally as an individual.
>
> In this unit you will learn:
>
> ❑ how to agree and carry out your role and responsibilities within the team
>
> ❑ how to participate effectively as a team member.

★ KEY WORDS

TEAM	A group of people who work together to achieve a set of common aims and objectives.
MULTI-DISCIPLINARY TEAM	A team consisting of different professionals, such as physiotherapists, nurses, carers and doctors.
MULTI-AGENCY TEAM	A team made up of people from different organisations such as social services, the health service or voluntary organisations.

Agree and carry out your role and responsibilities within the team

To help you meet the requirements for this section of the unit you will need to know and understand how to:

❑ review information and seek advice about the team's objectives and purpose

❑ clarify your own and others members' roles and responsibilities

❑ carry out your own agreed role within the team

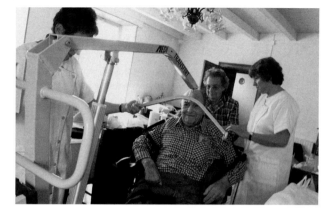

Fig 5.1 Teamwork – central to the work of a carer.

❑   evaluate and use feedback constructively

❑   take responsibility for your own development and learning

Review information and seek advice about the team

A team is a group of people who share a common purpose and work together to achieve that aim. This does not mean that everyone does the same job, but that everyone works together within their role to achieve the same goal. For example, a team of footballers all have different tasks; some may be defenders, some scorers and some goal-keepers. Despite their different roles, they all have the same objective – winning the game – and so they work together in order to achieve that aim. It is the same within the area of care work. Each member of staff may have a different role; some may be care assistants, some trained nurses and others administrators. However, they all share the same aim or goal – of providing high-quality care for individuals.

Teams may also be multi-disciplinary or multi-agency. Each person may have a very different role from the others, but they still work together with a shared aim of improving the health and wellbeing of the service users in their care.

All members of the team need to be clear about the purpose and objectives of the team as a whole. If someone does not know the reason why they are doing a job, or the purpose of their role within the team, it will be more difficult for them to feel that they can contribute towards the overall aims of the organisation. This might have an effect on the success of the team as a whole, and result in team members not fulfilling their potential. If you do not know what your team's objectives are, you need to find out by talking to your supervisor or manager.

Clarify your role and responsibilities

Your role within the team will depend on several factors;

❑ what expectations other people have of you

❑ your written job specification agreed at interview or appraisal

❑ how you see yourself developing within your role.

It is important that you are able to identify, agree and clarify your role and responsibilities, and how they contribute towards the overall objectives and purposes of the team. Think about what type of job you are required to do, or which areas you are responsible for at work. Are you responsible for getting individuals out of bed in the morning? Is it your job to record their menu choices? Are you required to contribute towards keeping written records of individuals up-to-date?

You may find it helpful to write down the different responsibilities within your job, and discuss them with colleagues and your manager for clarification. However, you must remember that while some aspects of your role will be easy to identify, others may not be so clear. You also need to take care not to be inflexible about what is and is not your role or responsibility. Good team work requires you to be willing to help others where necessary, and cooperate with other team members in order to achieve the overall purpose of the team.

👍 POINTS TO NOTE

These three issues are important when examining your role and responsibilities:

1 Identify – understand your role and responsibilities. What are you expected to do, and what the underlying purpose is?

2 Agree – once you understand what your role involves, you need to be in agreement with what is expected of you. If you do not agree, you need to talk to your manager or supervisor about it.

3 Clarify – make sure that you are clear about what is expected of you. If you are confused about your role, it can result in unnecessary conflict. You may need to ask for further clarification from your supervisor.

The roles and responsibilities of other team members

For a team to work well and be effective, there will be a mix of different roles and responsibilities within the team. Different people will bring different skills and characteristics to the team. Some people may have particular leadership qualities (such as motivating others) and therefore work in a leadership role, while others may be good at creating new ideas or being organised and practical. Many things will influence these different roles, eg:

❑   level of training or qualifications

❑   extent of experience

❑   personal skills and knowledge.

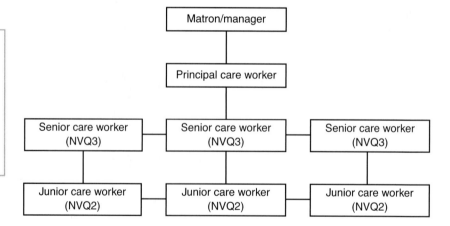

Fig 5.2 How does your organisation compare to this chart? Where does your job role fit?

Although there may be many different roles within your team, it does not mean that they are less or more important from any other. For a team to be effective, each person's role needs to be equally valued and respected by the other members of the team. It can sometimes be helpful to think about these different roles like the parts of the body. Each part of the body has a different function; even though the eye has a very different purpose to the leg, each is important to the overall functioning of the body.

Contributing to the team and its activities

In order to be an effective team member, you not only need to know what your own role is, but also how you personally contribute towards the objectives and purposes of the team. A team is only successful in terms of meeting its objectives and achieving its purpose when every member of the team carries out their own role and responsibility effectively, and shares the same aims and vision.

John Adair, an expert on leadership, used a Venn diagram to demonstrate the importance of both individuals and groups in producing an effective team.

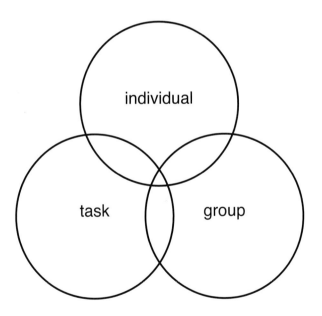

Fig 5.3 Notice how the different aspects interlock with each other.

From this diagram you can see that an effective team needs all three aspects to be functioning well. If you only have two pieces working the following might happen:

Group and task	The job might be completed, but individuals within the team may feel their personal contribution is not valued and therefore may lose motivation.
Group and individual	This may result in a happy and first-rate working environment, but the jobs may not be completed.
Task and individual	The consequence of ignoring the group is that people might do their own thing and pull in different directions, causing conflict.

REFLECT

Consider the advantages of working as part of a team. What difference does it make to your working life?

You can contribute towards team activities, objectives and purposes by:

- ❑ showing willingness to help and contribute to the team
- ❑ working in a way that respects others
- ❑ communicating with others effectively
- ❑ dealing with any problems promptly and appropriately
- ❑ being keen to learn and develop in your role
- ❑ having an awareness of how your role contributes towards the overall objectives of the team.

Carry out your agreed role within the team

Once you have identified, clarified and agreed your role within the team, you need to be able to carry out that role effectively and willingly. If you do this, the team is more likely to be successful in terms of providing the best possible care for the service users and creating a place where individuals feel respected and valued.

How you carry out your role is very important. If you do your job reluctantly or constantly complain about what you have to do, you may still complete the task but your attitude will contribute towards an unpleasant atmosphere to work in. You need to make sure that you work in a way which shows you to be enthusiastic, eager to help, reliable and trustworthy.

A successful team where all members carry out their role and responsibilities effectively might have the following characteristics:

- ❑ a common purpose and shared objectives which are known and agreed by all members
- ❑ each member knows and agrees their own role and those of other members

❑ ability to support each other in achieving the common purpose

❑ trust and communication with each other in an open and honest way

❑ a leader whose authority is accepted by all members.

Evaluate and use feedback from others constructively

It is not always easy to accept feedback about our performance. Can you remember how you reacted to a particular grade you were given at school for some work you completed? Do you remember receiving your school report which highlighted an area of your performance that needed improvement? Did you protest and complain, or did you accept the remarks graciously and try to improve your work, taking into account the comments made? Feedback is an important part of professional development, and without it we would find it very difficult to know how well we are performing or what we could do to improve.

Feedback can be either informal, such as discussing issues as they arise with your colleagues or supervisor, or be a more formal process, as in a written review of your performance or appraisal. Your manager or course tutor will be involved in this process.

Whether feedback is informal or formal, you should welcome any comments about your performance as it can help you to know how well you are doing and what you need to do to improve. We may feel that we have done a good job, but it can be beneficial if another person tells us what they think we did well. Likewise, it can be helpful for highlighting areas of our performance that need to improve, in order to achieve our individual targets and goals. This might include learning a new skill or achieving some other area of personal development.

It is important that you see feedback as a positive experience and learn to accept feedback about your performance graciously. Here are some points which may help you:

❑ Try to listen without interrupting – do not try to defend yourself. Allow the person to tell you how they feel.

❑ Keep an open mind.

❑ Try to learn as much as possible.

❑ Take action on the areas where you agree with the feedback. Think about the consequence of your actions, whether there have been misunderstandings,

> **REFLECT**
>
> Think about an occasion where you were given feedback. In what way did it help you?

> **FIND OUT**
>
> . . . about what system is used in your workplace to provide feedback about your performance.

and how you might want to approach situations differently in the future.

❑ Give feedback in return.

☑ ACTION

Meet with another colleague you work closely with, and practise giving constructive (helpful) feedback to one another.

• What did you find helpful about this process?

• Did you find it easy to do this? Discuss the reasons why.

Take responsibility for development and learning

Good team work is not only about being able to work as a part of a team, but about developing as an individual. Work in care requires constant change, and this means that you will be continually developing new skills and understanding. You may be required to take on new roles and responsibilities, or gain expertise in a different area, or you may need extra support to carry out an existing responsibility.

Identifying your strengths and weaknesses

In order to monitor your personal development, it is important to evaluate how well you feel you are doing in terms of carrying out your roles and responsibilities. It is useful to carry out this process with your supervisor or manager who will be able to offer you any extra help you might need.

❑ Identify your own strengths – particular aspects of your work where you feel competent and knowledgable.

❑ Identify areas for further development – this may be an area where you feel inexperienced or find difficult, eg a certain task you want to be able to accomplish more effectively.

❑ Set a goal or target – set out what you actually want to achieve; eg do you want to deal with an area of conflict with another team member more effectively?

❑ Make a development plan of how you will achieve your goals and what help you might need in order to carry out your responsibilities more effectively. This might involve some sort of in-service or external training.

You might want to use a chart such as this to help you with this process:

STRENGTHS	AREAS FOR FURTHER DEVELOPMENT	GOALS OR TARGETS	DEVELOPMENT PLAN – How you will achieve your goals

It is important that you evaluate this process regularly to assess your development and progression. It can be very encouraging to feel that you are achieving a goal.

Participate effectively as team member

To help you meet the requirements for this section of the unit you will need to know and understand how to:

❑ inform other members of the team of your activities

❑ ensure your behaviour to others in the team supports the effective functioning of the team

❑ accept and use suggestions and information offered by others constructively to improve your practice

❑ manage your time effectively

❑ offer ideas and information to improve team working

❑ deal with differences of opinion and conflicts constructively

Inform other members of the team of your activities

When you are working as a part of a team, you need to remember that you are not working on your own in isolation. This means that you will need to develop certain skills in order to communicate constructively with other team members and let them know what you are doing. Communication is dealt with in more detail in Chapter 1.

Informing other people of your activities helps to:

❑ build an effective team where each member is respected

❑ solve potential problems

❑ show you are committed to the team and to the overall objectives of the team

CARE VALUES

Being able to recognise what your strengths are and where you best fit into a team will help you to fulfil your potential and feel valued as a team member. When people feel that they are developing and achieving personal goals and ambitions, their self-esteem and confidence increases. This results in a more effective team and a better service for the individual.

REFLECT

Think about the team you are working in. What works well and what hinders effective team-working?

❑ provide effective care to your service users, and ensures that each person's needs are addressed effectively

❑ maintain your own safety and protection.

Each person has a different way of communicating; some styles are helpful, others are less so. If you are secretive or unwilling to share information with your colleagues, this is likely to have a detrimental effect on the team. People may feel you are withholding important information, which may result in lack of trust. Others may feel that they have nothing to say because they do not feel very confident in their role, and that what they say will be unappreciated. It is important to remember that every person in the team is vital to the effective functioning of the team, and that each role is equally important.

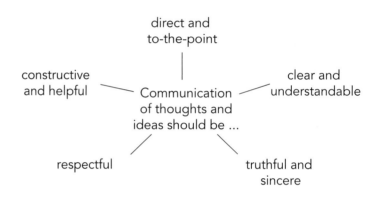

Communication within a team takes place either informally or formally. Informal communication involves everyday conversations that happen while carrying out your routine responsibilities. Formal communication involves communicating relevant information as part of the organisational procedures, such as team meetings or writing up care plans.

Fig 5.4 Handover meetings are essential to the smooth running of the team and seamless care for the individual.

Fig 5.5 Active listening – central to effective team-working.

There is often a set time to communicate important information about individuals with other members of the team. An example of this is when there is a changeover of staff. It is essential that those coming on duty know what has happened while you have

---

✎ CASE STUDY

You have noticed that when you work on the same shift with Brenda, she appears reluctant to work with anyone else or discuss anything with the other members of the team. She often cannot be found, as she never tells anyone what she is doing or where she is. When you mention this to her one day, she tells you that she does not understand why everyone should know her every move and what she is doing all the time.

- What might be the consequences of Brenda's behaviour?

- How would you respond to Brenda?

- What would you do to emphasise the importance of communication within the team?

Legislation and organisational policy and procedures

Whatever method (written or spoken) is used to communicate information, it is important to consider which information to share, to whom and what basis. Confidentiality involves sharing information on a need-to-know basis, which means that you only tell certain information to the people who really need to know it. It is your responsibility to ensure that you work within the bounds of confidentiality, and respect your service user's rights to have personal information about them only shared when there is a legitimate reason to do so.

All care organisations have a confidentiality policy that sets out the legal requirements for keeping information safe. Make sure you have read your organisation's policy on confidentiality.

FIND OUT

The Data Protection Act 1998 is the main piece of legislation relating to confidentiality, and refers to any information relating to individuals, whether it is written, spoken or held on a computer.

- Find out about and make a note of the main principles of this Act.

- Work out how these principles affect your role.

CARE VALUES

Principles that underpin effective team-working:

- trust and support
- shared objectives
- good communication
- reliability, commitment and cooperation within the team
- motivation and accountability of individuals
- individuals who know their own roles and responsibilities, and how they fit in to the overall objectives of the team
- respect for other people's ideas and opinions.

It is clear that this type of team will work well together and produce a positive, supportive and encouraging environment to work in. It is also more likely that the team will achieve its goals and objectives, and be a team where people can develop to their full potential.

REFLECT

Think about and list all the different types of unhelpful behaviour there can be within a team.

been working. This will include any significant happenings that have taken place with the individuals for whom you have been caring. It is important that at these meetings each member of staff is encouraged to contribute their ideas and thoughts. Written records are another way of passing on important information, such as documenting incidents or important events.

Support other members of the team

The way you behave within the team is important to the effective functioning of the team. Team work involves building good relationships for working effectively with other team members. You need to understand and respect the feelings and views of others, even if you do not share those feelings and views. This is known as 'empathy'. Your behaviour also needs to demonstrate that you respect the other team member's views and roles, and that you treat others with consideration, understanding and courtesy.

However, it is a sad fact that not all behaviour within teams is constructive. You may find that the way some people behave or act is unhelpful or detrimental to the overall effectiveness of the team.

A list of unhelpful behaviours might include:

- ❑ aggression – being bad-tempered, abrupt with people
- ❑ easily offended – excessive seeking of sympathy
- ❑ domination – being self-centred and power-led
- ❑ competition – always wanting to be first or the best
- ❑ fooling around – being silly and joking all the time

People behave in unhelpful ways for many reasons. Sometimes they may feel that they are not a valued member of the team, which can lead to frustration and a lack of cooperation. Some may not fully understand the objectives or goals of the team or where their particular role fits into the overall picture; others may not like a fellow team member.

We all bring our own personalities, characteristics and ways of behaving to a team. Often, these are formed from our past

☑ ACTION

Look at the diagram and discuss how each style of interaction might affect the overall functioning of the team.

experiences. Although some aspects of our behaviour may be difficult to change, as care workers and team members you have a responsibility to ensure that you act in a way that is positive and constructive to the team as a whole.

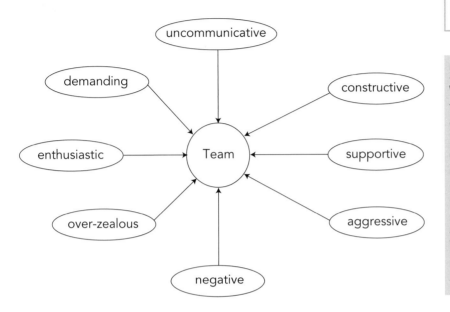

Fig 5.6 *Many of these styles are present in a team at the same time. How could you handle each one?*

Improve your practice within the team

As we saw earlier in the chapter, feedback is a very important and useful process for helping us to improve our performance and role within the team. To be a good team worker and in order to develop your potential, you will need to accept and make the most of any suggestions you are given by others to improve your practice.

CASE STUDY

In team meetings, David always seems to have an answer for everything and does not allow anyone else to contribute to discussions. When someone does offer any suggestions, David frequently undermines them. When working with other colleagues, he regularly takes charge and makes all the decisions, even when the other person is more senior.

- In what way is David's behaviour unhelpful?

- What effect might David's behaviour have on the effective functioning of the team?

- Why do you think David is behaving in this way?

Some people may find that they are given feedback regularly; others may find that feedback is infrequent and insufficient. Do not wait to be given feedback if you are unsure about how you are doing; you should actively seek feedback about your performance. However, you will need to take care that you are not continually seeking feedback, as this might suggest that you are lacking confidence and unsure of yourself.

Remember that feedback is most useful if it is specific or focused on one particular aspect of your work. You could ask questions such as:

❑ What do you think my strengths and weaknesses are, in terms of communicating with people?

❑ Could you tell me how well you think I performed with bathing that individual?

❑ How well do you think I deal with relatives?

Feedback is not really useful until the issues raised are dealt with, and you use it to improve the way in which you practice. This process is an important part of being a reflective practitioner. This means that you reflect or think about the suggestions you have received and work out a plan to address those issues. It can be useful to write down the suggestions you have been given in your feedback and make a record of your professional development. This will help you to see the skills and knowledge that you have developed and what your priorities are for the next few weeks or months.

CASE STUDY

Rachel is a new member of staff and has been asked to make an appointment with her supervisor to talk about her performance at work and any issues of concern. She tells you that she is worried about this meeting.

- Why might Rachel be worried?

- What would you say to Rachel to reassure her?

Offer supportive and constructive assistance to team members

Working as a part of a team involves being flexible about what is and is not your job. For example, if a colleague needs your help with a particular task, you need to be willing to offer help and support in whatever way you can. If you refused to provide assistance, this would not contribute towards a good working environment and might result in anger or frustration; this would have a negative impact on the overall effectiveness of the team. A refusal to help you could also have a negative impact on the care being provided to individuals.

Being mutually supportive when necessary will help to build the team spirit, and raise morale and confidence in one another.

REFLECT

In what way do you offer support and assistance to your team members? Is there anything else you could do to be more helpful and considerate?

CASE STUDY

Jo finds it difficult that she has to do all the practical work while Mary sits in the office, according to Jo 'doing nothing all day'. One morning, Jo passes the office and hears the phone ringing. Mary is not there because she is dealing with some relatives. Jo decides not to answer the phone because it is 'not her job' and 'why should she have to do other people's jobs for them, when she has enough to do already?'

- Is Jo working in a way that supports others and is constructive to the team?
- What are the consequences of having this type of attitude within a team?
- How would you help Jo to change her attitudes?

There are many ways you can offer support to your colleagues, but essentially it requires you to observe what is going on around you and recognise the situations where people may need help and encouragement. For example, you could offer help in the following situations:

- ❑ if someone is overwhelmed by the amount of work they have to do
- ❑ passing on any information you have which will help team members
- ❑ where a new member of staff is nervous or lacking in confidence
- ❑ encouraging someone who has achieved a new task to develop even further
- ❑ where someone is struggling with their work because of a personal problem.

Sometimes offering help can be taken in the wrong way. Some people may feel that you are undermining them and that you do not believe they are capable of performing a certain task. It is therefore important that you use your communication skills well when offering support, and think carefully about the words you use with some people. However, if you act in a way that shows you genuinely want to help your colleagues, you are not likely to cause offence.

Complete your commitments to other team members

Work in the caring profession can often be demanding, and teams of carers will often have a heavy workload. It is important that you share this load with your colleagues and do not shirk your duties. Being reliable is an essential requirement for a good team worker and you can do this by:

❑ being punctual for work – if it is unavoidable that you arrive late, apologising for any delay will convey the fact that you are committed to the team.

❑ phoning promptly to report any sickness

❑ not objecting when asked to do something which is a reasonable part of your role.

❑ always finishing a task even if it means finishing work a few minutes late.

CASE STUDY

Andrew has arrived late for the third time this week, and when asked why by the manager, responds abruptly saying that he does not know. The manager suggests that he quickly joins the rest of his colleagues in carrying out the morning tasks, and he grumbles as he starts work.

- What effect might Andrew's behaviour have on the rest of the team?
- What could Andrew do differently so that the team works effectively?

REFLECT

Do you manage your time well? If so, how do you do this; if not, why not?

REFLECT

You need to be responsible and know your own work role. You are accountable to both your line manager and your service user.

Time management and accountability

How you manage your time is crucial to the effective working of the team. Sometimes this can be difficult, especially when you have a heavy workload. There can be many demands made upon your time from other colleagues, service users and your manager. How you respond to these different expectations is important if you are to be an effective team worker and accountable for what you do.

❑ Define the priorities – work out what needs to be done first. It is important that in doing this you also consider the individual needs of service users and treat each person equally.

❑ Know your boundaries – working with your line manager decide what you are responsible for within your work role and what tasks fall outside this; eg what you are not expected to do, such as dressings or giving out medication.

❑ Personal reflection – if you are finding it difficult to manage your time well, there may be a good reason. Think about why you are finding it difficult, and talk to your manager about it.

Running out of time

Rushing through your tasks might mean that the level of care you give is unsatisfactory. For example, you might be tempted to leave someone in the bath while you go and deal with another person. This might save you time, but it is potentially dangerous and does not show a very good level of care. Carers have to balance caring for the individual needs of all service users with the amount of time they have. This might mean that you are not able to complete some tasks.

It is important that when you feel that you cannot complete a specific task within a certain time, you immediately inform the relevant people – your colleagues, and sometimes your manager – before the situation becomes worse. If you identify that there is a problem, there may be something that can be done to help. If you struggle on alone and delay calling for assistance, it may be too late and someone may even be harmed.

CASE STUDY

One of your colleagues has just phoned in sick, and your manager tells you that extra help will be available but only after lunchtime. You are responsible for helping eight service users to rise, washing and dressing them and giving them breakfast.

- What would you do?
- How would you prioritise your time in a way that is efficient but also puts the needs of service users first?

Offer ideas and information to improve team-working

As a team member you are responsible for contributing towards an effective team. This involves offering suggestions or ideas about how to improve the performance of the team. You should be willing to contribute towards the team in this way, and regard yourself as a valuable member of the team. Even if you feel less experienced than others and therefore feel that you have nothing to contribute, you can still offer helpful ideas. Sometimes new members of the team can see things in a more objective or detached way. When you have worked somewhere for a long time, it can be difficult to see the things that need to be changed.

When you are offering suggestions, remember that information is most useful when it is:

- ❑ clear and direct
- ❑ realistic and achievable
- ❑ relevant to the objectives of the team.

Fig 5.7 When trying to change a method of working, remember positive – negative – positive.

It is important when suggesting ideas that you do so constructively and in a way that is positive and benefits the team. Sometimes you may want to suggest a course of action because you think the present way of doing things is unhelpful or harmful in some way. However, if you criticise or pick holes in the present process, you may upset someone unnecessarily. You should always try to say something positive before and after you disapprove of something. It can be helpful to see this process as being like a sandwich, with the positive feedback as the bread surrounding the middle section of negative feedback.

☑ ACTION

Try giving some suggestions for improving something where you work. Use the format identified above to help you to do this in a positive way.

CASE STUDY ✍

Farad, a care worker, has noticed that two members of staff are always arguing. This has been going on for several weeks, and the service users are starting to notice. He wants to do something about it, but does not know what to say.

- Using the illustration of a feedback sandwich, how would you offer suggestions or help in a positive way to these members of staff?

Deal with differences of opinion and conflicts constructively

A good team does not just happen; it needs to be led well and requires all team members to be committed to working together. Because people are different, within any team there is likely to be a range of opinions and views. If these are valued and respected the team can work well together. However, if differences of opinion are not handled well, conflict can arise.

Identifying that there is a problem is very important and a necessary first step in finding a solution to the problem. When we find someone difficult, there is a tendency to concentrate on all their negative characteristics and ignore any positive attributes they may have. It can be helpful with people you either do not like or have little in common with to make a special effort to think about those aspects of their personality or character that are positive. You can focus on the things that are helpful by:

❏ making a list of all the positive things about the person – are they good at a certain task, or particularly kind to someone?

❏ complimenting them for something that they did well, or perhaps for a new hairstyle or outfit.

Because relationship problems tend to be very emotional, it can be useful to think more objectively about a resolution. The following diagram shows the process you can work through to solve any problems you may have with others.

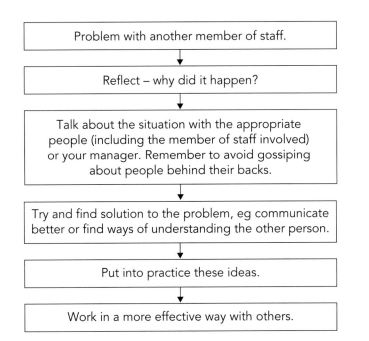

Fig 5.8

CARE VALUES

In any team there may be relationship problems or areas of conflict between some members. These might manifest themselves as:

- personality clashes
- poor communication
- disagreement
- rivalry or competition between colleagues.

It is important to deal with problems quickly before they have an influence on the effective functioning of the team. When there is conflict, it is important to stop and reflect on what has happened and why. Is there anything you could have done differently to avoid the problem? It is important to learn from your experiences so that you can address the issues involved and become a more effective team member.

REFLECT

Think about the members of your team. Which members do you work well with, and which do you find difficult? What do you notice about these two lists? Why do you work better with some people more than others? Is there anything you can do to improve your relationships with those you find difficult?

FIND OUT

Think of a another member of staff that you either do not know very well, or do not get on well with. Take time to find out their likes, dislikes and interests. You may find that you have something in common!

Take care not to be too intrusive, especially if you have not talked in any detail with them before, otherwise they might just think you are being nosy!

REFLECT

At which stage is your team at? If you are not at the performing stage, what steps could be taken to move the group forward? You may want to discuss this with your colleagues and manager.

Dealing with conflict

Conflict is seen as one of the stages in the development of a normal team, which means that if there are disagreements within the team, it can be beneficial *if* they are handled appropriately. There are four stages to team progression and growth, which have been identified as: forming, storming, norming and performing.

Forming
Individuals within teams meet each other and learn the objectives of the team and the roles and responsibilities of the team members. (Remember, if the team members change, there will be a new team)

↓

Storming
Team members may disagree and argue with each other and evidence of personality conflicts may emerge as people get to know one another. This stage can feel like everything is going wrong, but if handled well, can be helpful in building a strong team where issues can be aired and dealt with effectively.

↓

Norming
The team begins to settle down, learns to accept each other's roles, is able to make shared decisions and compromise where there is an area of disagreement.

↓

Performing
The team starts to work effectively; individuals feel confident about their roles and the group becomes more supportive of each other. This is the stage where the team objectives can be achieved.

Fig 5.9 Storming can be a useful part of team development.

CASE STUDY ✍

The Claremont Residential home has been open for six months. There are 13 members of staff and a few vacancies to fill. Even though the team members do not know one another very well, things appear to be settling down and each member of staff seems to be aware of their own roles and that of the other team members. The manager is pleased that the home is functioning well and that there are no difficult problems to deal with regarding staff relationships.

- At what stage of development is the team at Claremont Residential home?

- What might happen as the team develops and grows together?

Stress

When any member of a team is stressed, it can be both upsetting and harmful. However, if the whole team suffers from stress, the effects can be disastrous.

In order to recognise stress in any member of the team or even yourself, it is important to be able to recognise the symptoms of stress. These may include:

- ❏ low standards of work

- ❏ illness and frequent absences from work

- ❏ hostile, intimidating or unfriendly atmosphere

- ❏ specific targets or deadlines not met

- ❏ lack of effective communication and cooperation

- ❏ members not trusting one another

- ❏ gossip, infighting and cliques

- ❏ poor timekeeping – lateness for work, long tea and lunch breaks

- ❏ low morale, poor self-esteem and lack of confidence.

CARE VALUES

There are many potential barriers which prevent teams from working effectively together. These include:

- unhelpful behaviour (aggression or argumentativeness)
- unfair workloads
- factions or cliques
- stress (either individual or group stress).

REFLECT

Think about your workplace. Can you think of any potentially stressful situations? How do you know that people are stressed (what evidence is there)? What do you think is the cause of the stress? What could be done about it?

CASE STUDY ✍

Mohamed is not looking forward to going to work today. Everyone is always stressed and irritable, and this makes him feel worse. Several colleagues have gone off sick with stress-related symptoms, and this has meant that agency staff have to come in each day to help. He never knows who he will be working with. He cannot even talk about it to his manager, because she is always shouting and showing that she to is under pressure.

- What might be the problem here?

- If you were in charge, how might you deal with this situation?

Controlling stress

The most important way of reducing stress is to identify its cause. Stress can be caused by many different factors, although one of the most common causes of team stress is lack of direction: no one knows what they are meant to be doing, so the team drifts aimlessly. Here the team needs to be reminded about the team objectives and their individual roles and responsibilities within the team. Whole team meetings may be helpful in order to highlight any particular problems, and individual team members may need extra support.

Resolving conflict

Some people are better at dealing with conflict or difficulties than others. Use the following checklist to identify how well you deal with difficult situations:

STYLE	BEHAVIOUR
Avoidance	• avoids talking about the problem • ignores the problem • denies that there is a problem
Accommodating	• tries to cooperate even when they may not meet their own personal or team goals • non-assertive behaviour
Win/lose	• confrontational and aggressive • must win at any cost, even if it means that relationships will be harmed
Compromising	• cooperative • suggests a compromise between team members in order to achieve objectives and maintain good relationships
Problem-solving	• acknowledges that all members have valid needs • openly confronts the problem • encourages everyone to deal with disagreements and to express opinions • actively looks for a solution to the problem

It is important to remember that it is illegal to discriminate against another person, and this is true for other team members. Specific legislation that relates to the rights of those working in teams includes:

❑ equal opportunities policies

❑ policies relating to bullying and harassment

❑ anti-discriminatory legislation.

As a member of a team it is helpful to be aware of these policies, but there are other things you can do to challenge inappropriate behaviour in the workplace:

❑ Do not join in with racist jokes – they may seem harmless at first, but they can provoke tension, offend others and are against the law.

❑ Avoid arguments about controversial issues.

❑ Set a good example to others by respecting each member of the team equally.

Seek appropriate advice and guidance when you experience problems

It is important to remember that not all problems are easily solved; this is especially true for personality clashes. However, even though you might not get on with someone personally, it does not mean that you cannot respect them for the job they do, and work together effectively. If you have worked through the process identified above and still cannot resolve the problem, you may need to put the issues aside for the sake of the team and 'agree to disagree', bearing in mind that if the situation deteriorates, you may need to have further help.

If you still experience problems with another member of the team, it is important that you know where you can go for extra support. The first step is usually your manager or supervisor, and it is important that you talk to them as they should be able to offer you the support you need and help you find a solution to the problem. They may be able to provide any training you require to help you work more effectively within the team.

If the manager is the person with whom you are having trouble, you may need to go elsewhere for help, especially if there is evidence of bullying or discrimination. If there is a senior manager you could contact them, or if you are a member of a trades union or professional body, you can seek advice from them.

A person who reports wrongdoing at work is known as a 'whistle-blower'. There needs to be *clear* evidence of misconduct or illegal behaviour before action is taken to deal with it. Often people are afraid to report abuse or wrongdoing in the workplace for fear of being found out and being punished as a 'whistle-blower' by the organisation. However, the Public Disclosure Act 1998 was designed to offer protection to whistle-blowers so that they are free to report problems.

CARE VALUES

Sometimes problems such as inappropriate behaviour may arise because of prejudice or discrimination; eg making discriminatory remarks about someone. There are various kinds of prejudice at work; see chapter 4 for more information.

FIND OUT

Write down the main points of the equal opportunities policy and procedure in your workplace.

Fig 5.10 Sometimes becoming a 'whistle-blower' is the only way to protect your service user and the organisation you work for.

Summary

In this chapter we have looked at ways which can enable you to be a more effective team member. You should know how to:

❏ identify, clarify and agree your own roles and responsibilities and those of the other team members

❏ recognise how these can contribute towards the overall objectives and purpose of the team

❏ evaluate and use feedback about your performance constructively

❏ seek support from other people to help you to develop in your role

❏ ensure that your behaviour is constructive and contributes towards supporting the team

❏ manage your time well, ensuring that you complete your commitments within specified timescales

❏ make a positive contribution to the team by offering suggestions, ideas and information

❏ respect the opinions and beliefs of other team members, even if they differ from your own

❏ ensure that you deal with differences of opinion or conflict constructively, and seek help where necessary.

Contribute to the moving and handling of individuals

→ Introduction

As a worker in the care sector, you will be actively involved in the moving and handling of individuals, and you will need to recognise the importance of maximising a person's independence. Every task that the care worker does for their service users and the way that they carry out the task is important, but the need to ensure that moving and handling is carried out correctly is essential, both to the carer and the person for whom they are caring.

The care we provide today should be person-centred and tailored to each individual's needs.

As a care worker, you need to build up a relationship whereby the individual begins to trust you and accept the support they are being offered. You can do this by always treating your service users with respect and dignity. However, you also need to be aware that you have a responsibility under health and safety to follow your organisation's policies and procedures with regard to moving and handling. The consequences of not following correct moving and handling techniques can be severe:

❏ You can cause injury to the individual.

❏ You can cause injury to yourself and others who work with you that may result in litigation.

By not following correct procedures, you may cause your service user to experience pain and discomfort, which will greatly reduce their independence and feeling of wellbeing.

In this unit you will learn:

❏ how to prepare individuals, environments and equipment for moving and handling

❏ how to enable individuals to move from one position to another.

The level of assistance required by individuals to move may vary; eg helping them to get out of their chair, to being fully dependant on care staff to carry out all moves. You may work with:

❏ individuals who will cooperate with the move

❏ others who will not have the understanding to cooperate

❏ others who may be unconscious.

★ **KEY WORDS**

INDIVIDUALS	The people who require services.
MOVING AND HANDLING	The process of assisting individuals to move from one position to another.
RIGHTS	The rights of an individual to be respected, treated equally, treated as an individual, have dignity and privacy maintained, and cared for in a way that meets their needs and protects them from harm.
HAZARD	The potential to cause harm.
RISK	The probability of a hazard occurring.
RISK ASSESSMENT	Assessing risk so it can be reduced to the lowest level possible.
LEGISLATION	The law relating to moving and handling policies and procedures.
SERVICE USER	An individual who receives care and support from your organisation.

CARE VALUES

In promoting independence, the carer should seek only to assist an individual to do what they cannot do for themselves. You need to be aware that the approach you use will send messages to individuals, and you want to be sure that the right message is received to make sure that you get full cooperation from the service user.

Prepare individuals, environments and equipment for moving and handling

To help you meet the requirements for this section of the unit you will need to know and understand about:

- ❑ infection control
- ❑ principles of safe moving and handling
- ❑ what is a hazard
- ❑ how to carry out a risk assessment
- ❑ how to promote independence
- ❑ the consequences of not moving and handling safely.

Infection control

Prior to commencing any moving and handling activity, carers need to be aware of the risk of cross-infection (passing diseases or organisms from one person to another) to the individuals we care for. You can minimise this risk by following your organisation's guidelines on personal hygiene.

Uniforms

Uniforms are a form of protective clothing. They protect both the service user and the carer from cross-infection. However, if the uniform is not laundered correctly it can become the cause of cross-infection.

Uniforms are also used as a means of identification; they identify carers to service users, relatives and other professionals who may be in need of assistance. Uniforms need to be of a suitable design to allow the carer to move freely with no restrictions.

Footwear

In a care environment, footwear is very important. Wearing the correct type of footwear affords protection both to the service user and the carer. Shoes should be comfortable, toes and heels enclosed with a flat or low heel to provide stability when moving and handling; this should reduce the risk of strain or injury to the back.

Jewellery

Minimum jewellery in a care environment should be worn. Jewellery can cause injury both to the service user and the carer; the skin of vulnerable elderly individuals can tear easily, so care should be taken to reduce this risk.

Jewellery can also harbour bacteria, which can be passed onto to others within the care setting.

Hair

Hair should be neat and tidy at all times. It can harbour bacteria, so should be washed frequently and tied back if long.

Skin

Cuts and grazes should be washed and covered with a waterproof dressing to prevent infection.

Hands

Hand hygiene is a most effective way of reducing cross-infection. Hands should be washed using correct hand-washing techniques and cleansing solution. This should occur prior to commencing any activity within the care setting, and after completing tasks.

Risk assessment

When preparing to carry out a moving and handling task, there are specific things you must be aware of before starting. You need to know if:

- ❑ the task has been risk assessed
- ❑ you are aware of the risk assessment results
- ❑ any equipment is required to complete the move.

FIND OUT

What policies does your organisation have in regard to personal hygiene? Where are they kept? Do they cover all of the above? What suggestions could you make to improve them?

When commencing a task, how do you assess the situation? There is a simple format that can assist you to risk assess the task, called TILEE. This stands for:

❑ **T**ask

❑ **I**ndividual capability

❑ **L**oad

❑ **E**nvironment

❑ **E**quipment.

As carers you will be risk-assessing situations all the time, although you might not be aware of it. When assessing any situation, ask yourself the following:

Task

❑ Does the task need to be undertaken?

❑ Will the load require holding away from the body?

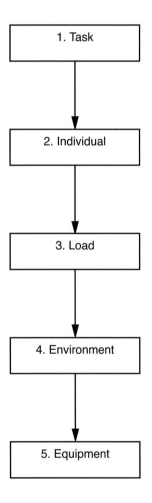

Fig 6.1

❑ Does the task involve twisting, stooping, stretching, pushing or pulling for long distances?

❑ Are you working at different heights, eg commode, bed or chair?

❑ Is the task repetitive? Is there time for rest and recovery?

❑ Do you have to carry or hold the load for long periods?

Individual capability

❑ Have you and your team members been trained in moving and handling?

❑ Do you or they have any previous injuries?

❑ Are you of the same height and ability?

❑ When working with another colleague, do you both understand the issues involved to coordinate the task?

❑ Are they/you wearing suitable clothing and footwear?

❑ Are they/you aware of your limitations?

Load

❑ What can the individual do for himself or herself?

❑ Is the individual tall, heavy, unpredictable, uncooperative, confused, agitated or nervous?

❑ Is the individual unwell, in pain, tired?

❑ Can the individual communicate or understand?

❑ Is the individual's clothing hindering the task?

❑ What is the individual's skin condition?

Environment

❑ How much space is available?

❑ Are the floors uneven, slippery or unstable?

❑ Consider the lighting (very important for night staff).

❑ Consider the access.

❑ Is the bed too low, up against the wall, heavy to move?

Equipment

❑ What equipment is available?

❑ Is the equipment fit for the purpose?

❏ Has it been well maintained?

❏ Have you been trained to use it?

❏ Is the equipment accessible?

❏ Do you have to wear protective clothing, gloves and aprons?

The risk assessments that your employer carries out are general risk assessments, usually completed at the initial care planning stage. However, risk assessments should be reviewed at regular intervals as although the environment may not change, the person or persons involved will. No two moves will ever be the same, so it is important that you use the checklist each time you carry out an activity.

Carers working within the health care sector are at significant risk of injury from manual handling tasks. In order to reduce the risk, legislation exists to protect employees from manual handling injuries. However, welfare legislation such as the National Health Service and Community Care Act 1990 and the Care Standards Act 2000 place duties on care organisations to meet the individual needs and requirements of service users with dignity and respect. Under the Health and Safety at Work Act 1974, employers not only have a duty to protect their workforce from injury, but they also have duties towards non-employees including service users, which include 'not exposing them to risks arising from their employees' activities'.

Using risk assessments

Your employer should have their own care plans and risk assessments for all aspects of the organisation. However, if required, there should be specific risk assessments for manual handling. These risk assessments will usually be found in the individual's care plan. Care should be taken to check care plans prior to starting any moving and handling activity. This helps to ensure that you have up-to-date information such as:

❏ the individual's capabilities

❏ any assistance required

REFLECT

Risk assessments should be completed within 24 hours of admission, and reviewed as often as necessary. Does this happen in your care establishment? How do you know? How do you find out the results?

CASE STUDY

Mary is a resident at the home where you work. She had a stroke two years ago and cannot move the left side of her body. She has asked you to help her get out of bed, as it is nearly time for breakfast.

• How would you prepare Mary for the move from her bed to a chair?

• Think about TILEE. How would you prepare the environment?

- ❏ how many carers are needed
- ❏ any equipment you might need to use.

All risk assessments are a working tool. This means that although the risk assessment was relevant at the time of completion, they can be subject to change, depending on the condition of the individual. This means that as a carer you need to be aware that although you have checked the individual's risk assessment, you must *still risk assess* the present situation.

Moving and handling of individuals

Manual handling is the movement or support of any load by physical effort. It includes:

- ❏ lifting
- ❏ putting down
- ❏ pushing
- ❏ pulling
- ❏ carrying or moving.

RISK ASSESSMENT FOR CLIENTS WHO REQUIRE MANUAL HANDLING

Name

Weight

Height

Mobility	good	fair	poor
History of falls	yes	(no)	
Assistance required	(yes)	no	sometimes
Can the client weight-bear	(yes)	no	sometimes
How many carers are required	none	(one)	two
Understand instruction	(yes)	no	sometimes
Ability to participate	(yes)	no	sometimes
Require walking aids	(yes)	no	
Which aids are required	walking stick	(Zimmer frame)	wheelchair
Is any equipment required	yes	(no)	
Which equipment required	hoist	slide sheet	banana board
Requires assistance with	walking	(standing)	toileting
	Transferring		bath
	in/out of bed		
Handling constraints	skin	pain	catheters
Other			

Control measures   *carer to assist service user when rising from a chair or bed*

FIND OUT

The example risk assessment, is easy to complete. Compare it with one from your own establishment. Consider the following:

- Is the information covered comprehensive?

- Does it inform you of what you need to know to carry out moves successfully, without putting either yourself or your service user at risk?

- How could the format be improved (if necessary)?

REFLECT

Imagine how you would feel if a complete stranger approached you and started touching your body. What would you think the person was doing? What would your reaction be? Would it be any different from your service user who has dementia?

CARE VALUES

When providing care, always look beyond the label of the disability. Speak to people as you would wish to be spoken to yourself. If conflict arises about the way you are expecting to move someone, explain and negotiate with them to ensure compliance with the requirements of your organisation.

Respect for the individual

The individual who is going to be moved is the key person to consider and should be actively involved in decisions about the best way to carry out a move. Unless the person is unable to contribute at all due to mental or physical illness, you should consult with them and discuss the most comfortable way of completing the move. Remember that many individuals will have had a disability for a long time, and will be very experienced in how to deal with it. They will know the most effective way to move which will cause them the least pain and discomfort, so it makes sense to ask them.

It is important to remember that you tell the individual what you are going to do each time you assist them. As we get older we can experience problems with our short-term memory, so do not assume that because you completed the task at lunchtime, the individual will understand what you are going to do at teatime. You should communicate with your service user in a way that makes it easy for them to understand. If you are using equipment, explain what the equipment is for, and demonstrate it to them if necessary; this helps to allay fears. Often when carers think that individuals are being uncooperative, it is because the individual does not understand what is happening to them. For people who are experiencing some form of dementia, each time you approach them you might be seen as a stranger who is trying to do personal things; naturally, this will alarm them.

Fig 6.2 Mutual understanding helps to keep everyone involved in the movement safe.

Safety of the Carer

When completing risk assessments, account must be taken of the carers as well as the service users. If the preferred way of moving for the individual puts the carer at risk, then other ways of completing the task must be explored. As a carer, you have a duty of care towards your service users, but your employer also has a duty towards you. This means that if the individual requires a hoist to move them and they refuse to use it, your employer has to find a solution. It is not good enough to expect you to lift someone because an individual refuses to acknowledge the risk assessment and the risk involved.

Working Together

Once you have carried out all the necessary assessments, you should then explain to the individual exactly what you intend to do and how you expect them to contribute towards the move in a safe way. This will vary according to a person's ability, but most people will be able to contribute in some way; care should also be taken to communicate with people who appear to have no understanding due to mental disability or who are unconscious – you should still explain what you are doing and why.

Safe Environment

When assisting someone to move, care should be taken to ensure that the surrounding environment is free from obstacles and hazards, so that the move can be completed safely. When the move is complete, the environment should be tidied and anything which was moved returned to its familiar place to make sure that individuals are not confused by changing environments. Before moving items that belong to one of your service users, always seek permission first.

CARE VALUES

Every person has the right to be treated with dignity and respect, and to have procedures explained to them rather than have things done to them which the carer thinks are best. Each stage of the move should be explained to individuals in a manner, level and pace that they understand. Time should be given for the information to be absorbed. The consent of the individual should be obtained before commencing the move. Moving an individual when they are unprepared can lead to unsafe practice and could be deemed as abuse.

CASE STUDY

The individual's risk assessment says that a hoist is required to transfer the individual from bed to chair. The bedroom that the individual uses is a small one, which has a bed, wardrobe, dressing table, chair, television and a small table in it. As carers, you can manage to get your service user from the wheelchair into bed without the hoist, and the individual is happy with this. However, although you can manage, it does mean that one of the carers has to climb over some of the furniture, and the other carer has to stretch over the bed.

- What could you do to resolve the issues raised?

Now think about a service user being cared for in their own home with the same issues.

- Would the procedure that you follow be the same?

- Could you enforce changes under health and safety?

- Find out what the law says about working in someone's own home.

FIND OUT

All organisations have procedures for recording and reporting faults. Find out your organisation's policy and your responsibility in relation to this. Keep a copy in your portfolio.

Equipment

Within your place of work you may use many different kinds of equipment, including several different types for lifting and moving. It is important that you check each time you use the equipment that it is safe for its intended use, and that it is suitable for the individual you are going to use it with. If you find that equipment is unsafe by being worn or damaged then you should:

- ❏ stop using it immediately
- ❏ take it out of service
- ❏ report it to your manager
- ❏ put a notice on the piece of equipment to inform others that it is unsafe
- ❏ record it in your communication book.

It is important that you do this, even if it means you have to reassess the situation and look at other ways of moving the individual. If the individual is non-weight-bearing and it is the hoist that requires attention, it may mean that the individual has to be cared for in bed until the equipment is repaired, rather than everyone involved being exposed to risks from unsafe equipment.

CASE STUDY

Mrs Smith, who is normally physically independent, is sitting in her chair in the lounge. It is lunchtime, and as you walk by, she asks you for assistance to get up out of her chair. What would you do?

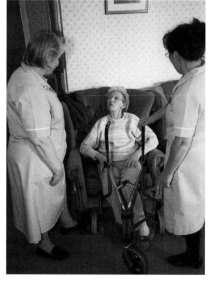

Fig 6.3

Points to think about:

- What is the individual normally capable of?
- Has anything happened that day?
- Where can you get information from?
- Who can you get information from?
- Are there any changes to the environment?

Now think of Mrs Smith living at home – is there anything different you would do?

- Would you know what the individual was capable of?
- Would you have as many sources of information?
- Are there enough resources to help you?
- Would you need to seek medical help?

> ### 👍 POINTS TO NOTE
>
> When you have looked at the previous case study and identified what might have happened, where to get information from, and what to do next, you will have completed a risk assessment!

Seeking help

After assessing the situation, remember to think about your own capabilities. Are you trained to be able to complete the task competently? If not, you should seek the help of an appropriate person to assist you. Do not feel that you are letting anyone down by admitting that you need help; you have a responsibility towards yourself and the people you care for to provide care in a safe way.

> ## REMEMBER   ☺
>
> When completing a manual handling task:
>
> ❑ check the risk assessment
>
> ❑ consult with your service user
>
> ❑ encourage them to participate as much as they can
>
> ❑ ensure equipment is safe to use
>
> ❑ stop the activity if the individual requests, or if there are indications that the moves are now unsafe due to changes within the environment or to the individual.

Enable individuals to move from one position to another

To help you meet the requirements for this section of the unit you will need to know and understand about:

❑ how to promote independence

❑ equipment used in moving and handling

❑ policies and procedures which relate to manual handling

❑ how to record and pass on information.

Promoting independence

When completing an individual's care plan and risk assessment, it is important to include as many people as possible in the discussions and decisions. Some of these are included in the diagram:

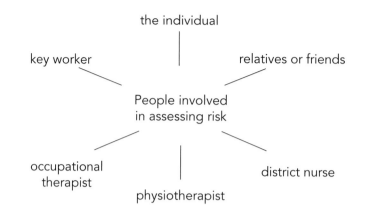

On admission to care establishments, people can experience a sense of loss of:

- ❏ home
- ❏ partner
- ❏ personal belongings
- ❏ identity
- ❏ independence.

This can lead to depression, which can cause them to lose interest in their surroundings and daily life. This is when carers can play an important part in providing person-centred care and making the individual feel that they and their wishes are important, giving them choice in all things and empowering them with decisions which affect their lives.

👍 POINTS TO NOTE

Once the risk assessment is complete, the care team will then have the required knowledge on which to make a decision about the best way to move the individual. They should have identified:

- any physical condition which might have an affect on the way the individual is moved
- any mental disability which might have an affect on the way the individual cooperates with the move
- any changes which might be needed to the environment
- any equipment that may be needed for assistance.

Equipment used for moving and handling

There is a large variety of equipment available to help us in completing moving and handling tasks safely. These include:

❑ hoists and slings which must be used if the individual is not weight-bearing

❑ transfer boards, designed to assist in the move and take some of the weight

❑ lifting handles, eg to enable the individual to pull themselves up the bed

❑ slide or glide sheets, enabling individuals to be moved whether or not they can assist

❑ wheelchairs which are used to move individuals from one area to another.

Hoists

There are many hoists on the market, which can assist service users with different needs. These include:

❑ Mobile sling hoist – eliminates need for any moving and handling, used for moving individuals (eg bed to wheelchair), should not be used over long distances.

❑ Toileting and standing hoists – enable an individual to be lifted or transferred from sitting to standing.

❑ Mobile seat hoists – enable an individual to be lifted and transferred in a seat as opposed to a sling; they are usually found on baths.

❑ Mobile stretcher hoist – enables an individual to be lifted or transferred while in a semi-reclined position.

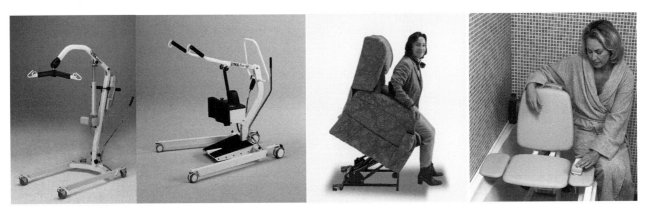

Fig 6.4 Before using any equipment – risk assess and make sure that you can use the equipment safely.

When using hoists, remember to make sure that you use the correct sling for the hoist and the weight of the individual. Each

REFLECT

Many individuals will be upset by the thought of having to be moved with a hoist. This may have a negative effect on the way they contribute to the procedure.
What do you say or do with your service user when using a hoist? How do you avoid upsetting service users?

individual should have had an assessment and the correct sling made available to him or her.

Ensure that you follow the manufacturer's instructions for the use of the sling and hoist. Only attempt to move the hoist using the steering handles, to ensure stability. Place the sling around or under the individual (making sure you use the correct loops) and attach to the hoist. Raise the individual just enough to allow movement (you do not have to raise them to a great height), and move or transfer as appropriate.

You should be aware that to use a piece of equipment correctly, you need training; you should not use any equipment if you are unfamiliar with it. If you are unsure about what to do, seek advice from a senior member of staff.

Slide boards

These are used to slide an individual from one level to another (eg bed to wheelchair, and visa versa). They are designed for use by individuals who only need assistance to transfer, although the care worker may need to reassure and encourage individuals to make good use of them. Slide boards are built to various designs and colours.

Slide sheets

These require the assistance of at least two people standing on opposite sides of the bed. Slide sheets allow individuals to be moved up and down the bed with assistance, or sometimes the individual can use it themselves under simple instruction. They can be used regardless of the level of consciousness of the individual.

Fig 6.5 *Service users may need plenty of reassurance during transfer with a slide board.*

Fig 6.6 Never use slide sheets on your own.

Monkey pole or lifting handle

This is a handle which is fixed above the bed. It is for use by individuals who can help themselves. They will need to have some upper arm strength to be able to pull themselves up and change position.

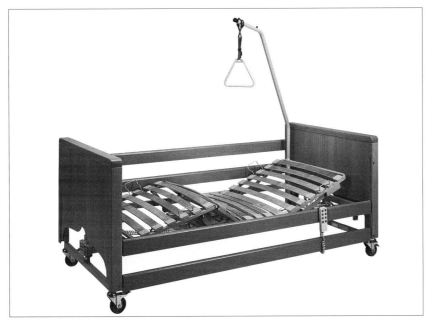

Fig 6.7 Service users with limited arm strength cannot easily use this equipment.

Wheelchairs

When using wheelchairs, it is important to remember that individuals should have been assessed and supplied with their own wheelchair. Problems can arise if you are using a wheelchair designed for someone 5ft 2in tall, with an individual who is 6ft tall; you would have difficulty placing their feet on the footrests, and may cause them pain and discomfort in the process. Wheelchairs also need regular servicing, and footrests and safety belts must be in place at all times. Remember that if you remove footrests from the wheelchair without a risk assessment in place, you would be accountable if individuals injured themselves. Always ensure that the tyres are pumped up, otherwise the brakes could potentially fail.

REMEMBER

When you are assessing how to move someone with equipment, you need to:

❑ look at the risks

❑ look at individual capability

❑ discuss options with the individual.

If conflicts arise between you and the individual about the way they could be moved, try to explain the risks, making suggestions on how best to move them. If you cannot reach an agreement, seek assistance from a senior member of staff.

FIND OUT

Make a list of the equipment that you have in your care setting. Make a note of where it is kept. Check to see when it was last serviced, and that you know how to use it. Take time to read the manufacturer's instructions.

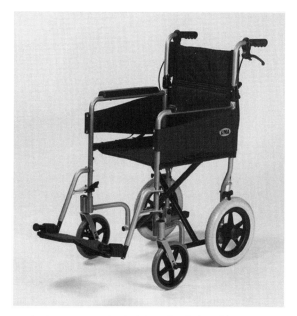

Fig 6.8 When was the last time you checked the safety belt and footrests on your equipment?

Moving and handling techniques

This next section should be used alongside formal, practical training. Never attempt to move or handle anything without the appropriate training first!

As a worker in a health care environment, your organisation has a duty to ensure that you are working in a healthy and safe environment. There will be policies and procedures in place regarding the moving and handling of individuals, which advocate no lifting. There should be very few situations in which a care worker would be expected to lift, unless there was an emergency situation. In stating that individuals are never lifted manually, the policy refers to lifting the whole, or a large part, of the weight of the individual. The policy should not prevent a carer from giving assistance to an individual, or from using pushing or pulling movements, or upward or downward force in order to achieve the move. However this is only acceptable if such forces are as low as is reasonably practicable, taking into account alternative methods and equipment. A safer handling policy often adds to the quality of care which an individual receives. Encouraging self-help stimulates individuals both physically and mentally. It can clearly reduce the effects associated with immobility, and can contribute towards the individual's physical rehabilitation where appropriate.

Principles of safe moving and handling:

Position of feet

Get a strong base to move from. The knee should point in the direction of the move, as this is the natural way in which the foot moves.

Position of the back

Keep it straight, in natural curved position.

Use leg muscles

These are the biggest and strongest muscles in the body. Practice makes perfect – develop good habits and increase flexibility.

Use a suitable grip

Take into account clothing and the service user's skin condition. Be aware of jewellery or watches which could cause injury.

Use momentum

Once an object is moving it is easier to move. The hardest part of pushing a wheelchair is actually starting to push; once moving, it is quite easy to maintain.

Keep object or individual close

The nearer to yourself, the lighter the object is (HSE Guidance, Manual Handling Operations Regulations, 1992).

Do not twist or bend

Use leg muscles and reposition feet rather than turning or twisting, which could cause serious injury to your back.

You only have one back

Medical science has not managed to replace this yet, so once it is broken, it is virtually impossible to repair. Look after it and develop good habits.

Assisting someone to move or transfer can be done with either one or two carers; this will be indicated on the individual's care plan. To assist a single carer, the individual will need to be able to contribute to the move or follow simple instructions. A slide board can be used, but if there are any complications, consideration should be given to using a hoist.

If you are assisting an individual who cannot assist with the procedure either because they are unconscious, confused or seriously ill, there should always be two carers present. Roll the person using the slide sheet onto their side and support them with pillows.

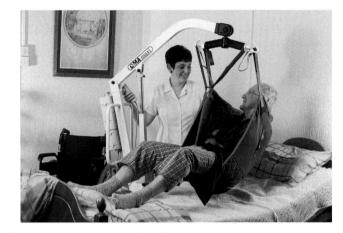

Fig 6.9 Keep your service user involved at all times.

> ## REMEMBER ☺
>
> If a move or procedure requires two carers, one carer must coordinate the move, while the other carer must follow the lead carer's instruction.

Recording information

A person's care plan should contain the required information on their moving needs. This includes:

- ❑ information about the most effective way of moving them

- ❑ any equipment required

- ❑ any technique which is used to enable the individual to move themselves.

This information should be recorded in a format which is easy to understand and readily available for carers to read. However, if you notice any changes which could have an effect on any of these points, it is your responsibility as a care worker to record the same and inform your senior that you have done so. Some of the things that might have an effect on the usual moving techniques used with an individual are as follows:

- ❑ The individual is unwell or in pain.

- ❑ There has been an improvement in the level of assistance needed.

- ❑ The individual has lost their confidence and feels unable to assist.

Any changes which you notice should be recorded in a clear and legible manner.

FIND OUT

What records are available to you in your organisation for recording your observations of a service user's mobility needs

REFLECT

How have you recorded changes to a service user's mobility needs? What changes could you make to improve your records?

> ## REMEMBER ☺
>
> Whether you are working in a care setting or in an individual's own home, it may be necessary to move items of furniture to enable you to complete the move safely. However, it is important to remember that you must return items to their original place to ensure that individuals can find personal items which are important to them, and feel reassured by their surroundings. This is especially important for individuals with mental disabilities. Consideration should also be given to infection control. Do not forget when giving care to individuals that it is always important to wash your hands and use protective clothing to prevent the spread of infection.

Example of observation record

DATE	OBSERVATION	OUTCOME	SIGNATURE
1.11.05	Mrs Smith has needed assistance to get out of her chair today.	Staff to encourage Mrs Smith to remain independent. Give simple instructions to Mrs Smith to enable her to get out of her chair. Staff to observe and monitor on a daily basis.	A.N.Other
2.11.05	Mrs Smith is still having problems getting out of her chair. I have tried her in a higher chair and this has solved the problem. However, Mrs Smith prefers to sit in her original chair.	An OT assessment has has been requested to higher Mrs Smith's chair. Until then, please encourage Mrs Smith to sit in another chair, and reassure Mrs Smith that she will be able to use her own chair when it has been raised.	A.N.Other
8.11.05	Mrs Smith's assessment has been completed and her chair has been raised.	Mrs Smith is now able to get up out of her chair without assistance.	A.N.Other

CASE STUDY

Mr James is being admitted to a residential home. He requires transferring from a wheelchair to an armchair. How would you proceed with this move?

Think about:

- information available at this time
- where might you access information
- factors you need to take into account
- communication.

Scope

In completing this unit, you also have to provide evidence that you have taken into account the communication needs of your service users (see chapter 1 for more information on this topic). You need to be aware of the limitations that some individuals may have, and strategies that you can use to overcome these. When completing an individual's care plan, attention should be given to the individual's preferred spoken language and the terminology used.

Think about what happens when we meet new people; we assess them by finding out about them, their families, their jobs and any other important life events. This way of working should also be applied to our service users. For example, one way of showing that we value our service users is by consulting with them. We need to explain what our role is, how we can work with them to achieve care goals, and of course we need to know that the individual understands this information. We can achieve this by being honest with our service users, having empathy and understanding and not using jargon. We should always treat service users on an equal basis with ourselves. We need to have good questioning and listening skills and know the difference between fact, opinion and hearsay. We need to know the difference between an individual's wants and needs, and the carer's wants and needs.

Only seven per cent of our communication is verbal; most of the information we receive is via body language. We also process information by the tone of voice that people use, and also the pitch and inflection. As carers, we need to be sure of the message being signalled. In sustaining relationships we need to be flexible enough to develop methods of communication that meet the needs of our service users. They should be encouraged to express their needs, wishes, and feelings towards ourselves and other care workers, as well as the organisation.

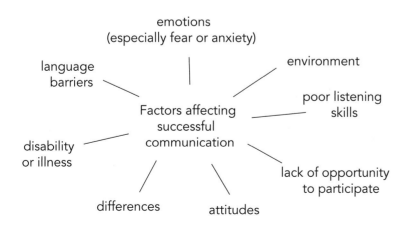

FIND OUT

The definitions of:
- fact
- opinion
- hearsay.

CARE VALUES

As care workers, we need to ensure that we value people. This can be demonstrated by:

- sitting down and being on the same level as the individual
- thinking about how we approach someone
- the tone of voice we use
- the body language we use
- our facial expressions
- the words and jargon that we use.

It is important to remember that to communicate effectively, everyone should be given an opportunity to participate. You will need to think of different ways which people have of communicating with each other.

CARE VALUES

Good practice means valuing people for their:

- individuality
- diversity.

Good practice requires you not to judge people by your own standards; you should be open-minded and work towards enabling individuals to resolve their own difficulties and make informed choices. We should be facilitators, rather than fixers. If individuals make decisions then they own them, they take responsibility for them and are accountable for them.

Once you have identified the barriers to effective communication, you can begin to do something about them. There may be practical issues to consider, such as the provision of a private place, the provision of an interpreter or just the presence and support of a staff member to encourage.

It is important to remember that being patient and taking the time to ensure service user understanding can lessen the chance of conflict arising.

Legislation and organisational policy and procedures

Your organisation will need to take into account legal and organisational requirements when moving and handling individuals. These should include personal beliefs and preferences which the individual may have in relation to the way they are moved. You as a carer need to understand that your organisational policies and procedures are a legal requirement and as such should be followed. If conflict occurs, you have a responsibility to help resolve any issues.

You should be actively supporting your service users by following the agreed plan of care and risk assessment when assisting your service users to move. When individuals require assistance with moving and handling, the care organisation will need to look at the management of other issues that this will cause; eg if individuals cannot move freely by themselves, this can have an effect on their continence. If the individual has no communication difficulties or mental disability, they can ask for assistance to use the toilet whenever they need to. However, if there are difficulties in communicating an individual's needs, this should be included in the care plan.

People working within the health care sector are at risk of injury resulting from manual handling activities. In order to control and reduce this risk, legislation exists which is designed to protect employees from injury. However, we still have a responsibility to ensure that individual needs and requirements are met while also ensuring that individuals are treated with respect and dignity.

Legislation related to moving and handling includes:

- The Health and Safety at Work Act 1974 (this places general duties on most people within the workplace, employers, employees, manufacturers, suppliers).
- Management of Health and Safety at Work Regulations 1999 (this places a legal duty on employers to implement suitable health and safety management systems).
- Manual Handling Operations Regulations 1992 (designed to reduce the risk of employees being exposed to those manual handling activities which present a significant risk of injury).

- Provision and Use of Work Equipment Regulations 1998 (states that equipment should be suitable for its intended use, be safe and maintained regularly, only be used by people who have had suitable training and be accompanied by appropriate control measures).

- Lifting Operations and Lifting Equipment Regulations 1998 (states that there is an absolute duty to carry out lifting operations safely and that equipment must have adequate strength and stability for its use, have the safe working load clearly indicated and be inspected by a competent person every six months).

Other legislation which you will need to be familiar with includes:

- Data Protection Act 1998

- Access to Medical Records Act 1988

- Access to Health Records Act 1990.

(All these acts relate to the confidentiality of information, which is the cornerstone on which we provide our services. Confidentiality must be maintained unless we feel that the information that individuals give us puts them or others at risk.)

- Control of Substances Hazardous to Health (COSHH 1988)

- Infection Control Guidelines (COSHH 2002)

These two regulations provide information on infection control.

Seeking help

If you are caring for an individual and are experiencing problems in following the risk assessment, you need to turn to other professionals for advice and guidance. Providing care to your service user in a safe way is central to everything you do.

It is important when caring for others to understand why we should encourage them to move to different positions. Individuals who cannot move freely can be prone to circulation problems, which can lead to pressure sores. Relieving pressure protects the skin and allows blood to flow freely.

FIND OUT

. . . where your organisation keeps their policies and procedures, individual care plans and appropriate risk assessments. Make notes on how to access these. Find out how access is achieved if you are working in the community.

CARE VALUES

Moving and handling techniques change over time; care organisations have a duty to update their staff on techniques which can be safely used, and to inform their staff of dangerous techniques.

👍 POINTS TO NOTE

The following techniques have all been banned:

- orthodox lift
- neck lift
- drag lift
- pivot lift/transfer
- Australian lift
- thru arm lift.

These lifts have all been proven to cause distress, pain and injury to individuals and carers. Some of the lifts are contributing factors in the development of pressure sores, and must not be used at all.

Summary

In this chapter we have looked at areas which should ensure that you move and handle individuals in a safe way. In order to support your service users in the best possible way and to keep yourself safe, you should always:

❑ wear appropriate footwear and clothing

❑ identify and assess any immediate risks to individuals

❑ work with individuals to ensure their understanding of the need to move and handle in a safe way

❑ provide active support to enable individuals to use their strengths and potential

❑ understand the different types of equipment and why they should be used

❑ identify and take appropriate action when behaviours and practice discriminate against individuals

❑ ensure that individuals have appropriate information about how to offer comments about their care.

7

Support individuals with their personal care needs

> ## → Introduction
>
> This unit applies to people who work directly with individuals to support washing, dressing and going to the toilet, whether in domiciliary, residential care or hospital settings.
>
> There are many reasons why people require help with their personal care needs. Whatever the reasons, your approach and attitude towards personal care is extremely important in maintaining an individual's dignity and self-esteem.
>
> In this chapter you will learn:
>
> ❑   how to support individuals to go to the toilet
> ❑   how to enable individuals to maintain their personal hygiene
> ❑   how to support individuals in personal grooming and dressing.
>
> You may find it helpful to read this chapter along side chapter 2. Both chapters highlight the importance of action to prevent cross-infection and other health and safety issues.

Fig 7.1 Providing personal care is a sensitive issue. For many service users the need to ask for help and support in this area of their life is 'the last straw' and the last thing they want to do. Your role is to support the individual's dignity and self-esteem whilst encouraging and enabling independance as much as possible.

★ **KEY WORDS**

ACTIVE SUPPORT	Support that encourages individuals to do as much for themselves as possible to maintain their independence.
COMMUNICATE	Methods of communication include the individual's preferred spoken language, the use of signs and symbols; pictures; writing; objects of reference; communication passports; other non-verbal forms of communication; human and technological aids to communication.
HAZARDOUS WASTE	Includes biological waste (eg bacteria, micro-organisms), chemical waste (eg cleaning agents) and human body waste (eg blood, urine, faeces, vomit), which could cause a risk to human health.
INDIVIDUALS	The people requiring health and care services. Where individuals use advocates to enable them to express their views, wishes or feelings and to speak on their behalf, the term 'individual' covers both the individual and their advocate or interpreter.
INFECTION CONTROL	Procedures for preventing or minimising the spread of infection from one person to another.
PERSONAL GROOMING ITEMS	Includes toiletries such as soap, shampoo and shaving items; make-up, hairbrush or comb and perfume.
PERSONAL HYGIENE	Maintaining personal cleanliness through washing, bathing and showering.
PROSTHESES	Replacement of a part of the body with an artificial substitute, such as artificial limbs.
SERVICE USER	An individual who receives care and support from your organisation.
TOILET FACILITIES	Could include toilet, bedpan, commode or urinal.

Support individuals to go to the toilet

To help you meet the requirements for this section of the unit you will need to know and understand how to:

❑ encourage individuals to communicate when they need to use toilet facilities

❑ support individuals to understand which toilet facilities are available and choose which they prefer

❑ ensure individuals can call for help and that you respond immediately

❑ encourage individuals to clean themselves in a way which is acceptable and appropriate

❑ move and dispose of body waste discreetly, immediately and safely

❑ minimise the risk of cross infection

❑ measure and record body waste and report any problems and significant changes to the appropriate people

Encourage individuals to communicate when they need to use the toilet facilities

Good communication is vital to all aspects of care, including the use of toilet facilities and concerns about body waste. It is important to remember though that discussing personal issues such as this can be very embarrassing. It is your duty as a care worker to find ways of talking with the individual about their toileting needs, while at the same time protecting their dignity and minimising any feelings of humiliation. You may find it embarrassing to discuss these issues with individuals, but it is important that you do not show this, as it can make communication even harder. Approaching the situation in a matter-of-fact way will often help. While not always possible, another way of reducing embarrassment is to provide a carer of the same sex.

Communication difficulties

It is likely that some individuals in your care will have specific difficulties in communicating, and this may affect how they express their need to use toilet facilities. These include:

❑ language and cultural differences

❑ hearing or visual disabilities

❑ loss of memory, dementia or learning difficulties

❑ jargon (different terms or ways of referring to using the toilet)

❑ difficulty speaking (dysphasia), eg after a stroke.

There are many ways of overcoming such barriers, but perhaps the most important one is to get to know each individual in your care. For example, you may have a service user who cannot talk, but from their body language (such as being agitated, irritable or restless) you may understand that they need to use the toilet.

Other ways of helping individuals to communicate their need to use the toilet may include:

❑ pictures – card with a picture of a toilet on it, which they can point to

❑ gaining knowledge of the terms which different individuals use for going to the toilet

❑ observing behaviour which suggests someone wants to go to the toilet – particularly relevant when someone is confused and disorientated

❑ making sure that any hearing aids are switched on, with working batteries

❑ loop system – fitting these in the home helps individuals who are deaf.

👍 POINTS TO NOTE

Never guess or make assumptions about when individuals want to use the toilet facilities. Always ask the person themselves and respond accordingly, even if it does not fit into your busy routine.

Support individuals to understand which toilet facilities are available

Choice

Wherever possible, you should offer a choice of toilet facilities. Perhaps a service user wants to use a toilet which is furthest away, because it is quiet and there is less chance of embarrassment. While it may not be as convenient for you, the needs of the individual must come first. Sometimes it may be difficult to offer the individual their first choice, especially if someone else is using the toilet and they need to use the toilet urgently. However, you should still discuss these issues with the individual, including any alternatives so that they can make their own choices.

It is always preferable to use toilet facilities whenever possible, and individuals should be offered that choice even though it may be quicker for them to use a commode beside their bed. Toilets should be clearly signed so that individuals can find them easily, without having to constantly ask and draw attention to themselves.

Providing assistance

Individuals may need help with getting to and from toilet facilities safely. Assistance is often required due to the:

- ❑ individual's level of mobility – eg individuals with arthritis or having had a stroke may not be able to walk or stand without help

- ❑ level of continence (control over bodily excretions) – eg urgency (urgent need to use the toilet) or frequency (the need to use the toilet often)

- ❑ mental state of the person – people who are confused or suffer from dementia.

Questions you can ask yourself or others when considering the level of assistance required:

- ❑ Are there toilet facilities within easy reach of the service user's bedroom or living area?

- ❑ What level of assistance do they require in terms of mobility?

- ❑ Are there any aids or equipment which may help them, eg frames or walking sticks?

- ❑ Are they confused and therefore require additional assistance?

The level of assistance for each individual will vary from just needing someone there for reassurance, through to not being able to stand or walk without help. Often only a little help is required; eg ensuring that someone with poor eyesight wears their glasses might mean they can go to and from the toilet without assistance.

Environmental barriers

There may be environmental barriers to the safe access of toilet facilities. These can include: poor lighting, loose carpets or rugs, or chairs and tables blocking access. Although you may be able to get to the toilet safely, try to imagine how different it would be if you needed a zimmer frame or wheelchair, or could not lift your feet very high. Always try to see potential problems from the viewpoint of those in your care, and ensure that wherever possible you remove any potential barriers.

Clothing

Another area where individuals may need help is with their clothing. Buttons or zips may need to be unfastened, or underwear may need to be removed. This can be particularly difficult when individuals have limited mobility. For example, if a

REFLECT

Think about your workplace. What potential hazards might there be for individuals going to and returning from the toilet?

person needs to hold onto a zimmer frame for stability, they may not be able to let go of it in order to undo an item of clothing, without falling.

How to offer help

It is always important to discuss the level and type of help required with the individual in a discreet and tactful manner. You may also be able to observe how much an individual can do for themselves, and offer assistance when they are having difficulty. Remember to maintain privacy at all times and ensure that others do so too, even if this means challenging colleagues about intimate service user discussions held in public places or in a loud voice for everyone to hear.

Ensure that individuals can call for help

Incontinence or poor continence is common among older people and can be very embarrassing. Many people also take medication which means that they have to be able to reach a toilet easily and quickly. It is therefore important that individuals know that when they call for help with reaching the toilet, they will be heard and that someone will respond quickly. Often older people suffer from urgency (little or no warning about when they need to use the toilet) and therefore cannot wait very long. Although responding to a call for help immediately may be inconvenient to you, you need to be aware that often people do not wait until the last minute on purpose or to annoy you.

Some individuals only require help in going to and from the toilet, and are able to be left alone until they have finished.

> **REFLECT**
>
> Think about why individuals need to be able to call for and receive help immediately when needing to use the toilet.

Fig 7.2 Service users need to be able to call you back quickly and easily.

However, it is important that you do not go far away from the toilet during this time, so that when they call for assistance you can respond immediately. It can be very distressing for someone to be left alone sitting on the toilet for any significant length of time and having to shout for help.

Staying near the toilet may sometimes be difficult, especially if you are busy and someone else calls for help. Call buttons or bells are a useful way for individuals to call for assistance when they need it. You must make sure that the person can reach the button and also knows how to use it, and you must respond quickly to their call.

CASE STUDY

Faith has Parkinson's disease and needs considerable help with all aspects of personal care. One of the young care assistants took her to the toilet and told her to call when she had finished using the call bell which she made sure Faith could easily reach. The care assistant went to get another resident out of bed and forgot about Faith. Meanwhile, Faith had been using the call pull and even resorted to shouting for help. Eventually someone heard her and went to her assistance, but by this time Faith had been left for about half an hour.

- How might Faith feel about being left sitting on the toilet for so long?

- How could you as a care worker avoid such a situation happening to you and one of your service users?

Encourage individuals to clean themselves

It is important that you encourage individuals to carry out their own intimate procedures wherever possible, eg cleaning themselves after using the toilet. You must establish the level of help they need for this, and their preferred methods of cleaning themselves. Most people use toilet paper, but some individuals may prefer to use running water as well, or as an alternative. Some places may provide a bidet for this purpose and this should be offered if available.

Some cultures may require a specific procedure for cleaning; eg in Muslim and Hindu cultures, the left hand is traditionally used

---

CASE STUDY

Joseph is recovering from a stroke which has left him with speech difficulties and paralysed down one side. He is unable to go to the toilet without assistance.

- How will you find a way for him to clean himself that is both appropriate and acceptable for him?

POINTS TO NOTE

When encouraging individuals to clean themselves you will need to consider:

- the level and type of help they need
- the provision/availability of appropriate cleaning materials, eg toilet paper, running water
- any cultural requirements
- the individual's privacy and dignity at all times
- that women are encouraged to clean themselves from front to back to prevent the transmission of bacteria from the bowel.

---

for washing after using the toilet instead of (or as well as) using toilet paper. However clean or correctly the hand is washed afterwards, it is considered 'dirty' and therefore not used for eating with or shaking hands. This may present problems for some people who are not able to use the correct hand for washing due to a disability or impaired mobility.

Encourage individuals to wash their hands after using the toilet

You must always encourage individuals to wash their hands after using the toilet and where necessary, inform them of the reasons for doing so: to reduce the risk of infections spreading to others. For most individuals this will be part of the normal routine, but for others, particularly those who suffer from dementia or are confused, they may need extra support in washing their hands. Particular care should be taken to ensure that nails are clean, as bacteria can be trapped underneath them.

REMEMBER   ☺

Washing hands after using the toilet is an essential part of infection control, as it helps to prevent the spread of infection from one person to another.

REFLECT

Consider the reasons why hand-washing facilities should be close to the toilet. Design a poster to convey the importance of hand washing for individuals.

Hand washing facilities must be provided close to the toilet and be easily accessible with appropriate hand rails. Assistance should be given with cleaning if required. You will need to provide a bowl of water and towel for individuals using a commode or bedpan. Make sure that the individual's own materials (such as soap and towel) are used.

Ensure the toilet facilities are clean

No one likes to use dirty toilet facilities. Not only do they look very unpleasant, they are also potentially harmful to health. There are two reasons why it is important to ensure that toilet facilities are kept clean:

1 to protect staff and individuals from harm or the risk of infection

2 to provide a pleasant and comfortable environment.

Toilet facilities and any aids or equipment such as hand rails or call bells must be cleaned after use, with the appropriate cleaning materials. Your place of work will have procedures for which cleaning materials to use. Commodes are often not cleaned as regularly as toilets, but it is essential that these facilities these should also be cleaned after every use.

> ### Legislation and organisational policy and procedures
>
> The National Minimum Standards for Care Homes for Older People (2003) sets out requirements for 'premises to be kept clean, hygienic and free from offensive odours' (Standard 26.1).

Move and dispose of body waste discreetly

All care settings have their own policies and procedures for disposing of body waste. This usually means disposing of it in a toilet or sluice (a room or area specially designed to dispose of waste). As a care worker, you must know how to handle, move and dispose of body waste appropriately and safely.

It is important that you know how to handle these safely, in order to minimise cross-infection, and provide respect for the individual.

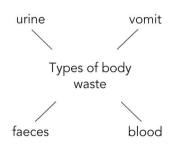

> ### REFLECT
>
> Think about a time when you had to use a public toilet that was dirty and smelly. How did it make you feel?

> ### FIND OUT
>
> What procedures are in your workplace for cleaning toilet facilities? Which cleaning solutions are to be used, and how often should facilities be cleaned?

REFLECT

The National Minimum Standards for Care Homes (2003) states that any soiled articles of clothing and linen must not be carried through into areas where food is stored, prepared, cooked or eaten. What are the reasons for this?

FIND OUT

. . . the procedures for disposing of body waste in your workplace.

REFLECT

How would you dispose of the waste in a bedpan or commode in a way which is discreet and respectful?

Minimising infection

Care taken when disposing of waste will help minimise any potential spread of infection to others. Accidental spillages of bodily fluids must be dealt with immediately using the correct protective clothing, eg gloves and apron. Antiseptic solutions should be used to clean equipment and surfaces according to policies and protocols, as these help to destroy bacteria. Soiled linen should be placed in an appropriate bag so that it can be laundered separately from other linen. These bags are often colour-coded such as red or yellow as identified in the workplace policies and protocols. Some bags are treated in such a way that they can be placed directly in the washing machine where they dissolve.

Methods of preventing infection include:

❑ ensuring that staff cover cuts or grazes with waterproof dressings before commencing work

❑ ensuring that staff maintain good personal hygiene standards, ie thorough hand washing after contact with blood and body fluids

❑ the maintenance of good environmental hygiene

❑ the wearing of latex-free gloves or disposable aprons for high risk or messy activities.

Respect the individual

While it is important to ensure good hygiene and minimise cross-infection when disposing of body waste, it is also vital that you do this as discreetly as possible, and that you show respect for the individual. It can be very embarrassing for individuals, especially if they need a lot of assistance with toileting. This is particularly important when someone is using a bedpan or commode which is next to their bed.

CASE STUDY

Joe, an 80-year-old man in your residential home, calls you over to where he is sitting in the residents' lounge. He tells you that he did not go to the toilet in time and has had an 'accident'.

- How will you deal with this situation in a way that maintains Joe's dignity?

Appropriate protective clothing for disposing of waste

It is the responsibility of all care workers to ensure that they work in ways which help protect both themselves and others from the

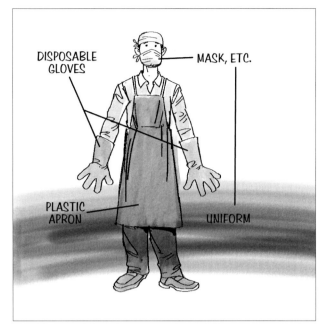

DISPOSABLE
GLOVES

MASK, ETC.

PLASTIC
APRON

UNIFORM

Fig 7.3 How accessible is protective clothing in your place of work?

spread of infection. This is especially important within the care setting where service users are often frail or ill and are therefore more susceptible to infection.

Using the protective clothing whenever you have any contact with bodily fluids (urine, faeces, blood vomit or soiled bed linen and dressings) will help protect you and others from cross-infection . Protective clothing must be changed between treating or caring for each individual.

Legislation and organisational policy and procedures

The infection control policy in your workplace should include:

- staff training in infection control issues
- procedures for safe handling of body waste
- use of personal protective clothing
- protocols on hand washing
- disinfection procedures.

Wash your hands after disposing of body waste

As you already know, you should always wash your hands before and after moving and disposing of body waste. The main reason for this is to prevent cross-infection by the spread of bacteria from one person to another. Our hands are covered with millions

Fig 7.4 Hand-washing is one way to help prevent the spread of MRSA (Methicillin-resistant *staphylococcus aureus*).

of micro-organisms (germs) which can spread through direct contact with others.

Hand washing is one of the most important ways of minimising the spread of infection. Hands need to be washed carefully using liquid soap and hot water and dried thoroughly with paper towels in order to reduce the number of bacteria. It is important to do this after:

❑ helping someone use the toilet, bedpan or commode

❑ disposing of bodily waste, eg emptying a bedpan, commode or catheter bag

❑ caring for someone who is incontinent

❑ handling bed linen, especially if it is soiled.

Measure and record body waste where required

There may be occasions where you will need to measure and record bodily waste. Often urine is tested when someone is admitted into residential care. This is in order to detect any abnormalities such as blood, which may indicate an infection, or glucose, which can be a sign of diabetes. The amount of urine which an individual passes is also important to monitor, as this may highlight potential problems; eg if someone has a poor urine output, they may be dehydrated.

For some individuals, it may be necessary to measure the amount and frequency of urine output using a special fluid

FIND OUT

More about MRSA and your role in preventing its spread

REFLECT

Why is it important to maintain your own cleanliness and hygiene prior to, during and following any activities involved in the personal care of others?

FLUID INPUT/OUTPUT CHART

NAME

DATE	TIME	FLUID INPUT	URINARY OUTPUT	SIGNATURE

Fig 7.5 Picture of a chart used for recording amount of urine.

input/output chart. This helps to keep a record of their urine output and will be written in their individual care plan. You may be required to measure the amount of urine before you dispose of it. Using a disposable bedpan in the toilet is one way of doing this, or if an individual has a catheter, the bag can be emptied straight into a measuring jug. A clean and clearly marked measuring jug used only for this purpose should be used, and this should be carefully washed after use.

Measuring and recording output and/or bodily waste is usually included in an individual's care plan to

❑   monitor a person's overall condition

❑   highlight a potential underlying illness or deterioration of a person's health.

Identifying underlying illness or change early can lead to a fast response in changes to treatment, medication or diet as necessary.

Report any problems and significant changes

You should report any changes or problems you observe as soon as possible to the relevant people, as this could indicate an underlying problem which needs further investigation. Problems to look out for include:

❑   difficulties in going to the toilet, eg continence level

❑   concerns about bodily waste, eg diarrhoea

❑ changes in an individual's mobility, eg ability to get to the toilet

❑ pain when using the toilet.

The following table shows some of the key changes or problems you may encounter:

BODY WASTE	*POSSIBLE* PROBLEMS
Urine	• cloudy or smelly – indicates possible infection • blood – possible infection, or something more serious • dark and concentrated – inadequate fluid intake • inability to pass urine (retention) – possible problems with bladder • incontinence • pain when passing urine – infection, kidney stones
Faeces	• constipation • diarrhoea • blood in stools – indicating an underlying problem • change in colour or consistency from normal pattern

Sometimes changes in body waste may be caused by something simple such as a change in diet, but they may also indicate a more serious problem that could require urgent medical attention. As a care worker, you must always report any changes in bodily waste immediately.

Legislation and organisational policy and procedures

When reporting or recording any problems or changes in an individual's condition, it is important to remember the legal requirement to maintain confidentiality. The Data Protection Act 1998 states that:

• records must be accurate, secure and confidential

• information should only shared with the relevant people on a need-to-know basis.

Information is handled in accordance with legal requirements, the home's written policies and procedures, and in the best interests of the individual.

CASE STUDY

Brenda has been feeling off-colour for a couple of days, and has stayed in bed. When emptying her commode, you notice that her urine is very dark and smelly.

• What action should you take?

Enable individuals to maintain their personal hygiene

To help you meet the requirements for this section of the unit you will need to know and understand how to:

❑ support individuals to communicate their preferences about personal hygiene care

❑ identify the degree of support needed

❑ wear appropriate protective clothing

❑ ensure room and water temperatures are safe and meet the individual's needs and preferences

❑ ensure toiletries, material and equipment are accessible and safe

❑ enable individuals to call for help

❑ minimise discomfort when assisting individuals

❑ maintain your own personal hygiene

❑ report any problems or significant changes in the individual's hygiene to the appropriate people

Personal cleanliness is very important:

❑ When skin becomes dirty, either because of exposure to the environment or through sweat or dead skin cells, it is a potential breeding ground for bacteria. This can lead to unpleasant body odours and infections which could spread to other people.

❑ People tend to feel more positive about themselves when they are clean.

A care worker can make a significant difference to an individual's morale and confidence by encouraging them to maintain their personal hygiene, and by offering appropriate support in order for them to do so.

Support individuals to communicate preferences about personal hygiene care

Everyone has different views and values about how often they wash and the way in which they carry out their personal hygiene requirements. Therefore, wherever possible you should offer choice to individuals. Choice can be offered in many ways:

❑ individuals may prefer to have a shower rather than a bath. This may be particularly relevant for those people

> **REFLECT**
>
> Think about how you feel after you have had a shower or bath. How might assisting with personal hygiene benefit individuals who are either ill, in pain, or feeling 'under the weather'?

whose culture and beliefs require running water for washing

❑ service users may prefer a carer of the same gender when washing or bathing. Again, this may be an important issue for people who follow the traditions and beliefs of the Muslim religion for example

❑ choices over how and when to wash their hair

❑ choices about the type of toiletries they want to use (eg shampoo, soap, toothpaste, talcum powder, bubble bath or bath oil etc).

CASE STUDY

Mr Smith is due for a bath this morning and is adamant that only a male carer assists him. Unfortunately, the only male member of staff is having a day off today and you (a female carer) have been given the task of caring for Mr Smith.

- How would you tackle this problem and demonstrate respect for Mr Smith's preferences and choices?

CARE VALUES

You should always talk about any concerns which individuals may have with them, as there is often something you can do to solve problems:

- offer reassurance about privacy
- suggest an alternative time
- offer choices.

It may be more appropriate for someone who is not feeling very well to have a wash or even a bed-bath. Offering alternatives and coming to a mutually agreed compromise such as these may help to reassure individuals.

You should encourage individuals to express their preferences about personal hygiene care and then respect their wishes. However, there can be conflict when an individual does not want to have a bath or shower and they really need one! Older people may be reluctant to take a bath because of:

❑ a previous bad experience

❑ feeling unwell or tired

❑ embarrassment about bathing in front of someone else

❑ feeling like they are a nuisance by asking for help.

These situations need handling carefully and sensitively. You should find observing the care values helps you to handle the situations successfully.

Identify the degree of support which the individual needs

The type of support which you may have to give individuals with their personal hygiene might include:

❑ hair washing

❑ mouth care and teeth cleaning

❑ having a bath or shower.

Individuals should be encouraged to carry out as much of their personal hygiene activities as possible. For example, someone who is unable to walk or stand without assistance may have no problem in using their hands and arms for washing and drying themselves. Never assume that if someone needs help in one particular area, they need help with everything else.

Time

People with reduced mobility often take a considerable amount of time to carry out their personal hygiene routines. It is important that you do not rush them as this may result in undermining their confidence and self-esteem, or even having an accident. Patience can be very difficult, especially when you are busy and it can be tempting to hurry people along, but respect for others means that you must allow individuals to move at their own pace.

Bed-bound individuals

When someone is confined to bed, it is still important that their personal hygiene needs are met. A bowl of warm water can be provided, but you must remember to change the water regularly and provide separate cloths for cleaning different parts of the body, eg face and genital area. The individual must be encouraged to do as much for themselves as possible, with you there to encourage and support where necessary. Make sure that the bowl of water is stable and within easy reach and that any toiletries needed are accessible. It is also important that you maintain privacy by closing the door or using a curtain (although sometimes total privacy is not possible, as voices and noise can

REFLECT

Make a list of all the reasons why individuals should be encouraged to help themselves as much as possible.

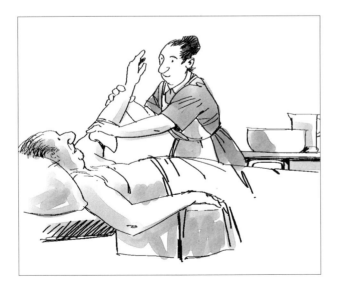

Fig 7.6 Encourage your service users to be as independent as possible. Don't assume you have to do everything.

FIND OUT

How much noise can be heard behind a curtain? Ask two colleagues to stand behind a curtain and have a conversation. To what extent does the curtain reduce the level of noise and protect privacy?

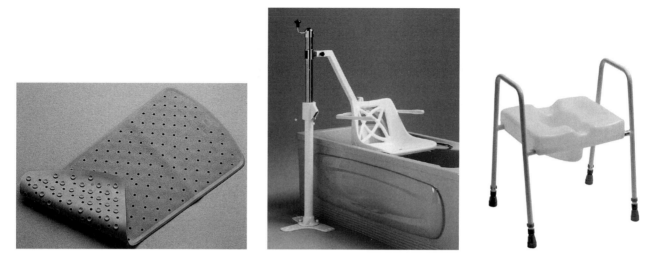

Fig 7.7 Useful equipment to aid personal care. What aids are available to your service users?

FIND OUT

The Disabled Living Foundation aims to provide the best possible choice for people who use equipment to live a more independent life. Find out about the various aids and equipment available from their factsheets at www.dlf.org.uk

CARE VALUES

As a care worker, you will need to understand the reasons for using gloves and aprons, and be able to help others understand this too. Vulnerable individuals who are perhaps confused or disorientated may feel anxious about seeing someone wearing protective clothing, and may be afraid of what might happen to them.

easily be heard behind a curtain). Make sure that as much of the body as possible is covered throughout the bed-bath, not only for privacy, but also to keep the individual warm.

Aids and specialised equipment

There are many aids and types of equipment that can be provided to help individuals maintain their independence and carry out many tasks for themselves. These aids vary significantly in cost, but include:

❏ bath lifts – these allow an individual to be lifted into the bath safely

❏ bath seats

❏ specially designed baths with doors to allow individuals to walk into the bath

❏ inflatable pillows and cushions

❏ non-slip mats

❏ plastic seats with holes in the middle, for use in the shower

❏ a variety of handles and grip rails for extra support

❏ adaptations for taps – useful for individuals with arthritic hands.

Wear appropriate protective clothing

As we have already said the main types of protective clothing which you are likely to use when assisting individuals with their personal hygiene are:

❑ plastic aprons – often white

❑ disposable gloves.

Protective clothing must only be used for helping one individual, and then removed and disposed of appropriately to prevent cross-infection. This may mean you need to take several changes of apron and gloves with you if you work in the community.

CASE STUDY ✍

Mrs Briggs has just been discharged from hospital and admitted to your intermediate care home. She has undergone surgery for a broken hip and suffers from early signs of dementia. You have been asked to help her to have a bath, but she seems rather distressed that you are wearing gloves and an apron, and says that she does not want another operation.

- Why might Mrs Briggs be distressed?

- How would you reassure Mrs Briggs and help her understand why you need to wear protective clothing?

Ensure the appropriate room and water temperatures

As far as possible, it is important when helping individuals to bath or shower that you make it a pleasurable experience. This means ensuring that the room is warm, secure and relaxing. Hypothermia (when the body temperature falls below 35°C) is a well known hazard for older people which can result in death, especially in the winter months or where there is inadequate heating and warm clothing available. It can be harder for someone with reduced mobility or a long-term illness to keep warm, and as a care worker, you should ensure that individuals in your care do not become cold. One way of doing this is by closing any windows to prevent drafts, especially when someone is having a bath or shower. Adequate heating is also important and you should make sure the radiator is turned on, even though you may feel that it is hot. This is because you are well, fit, active and fully clothed, whereas the individual taking a bath is sitting still, with no clothes on, and therefore more likely to feel the cold.

👍 POINTS TO NOTE

When bathing or showering old or vulnerable individuals, always check that the window is closed beforehand and if necessary that the radiator is turned on, as older people tend to feel cold easily.

When bathing individuals, it is very important that the bath water is at the correct temperature. There have been instances of frail and elderly people suffering serious injuries or even dying as a result of scalds from hot water. When water is above 44°C there is an increased risk of scalds; clearly, the higher the temperature, the higher the risk of burning or scalding.

Older people are particularly vulnerable to scalds because of:

❑ thinner skin – more susceptible to injury

❑ less sensitive skin – they may not feel the heat immediately, so do not pull away from the heat quickly enough

❑ less agility – may not be able to move away quickly

❑ slower reaction time due to dementia

❑ impaired feeling in a part of their body – eg individuals suffering from strokes can lose sensation down one side of their body.

Legislation and organisational policy and procedures

One of the National Minimum Standards for Care Homes for Older People published by the Department of Health (2003) sets out specific requirements for correct water temperature. Standard 25 states:

'Water is stored at a temperature of at least 60°C and distributed at 50°C minimum, to prevent risks from Legionella. To prevent risks from scalding, pre-set values of a type unaffected by changes in water pressure and which have fail-safe devices are fitted locally to provide water close to 43°C.'

There are several steps you can take to prevent scalds from hot bath water:

❑ When running a bath, always put the cold water in first.

❑ Use the 'elbow test' or special thermometer to check the bath water temperature. If water is over 43°C, it is too hot.

❑ Thermostatically controlled taps can be installed to ensure that water is the correct temperature.

❑ Do not leave a bath of water unattended – a vulnerable person may climb or fall into the bath and be incapable of getting out.

Whenever possible, always ask the individual what temperature they want the water. Preference for water temperature varies

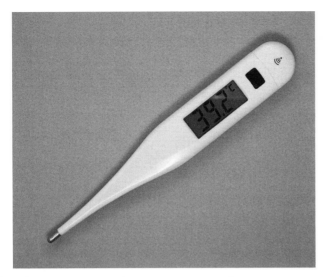

Fig 7.8 Use a thermometer to gauge the correct temperature of water.

from person to person, and you should never assume or guess what the individual needs. If possible, ask the individual themselves to check the water temperature before getting into the bath, so that is can be altered if necessary.

Toiletries, materials and equipment

Accessibility of toiletries and equipment

Some individuals may need very little support with personal hygiene; eg they may be able to wash themselves, but need assistance with climbing in and out of the bath. It is important

Fig 7.9 Keeping track of the soap can be easier if it is attached to something.

Fig 7.10 Bathrooms can be hazardous places. Make sure you store equipment and materials safely.

that before leaving an individual alone to carry out an aspect of personal hygiene, you make sure that they can easily reach any toiletries, materials and equipment they need. It can be very frustrating and even dangerous to be left alone when (for example) the soap is just out of reach, especially for someone who is unsteady; they may slip and injure themselves.

Soap can be difficult to hold especially when wet, therefore it may be more accessible if it is on a rope in the shower or on a specially designed tray for toiletries in the bath.

It is also important to keep the bathroom tidy; accidents can occur when items of clothing or equipment are left lying around. While you should try to ensure that an individual can reach aids such as hoists and lifts, or walking sticks and frames when they are needed, you should make sure that any such equipment is placed somewhere where no one else will fall over them.

Safe use of materials

There are many substances used in the care setting that are potentially harmful to health if used or stored incorrectly.

The effects from contact with hazardous substances range from mild eye or skin irritation, to respiratory problems and chronic conditions affecting the liver or kidneys. If these substances are not used or stored correctly, they not only pose a hazard to you, but also to those in your care. For example, if a resident had poor eyesight, they may not be able to distinguish between everyday toiletries such as shampoo, and more dangerous substances such as disinfectants. It is therefore essential that dangerous substances are stored in a safe place before and after use, and that you make yourself aware of the relevant policies and procedures in your workplace for their safe handling.

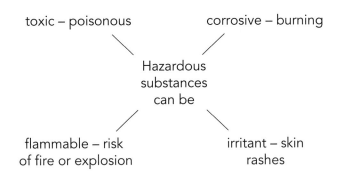

toxic – poisonous

corrosive – burning

Hazardous
substances
can be

flammable – risk
of fire or explosion

irritant – skin
rashes

> ### Legislation and organisational policy and procedures
>
> The Control of Substances Hazardous to Health (2003) (COSHH) regulations require all workplaces to regulate the storage and use of dangerous substances. In the care setting, these would refer to cleaning fluids, disinfectants or sterilising solutions.

Enable individuals to call for help

Bathrooms and toilets in care homes should be fitted with a call bell so that individuals are able to call for help urgently. You should make sure that this is within easy reach of the individual, and also that they know what it is and how to use it. Never rely totally on this method, as the individual may drop the call bell or slip and no longer be able to reach it. Always stay close by in case you are needed urgently, and keep checking that they are alright.

Support individuals in ways which cause little discomfort

Someone who finds it difficult to move without pain (eg with arthritis) will find it difficult to take a bath or even walk towards the bathroom without discomfort. When assisting individuals with their personal hygiene needs, you will need to find ways to minimise their discomfort as much as possible. One way of doing this is by treating them sensitively and carefully, and not rushing them merely because you are busy. You may also find that it helps for pain relief to be given before any movement or assistance, although it is important to allow medication sufficient time to work beforehand. Sometimes older people find it particularly difficult and painful to move early in the morning, and so may find it easier to have a bath or shower later in the morning or in the afternoon.

The provision of specific aids and equipment can be used to minimise discomfort. Someone with painful arthritis in their hands may find it more comfortable to clean their teeth with an electric toothbrush, instead of an ordinary one which requires more movement of the hands.

POINTS TO NOTE

When assisting others with an aspect of personal care, follow these points:

- Treat them with respect.
- Listen to their concerns, needs and preferences.
- Maintain privacy at all times (and ensure that others do the same).
- Show kindness and understanding – do not rush them or assist them in a rough manner.
- If appropriate ask for pain relief before bathing, etc.
- Offer baths or showers later in the morning to allow individuals with poor mobility to become more mobile as the day wears on.
- Provide suitable aids and equipment to alleviate avoidable discomfort.

CASE STUDY

Frank has problems with his balance and frequently falls. Yesterday he fell over in the dining area and severely bruised his left arm and hip. Today you are helping him have a bath, but he is in a lot of pain.

- What could you do to make this procedure as comfortable as possible?

Your own personal hygiene

As a care worker, you are required to ensure that you maintain excellent personal hygiene at all times. A care worker who does not look after his or her own personal hygiene is more likely to pass infections on to other staff and service users, and is more susceptible themselves to infections from others.

Infections may not always be obvious but are spread through:

❑ breathing in germs (coughs, sneezes)

❑ physical contact with others

❑ ingesting infectious organisms through the mouth.

Infection control

One of the easiest and perhaps best ways of preventing the spread of infections is by washing your hands regularly, but especially after using the toilet, before handling food, and after contact with other people's skin or bodily fluids. There has been much emphasis on the importance of hand washing in hospitals since the increase in the hospital superbug MRSA. General hygiene and cleanliness is also vital to infection control. All care workers should wash or bathe regularly and wear clean uniforms. Your hair should be kept clean, neat and tidy and if long, tied back. Do not cough or sneeze over others, as infection can be carried through the air on tiny droplets of moisture. Always use a handkerchief or paper tissue and dispose of it appropriately.

Methods of preventing infection

As a member of staff you are required to make every effort to prevent the spread of infection by:

1 washing your hands with warm water and soap:

❑ before and after caring for each service user

❑ after going to the toilet

❑ before preparing food

Fig 7.11 There used to be a health campaign that noted 'Coughs and sneezes spread diseases'.

2 making sure your nails are kept short and clean

3 washing (bath or shower) every day

4 keeping your hair clean and tidy

5 covering any cuts with clean dressings

6 not coughing or sneezing over other people, always using a handkerchief.

CASE STUDY

You have noticed over the last couple of weeks that Frances, one of your colleagues, has problems with body odour and is wearing dirty uniforms to work. Everyone is beginning to comment on this, but no one has said anything to Frances herself.

- Why is it important to talk to Frances about this problem?

- How might you raise the subject with Frances?

Legislation and policy

The National Minimum Standards for Care Homes for Older Adults (2003) published by the Department of Health defines the following standards for hygiene and control of infection in Standard 26:

26.1 Premises are kept clean, hygienic and free from offensive odours throughout and systems are in place to control the spread of infection, in accordance with relevant legislation and published professional guidance

26.2 Laundry facilities are sited so that soiled articles, clothing and infected linen are not carried through areas where food is stored, prepared, cooked or eaten and do not intrude on service users

26.3 Hand washing facilities are prominently sited in areas where infected material and/or clinical waste are being handled

26.4 The laundry floor finishes are impermeable and these and wall finishes are readily cleanable

26.5 Policies and procedures for control of infection include the safe handling and disposal of clinical waste; dealing with spillages; provision of protective clothing; hand washing

26.6 The home has a sluicing facility and, in care homes providing nursing, a sluicing disinfector

26.7 Foul laundry is washed at appropriate temperatures (minimum 65°C for not less than ten minutes) to thoroughly clean linen and control risk of infection

> 26.8 Washing machines have the specified programming ability to meet disinfection standards
>
> 26.9 Services and facilities comply with the Water Supply (Water Fittings) Regulations 1999.

Report any problems and significant changes

As a carer, it is important that you are always alert to any changes in your service user's condition. These changes may indicate either an improvement or deterioration in their health and wellbeing. Both must be reported to the appropriate people, usually your supervisor or manager. Often older people deteriorate slowly and you may not notice any significant change immediately. It is therefore important that you observe and report any minor changes that you note.

Problems could include:

❑ changes in the individual's health

❑ changes in the individual's skin condition

❑ changes in motivation for personal hygiene and grooming.

Reasons for monitoring individuals

❑ Problems may be addressed and any treatment required given as soon as possible.

❑ The individual care package may need amending (eg deterioration may mean additional assistance or different aids being required).

KEY CHANGES IN PERSONAL HYGIENE

AREA OF BODY	POTENTIAL PROBLEMS
Skin	• skin disorders such as eczema or dermatitis • unwashed sweat in folds of skin (eg underneath breasts) often looks red and spotty with broken skin – may lead to infection • pressure sores – ulcers often found on individuals who are bed-bound or immobile. They begin as red painful areas and if left untreated, the skin begins to break down and the ulcers grow deeper. At this point they are very difficult to treat, so prevention is very important • pale, cold skin (especially on limbs) may be due to poor circulation
Genital areas	• inflammation, discharge or swelling • incontinence • strong or offensive odour – may suggest poor hygiene or an infection

AREA OF BODY	POTENTIAL PROBLEMS
Mouth	• ulcers • bad breath (halitosis) – may indicate a more serious condition • tooth decay • thrush – white/cream patches on the tongue or lining of the mouth (a fungal infection common in older people, particularly those who are taking antibiotics or drugs to suppress the immune system)
Hair	• itching or scratching – may be due to dermatitis, impetigo or infection with head or pubic lice
Fingernails	• dirty fingernails can cause infections to spread • long or torn nails may cause injury through scratching

Support individuals in personal grooming and dressing

To help you meet the requirements for this section of the unit you will need to know and understand how to:

❑ support individuals to communicate their wishes and preferences about personal grooming and dressing

❑ provide appropriate support and encouragement in a way which maximises independence, respects personal beliefs, maintains privacy and meets safety requirements

❑ provide equipment and materials which are appropriate to the needs of individuals and meet safety requirements

❑ keep personal clothing and grooming equipment clean, safe and secure

❑ support individuals in their use of sensory equipment and prostheses

❑ report any problems or significant changes to the appropriate people

As a care worker, you will be caring for individuals who may need help with some aspects of personal grooming and dressing. This might involve help with the following areas:

❑ dressing and undressing

❑ make-up

❑ hairstyle

❑ manicure

❑ shaving.

Support individuals to communicate their wishes and preferences

The way we look, our hairstyle, and the type of clothes we wear say something about us: our type of personality and our individual characteristics. It is therefore important that we encourage service users as much as possible to make their own choices about how they look and the type of clothing they want to wear. Offering choice helps to promote independence and shows respect.

You should find ways to encourage individuals in your care to communicate their wishes and preferences about clothing and personal grooming. This means:

- ❏ offering a choice whenever possible

- ❏ respecting the individual's decision

- ❏ never making decisions for the individual based on what you would do, wear, want etc, without taking into account their wishes and beliefs.

Some individuals may find it difficult to communicate, possibly due to:

- ❏ loss of speech after a stroke

- ❏ hearing impairment

- ❏ dementia or learning difficulties.

It is important that you find ways to overcome such barriers; eg when helping an individual who has hearing difficulties to get dressed in the morning, always make sure that any hearing aid is fitted before you talk to them about what clothes they want to wear. Effective communication involves both verbal and non-verbal skills. If someone finds it difficult to speak, you can hold up different outfits and ask them to indicate in a way that is appropriate which one they want to wear.

CARE VALUES

One of the key principles of the care value base is to respect people's rights to their own beliefs and lifestyles, and to treat people as individuals. This means respecting their rights to:

- choice
- dignity
- effective communication.

Fig 7.12 We are all unique –this uniqueness is often demonstrated throught the clothes we choose.

Provide active support and encouragement

Active support means encouraging individuals to do as much for themselves as possible to maintain their independence within their level of physical ability. Older people often have problems with dressing or undressing. Painful conditions such as arthritis can make it difficult to fasten buttons or zips. Individuals with reduced mobility, due to a stroke for example, can find it hard to lift their arms up to remove an item of clothing, or bend down to put on shoes.

It is important that individuals are encouraged to do as much for themselves as possible and that you provide the appropriate support to enable them to do so. You can do this by:

- ❏ making sure that tasks are achievable
- ❏ asking the individual about the type and amount of help they need
- ❏ offering the appropriate help when required
- ❏ encouraging the individual wherever possible.

There may be occasions where you will need to provide specific aids and equipment which will help with dressing; eg:

- ❏ 'velcro' fastenings on shoes and clothing to replace buttons, shoelaces
- ❏ sock, stocking or tights aid
- ❏ long-handled shoe horns
- ❏ zip pullers
- ❏ elastic laces
- ❏ button hooks
- ❏ large buttons
- ❏ specially designed brushes and combs.

If these aids are used correctly they can result in individuals retaining maximum independence.

Maximise the individual's independence

Someone who feels weary or in pain may feel that it is easy to let someone else do everything for them, even if they are able to do things for themselves. Wherever possible, you need to find opportunities for individuals to do things for themselves, even if this involvement is only small. Maintaining independence is essential as it helps preserve a person's self-esteem and helps them feel more in control.

There are many ways in which you can encourage someone to be independent. Sometimes only a simple change is necessary, eg

---

FIND OUT

There are many organisations that provide aids and equipment to assist individuals with dressing and grooming. Find out about the types of equipment available for individuals who have had a stroke from the following website: www.patient.co.uk/ showdoc/12/

REFLECT

Place one arm behind your back and then try to carry out a normal routine using one hand only eg try unfastening and fastening your shoes, going to the toilet; eating a meal.

Think about what kind of problems you encountered. How did it make you feel?

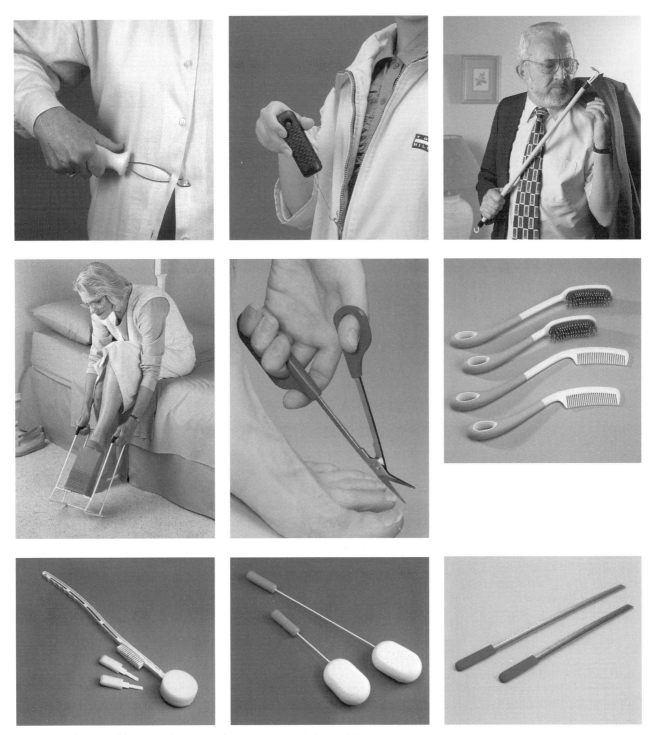

Fig 7.13 Make yourself familiar with a range of personal care aids that could be used to encourage independence in your service users.

when assisting with shaving. You may find that using an electric razor instead of a wet shave for someone who does not have very good control over his hand movements, means that he can carry out this procedure himself more safely, with just a little help.

CASE STUDY ✍

Winnie is 78 years old and fairly independent, being able to do most things for herself. However, one morning you go into her room and find her still in bed. When you encourage her to get up, she says she cannot be bothered getting up and dressed by herself, and asks you to help.

- How would you respond to Winnie?

- Why is it important not to do everything for Winnie?

REFLECT

Why might someone become reluctant to carry out their own care and maintain their independence?
What could you do to encourage them to maintain their independence?

Choosing suitable clothing

Suitable clothing needs to meet the choice and preferences of the individual wearing the items. However, you will need to be sure that the clothing also meets environmental requirements such as weather conditions and heating systems. Suitable clothing for many individuals might include:

- ❑ elasticated waistbands on skirts and trousers
- ❑ large buttons or velcro
- ❑ front fastening dresses
- ❑ shirts or dresses with wide sleeves.

Maintain the individual's privacy

When providing help with personal care such as dressing, it is important to show respect and ensure the dignity and privacy of individuals, to avoid them feeling embarrassed and humiliated. Simple things like closing the door when someone is getting dressed, not allowing people to interrupt, or maintaining service user dignity by taking care when exposing parts of the body, can be crucial to someone's self-esteem. Another way of showing respect for the privacy of individuals is by discussing any help they might require discreetly, and then provide that help in a way that is unobtrusive.

REFLECT

How would you feel if someone you did not know very well walked into your room when you were getting dressed?

CASE STUDY ✍

Anne is aged 68 and suffers from severe arthritis. She has recently been admitted to your residential care home because her family can no longer cope with her at home. She needs help with all aspects of personal care, including dressing and undressing. One day you find her sitting in the chair crying. She tells you that when Jim, one of the other care workers, got her out of bed that morning, he just took her nightdress off and left her sitting on the edge of the bed with nothing on. The door was wide open and everyone who walked past could see her. 'I was so embarrassed,' she said, 'I don't want him to help me again'.

- What could Jim have done differently to ensure Anne's privacy and dignity?

- How would you explain to Jim why Anne did not want him to help her anymore?

Legislation and organisational policy and procedures

The European Convention on Human Rights and Human Rights Act (1998) deals with many aspects of an individual's right to privacy, including the right to expect treatment with dignity during intimate care.

Respect the individual's beliefs and preferences

Individuals express themselves through the clothes they wear, their hairstyle, use of jewellery and make-up. These reflect the person's individual beliefs and preferences, and care workers need to find ways of supporting those in their care to dress or groom themselves in ways which respect their right to choose. When an individual has difficulty in expressing their preferences, care workers need to find ways of helping them choose what they would like.

Hair Care

For many people especially, having their hair washed and styled is important and helps them to feel good about themselves. Helping individuals to participate is very important. Although it is often seen as a less important part of personal care, men and women do not stop caring about their appearance as they become older. Professional hairdressers often visit residential settings or carry out home visists on a regular basis, and individuals should be encouraged to use the service.

Shaving

Shaving is important to most men, and those who are normally clean-shaven can often feel uncomfortable and distressed if facial stubble is left to grow. Helping male service users to

Fig 7.14 Providing a hairdressing service can promote feelings of health and well-being amongst service users.

CASE STUDY

Edith, an 82-year-old lady, has been feeling ill for several days and has been confined to bed, although today she is feeling a little better.

- What could you do to encourage Edith to choose how she dresses or grooms herself?

FIND OUT

. . . how a male relative, friend or service user would feel if they were prevented from shaving.

CARE VALUES

According to the care value base, individuals have the right to:

- be different – have their own beliefs and lifestyles
- make their own choices and still be respected
- not be discriminated against because of their beliefs.

shave in a way that they prefer can involve offering choices about:

- ❏ wet shave or electric shaving
- ❏ if they prefer wet shaving, whether they use shaving foam or soap, or how they rinse afterwards
- ❏ how much facial hair is removed
- ❏ how often they prefer to shave
- ❏ whether they use aftershave
- ❏ how much assistance is required.

Cultural beliefs and preferences

The word 'culture' refers to the different beliefs, behaviours, customs and religious backgrounds that exist between different groups of people. These can influence choices about personal grooming. It is important to make sure that all individuals have the opportunity to dress and groom themselves in a way which is consistent with their beliefs. The table below highlights some of these beliefs.

Meet safety requirements

Health and safety is an important consideration, both for yourself and those in your care. Employers and managers are now required

DRESSING OR GROOMING ACTIVITY	CULTURAL BELIEF OR PREFERENCE
Clothing style	Some religions require clothing to cover the entire body – any clothes provided need to take this into consideration.
Hair	Many Sikhs believe it is wrong to cut hair (both facial and head)
	Special hair oils may be applied to the scalp
Jewellery	Some jewellery has religious significance and should not be removed without the permission of the individual.

to assess risks and act in a way to reduce the risk of accidents, and it is necessary for all staff to comply with the health and safety policy in their workplace. It is your responsibility to ensure that individuals are protected from harm wherever possible.

As mentioned in Chapter 2, the Health and Safety at Work Act was introduced in 1974 and encompasses a number of regulations related to health, safety and security. These are:

- ❑ Manual Handling Operations Regulations 1993
- ❑ the Management of Health and Safety at Work Act 1994
- ❑ Health and Safety First Aid Regulations 1981
- ❑ the Control of Substances Hazardous to Health (COSHH) 1994
- ❑ the Reporting of Injury, Disease and Dangerous Occurrences Regulations 1985
- ❑ Fire Precautions Regulations 1999.

Moving and handling

(See Chapter 6 for a fuller examination of this aspect of care.) In the care setting, you will often be involved with assisting individuals to move. You need to attend recognised training to help you to do this safely, and in a way which prevents the risk of injury. The most important thing to remember here is that if someone requires assistance with their mobility, you

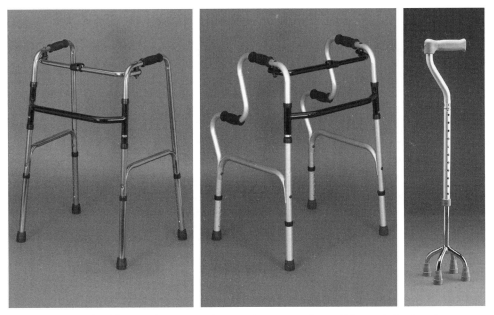

Fig 7.15 Find out the differences between each piece of equipment shown. What might be the advantages and disadvantages of each?

must avoid doing it manually. Serious injuries have been caused to care workers by lifting and moving people without using the appropriate equipment. Suitable equipment such as hoists and slings must be used, and it is your responsibility to use these correctly following the relevant guidelines and training on the correct use of equipment. Do not be tempted to use a piece of equipment unless you have had the correct training.

POINTS TO NOTE

Back injuries are a common form of injury amongst care workers – always use approved equipment correctly.

Legislation and organisational policy and procedures

The Manual Handling Operations Regulations (1993) requires employers to ensure that:

- all staff are trained in the correct use of equipment

- full instructions for using equipment are available

- equipment is in good working order, easy to use, move, maintain

- there are guidelines for appropriate cleaning and disinfecting of equipment.

Using appropriate and safe equipment

Assessment of needs

Equipment and other materials need to be suitable for the needs of the individual. An assessment of a person's abilities and needs is important in order to plan appropriate care to meet those needs. For example, a person who becomes frail and unsteady on their feet may require the use of a zimmer frame, wheelchair or walking stick, depending on the extent of instability. A variety of people are likely to be involved with this process, eg care workers and managers, through to physiotherapists and occupational therapists. Monitoring progress is an essential part of this process, in order to ensure that care and support remains suitable to the person's needs. Just because an individual uses a specific aid does not necessarily mean that they will always need it.

CASE STUDY ✍

Mary is a 76-year-old widow who lives on her own and has recently returned home from hospital after suffering from a stroke. She has reduced movement down the left side of her body and finds it difficult to eat.

- What specific problems with personal care might Mary face?

- What type of support might Mary need?

Safety

If equipment is broken or unsafe in any way, there is an increased risk of an accident or injury occurring. Equipment that is broken should never be used. All equipment must be serviced and maintained regularly according to the manufacturer's recommendations and the legal requirements.

Clothing can also cause accidents. It is important that clothing is well maintained and looked after properly. Badly fitting clothes can result in a range of accidents from burns to trips and falls. It is especially important to take positive action in the following cases:

- ❑ nightdresses or dressing gowns that are too long

- ❑ pyjamas with loose waistbands due to being too big or broken elastic

- ❑ torn clothing

- ❑ badly fitting shoes

- ❑ 'floaty night dresses or dayware.

Keep equipment and items clean, safe and secure

It is important to make sure that an individual's personal clothes and belongings are looked after and kept clean. These items might include:

- ❑ hairbrush/comb

- ❑ clothing, including underwear and nightwear

- ❑ shavers and electric razors

- ❑ make-up and perfume.

Personal clothing and other items should not be shared amongst individuals as this could result in the spread of infection. It also demonstrates a lack of respect and value for the service user. It has been known in places where there are many service users that personal items of clothing have been lost or given to another individual by mistake. One way of ensuring that this does not happen and that personal clothing is kept safe is by labelling all

FIND OUT

What aids and equipment are available in your workplace to assist individuals to dress and groom themselves?

REFLECT

What dangers may result from service users wearing inappropriate clothing as identified in the list?

items with the individual's name. Personal items should also be stored away in drawers and wardrobes when not being used.

It is important to make sure that clothing is clean and washed regularly. It is poor practice to encourage good personal hygiene and then allow an individual to continue wearing dirty or soiled clothing. Most care homes have their own laundry; however individuals being cared for in their own home should also be encouraged to wash their clothing regularly, or extra support obtained if this is necessary.

CASE STUDY

- Gillian, a colleague of yours, rushes into an individual's room where you are helping Hilda (who has dementia) to get dressed. 'Pass me Hilda's hairbrush, I need it to brush Gladys's hair because she has lost hers again,' she says.

- How should you respond to Gillian's request?

- Explain to Gillian why toiletries and other personal materials should not be shared.

Support individuals in their use of sensory equipment or prostheses

Older people and others and others often need specific aids and equipment to help them hear better or improve their eyesight, or use other aids such as dentures or false limbs. They may have concerns about using these aids which can easily be dealt with if addressed early enough. For example, someone may not wear their glasses because they are frightened of losing them; a simple process such as attaching a chain so that they hang round their neck, is often all it takes to encourage them to start wearing them again. Individuals may have concerns about the following aids:

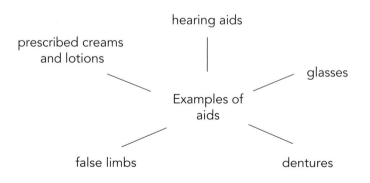

It is common for individuals who have been supplied with hearing aids not to use them. This may be because:

❑ They do not work – often because the battery needs replacing or it is not switched on!

❑ They are difficult to put in – older people find it difficult to do things that require small movements. This may be due to arthritis causing painful and stiff fingers, or perhaps a condition such as Parkinson's disease which causes tremors.

❑ They no longer fit well and are uncomfortable.

❑ They amplify background noise and can be irritating.

You should encourage individuals to wear their hearing aids, as this enables them to communicate more effectively. Always check that the battery works; replace if necessary and assist the person with putting it in if this is required.

CASE STUDY

Brian is hard of hearing and is constantly saying 'what?' and 'eh?' He often misses what people are saying. One day you find a hearing aid at the back of his drawer.

• What action should you take?

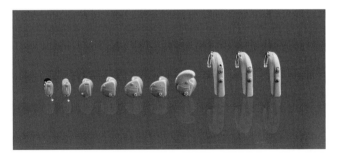

Fig 7.16 When did you last check the batteries in your service user's hearing aid?

If someone is reluctant to wear their dentures, it may mean that they no longer fit and need to be changed, or that the person has an infection which means that wearing dentures is painful. Professional advice needs to be sought so that any problems can be dealt with quickly. Individuals who have had a stroke may find it difficult to wear dentures because the muscle tone in their mouths has been affected and the dentures do not stay in. Make sure that dentures are kept clean as an individual would quite rightly be reluctant to wear them if they are dirty.

Fig 7.17 When did your service users last have a dental check-up?

Remember ☺

All service users, no matter their age or dental status, should visit the dentist regularly for checkups

Ensure that materials, equipment and facilities are clean and tidy

Clean

Infection can spread rapidly if strict cleanliness routines are not followed. It is your responsibility to ensure that any equipment or materials you use are cleaned appropriately after use and left in a suitable condition for the next person to use. All items of clothing should be removed and any soiled items cleared away appropriately. You must also make sure that any cleaning solutions are kept locked away, to prevent the possibility of harm or injury.

Tidy

It is always important to tidy up after yourself. The reasons for this are:

❑ to ensure safety – people may trip over items left lying around, or slip on a wet floor that has not been cleaned properly

❑ to respect others and promote good working practice – think about how you would feel if you constantly had to clear up after someone else at work.

Always check that any materials or equipment are left clean and tidy before someone else uses them. Many older people have poor vision, and are more likely to fall over something that is not in its usual place.

Legislation and organisational policy and procedures

The Health and Safety at Work Act (1974) places the responsibility on employers to provide a safe working environment and take reasonable care for the safety of themselves and others. It requires them to carry out risk assessments of their workplace and to find ways of minimising or eliminating any risks, which involves taking precautions to reduce accidents.

Ensure your own cleanliness and hygiene after supporting individuals

We have seen that hand washing and personal hygiene is important after all contact with individuals. It may seem obvious after helping someone to go to the toilet or when handling and disposing of body waste. However, infection can be spread through any contact, and you should take appropriate precautions such as wearing protective aprons and gloves, and washing your hands after every form of contact, even after helping individuals to get dressed.

REMEMBER ☺

Make a habit of washing your hands at all times!

Report any problems and significant changes

It is always important when assisting individuals with personal grooming and dressing to observe any changes and report these to the relevant people immediately. This is likely to be your supervisor or manager. The reason for this is that there may be an underlying problem that needs further investigation or treatment. Changes you may notice include:

- ❑ changes in motivation for personal grooming – this may indicate the onset of illness or depression

- ❑ changes in skin condition, eg bruises, swellings, discolouration, scratches or cuts. This may suggest that someone has been falling or injuring themselves, or indicate a serious health problem

---

FIND OUT

. . . about the procedure for reporting any concerns in your workplace.

❑ changes in mobility or ability to dress or groom themselves; eg a person who has previously been able to dress themselves but can no longer use one side of their body, may have had a stroke.

Summary

In this chapter we have looked at how to support individuals with their personal care needs. Enabling individuals to maintain their personal hygiene routines, grooming and dressing is central to the maintenance of self-esteem and feelings of positive wellbeing. You should:

❑ encourage individuals to communicate their personal care needs through the use of sensitive and inclusive communication skills

❑ find ways of overcoming communication barriers

❑ respond quickly and efficiently to the personal care needs of individuals

❑ encourage individuals to maintain their independence

❑ avoid the risk of contamination and cross-infection

❑ monitor and report any changes or unusual conditions in your service users' personal habits

❑ demonstrate respect and value for your service users' wishes and preferences.

Provide food and drink for individuals

→ Introduction

Food and drink is essential for life. We all know that we function better physically and mentally when we have adequate nutrition. Having said that, it is interesting to note that we can survive longer without food than fluid. The body can live off stored fat but does not store water well.

For many of us, mealtimes are the focal point of our day; breakfast, lunch and dinner are social occasions where we meet with family and friends and discuss the events of the day. When people become older and require assistance, mealtimes can become even more important. For many individuals, choosing their food may be one of the only things that they can take control over.

Eating and drinking should be an enjoyable experience for everyone. This unit of study is designed to enable you to help your service users make the most of the opportunities that mealtimes can offer by giving them choices over what they want to eat and drink, and then providing food and drink which is safe to consume.

In this Chapter you will learn how to:

❑ support individuals to communicate what they want to eat and drink

❑ prepare and serve food and drink

❑ clear away when individuals have finished eating and drinking.

Each of these issues is equally important in terms of meeting an individual's needs for food and drink.

★ KEY WORDS	
ACTIVE SUPPORT	Providing support that encourages individuals to remain independent.
INDEPENDENT	Encouraging people with disabilities to maximise their own potential, and to do as much for themselves as possible.
DIETARY REQUIREMENTS	Food and drink which provides a balanced diet to meet the nutritional needs of individuals.

FOOD AND DRINK	Food and drink which is to be consumed by the individual.
INDIVIDUALS	The actual people who are receiving care.
KEY PEOPLE	People who are essential to an individual's health and social wellbeing.
HYGIENE	Clean or healthy practice.
CULTURE	A group of people that share traditions, religion, age, era, which are defined by where and how someone lives.
ENVIRONMENT	A person's surroundings, both internal and external.
CONSUME	To eat or drink something.
NUTRIENTS	Substances that must be consumed as part of the diet to provide a source of energy and to maintain health.
NUTRITION	The intake of nutrients and their digestion into the body.
INTERACTION	The way in which two or more people respond to each other.
HIGH-RISK FOODS	Ready-to-eat foods which can support the rapid growth of bacteria, and usually intended for consumption without treatment, such as cooking.
RAW FOOD	Food which has not been cooked.
LOW-RISK FOOD	Usually dry stores (rarely implicated in food poisoning).
WISHES AND PREFERENCES	The choice of the individual in what they want to eat and drink.

Support individuals to communicate what they want to eat and drink

To help you meet the requirements for this section of the unit you will need to know and understand:

❑ factors which can affect choice

❑ what constitutes a healthy balanced diet

❑ The importance of the environment in care settings

Factors affecting choice

We all have preferences for the kind of food and drink we want to consume. Our service users are no different: there will be foods that they enjoy and others that they really do not want to eat. As good carers, we should fully understand the need for choices and support our service users to make their choices about the food and drink they consume.

When trying to find out what type of food and drink individuals prefer, it is important to remember that there are a number of things that might influence a person's choice, some of these are listed here.

Likes and dislikes

You will know for yourself that there are some things that you just do not like to eat.

Religious beliefs

These can prohibit people from eating certain foods; eg people who follow the Islamic faith choose to eat meat which has been killed and prepared following the rules of their religion; people who follow the Jewish religion do not eat pork, and may prefer to keep meat and milk separate; people who follow the Sikh religion are unlikely to eat beef. Many religions forbid the intake of alcohol.

Beliefs and values

Some people choose not to eat certain foods because of health, moral or ethical beliefs; eg vegetarians choose not to eat flesh, while vegans do not eat any flesh or animal products including eggs and dairy. Other individuals may choose to follow healthy lifestyles; eg eating low fat, low calorie foods.

Medical requirements

Some people may suffer from medical conditions or allergies which require them to avoid certain food items. There is a wide range of medical conditions that may affect dietary intake, including diabetes (where sugar needs to be controlled) and high blood pressure (hypertension) which requires a limited intake of salt in the diet. Common allergies should also be considered including:

❑ nuts (which can cause a severe allergic reaction, sometimes fatal)

❑ milk (in children it can cause eczema)

❑ gluten (which is found in wheat products such as flour).

Amount

In addition to the factors involved in choosing food, there are also factors which affect the amount of food we eat. Amongst caterers, there is a tendency to serve the same amounts to all customers, but individuals will have different appetites and needs. It is possible that in some cases men may eat more than women; someone of a large size may require more food intake than someone who is smaller; someone who is active may need more food than someone who is less active. It can be intimidating for someone with a small appetite to be given a large meal, while someone with a large appetite may go hungry if they feel unable to ask for more.

> **REFLECT**
>
> Think about your likes and dislikes in relation to food. Do you know other people who share the same feelings, or do your friends and family have different likes and dislikes? What do your service users like and dislike?

Fig 8.1 You are more likely to meet an individual's food choices if there is a variety of food and drink available.

Identifying an individual's food and drink choices

As health and social carers, we can obtain much of our information regarding a service user's dietary needs from the care plan. However, this is not all that we should use. It is important when attending an individual for the first time that you not only read the care plan, but that you also take the time to find out a person's likes and dislikes by asking them about their food choices or, if necessary, seeking information from key people involved with your service user.

When an individual enters residential care or attends a day-care centre, the menu in those settings will already be set and the

Fig 8.2 Ask your service user about their food likes and dislikes – no one will know better!

individual is often expected to choose from that menu. However, there may not be much on the menu that the individual likes, and you need to think about the appropriate action that you could take to support the individual if this is the case. When collecting dietary information for a care plan, it could be helpful to suggest a range of foods for the individual's consideration. Some people may respond well to prompting. However, care must be taken not to push someone towards a false choice.

When compiling menus either for residential care settings or domiciliary care, it is important to take the preferences and wishes of our service users into account. It can be useful to start this process by asking individuals about the meals already being provided for them, or about the meals they make for themselves. Once you have this information, you can take the discussion towards new food and drink items if necessary. Again, wherever possible try to include their suggestions on new menus.

Making choices about the food and drink we consume may seem an easy task to you and me. However, making a choice for some people can be very difficult; eg people who:

❑ are ill

❑ are uninterested

❑ have dementia or confusion

❑ have learning disabilities

❑ are 'fussy' eaters.

Fig 8.3 Pictures of food can be used to identify service users' preferences.

Individuals may struggle to let you know what they actually want, so, it will be up to you to find out more about their food choices. We have already said that you can read the care plan and you can supplement this information with questions and discussion, but what are you going to do in the situations listed?

If you are working with individuals who have communication difficulties, you will need to develop strategies to enable you to find out about individual preferences and offer choice. You will also need to be able to find out (evaluate) whether they have enjoyed their food or not.

There are many ways that you can approach this kind of situation; eg pictures of foods can aid an individual to choose and also record what they have eaten. Even leftover food can help to build up a picture of the individual's eating patterns and choices.

☑ ACTION

Working with another person, discuss how you would identify food choices with an individual who is profoundly deaf, and an individual who is deaf and visually impaired.

A visit to a restaurant or café can help to identify likes and dislikes, as can the use of the internet if this is available to you. Virtual shopping sites could offer you and your service user the opportunity to explore the issue of food in alternative ways.

Environment

When you are working with an individual to identify their food and drink preferences, you will need to take into account the environment in which you are working. It is far easier to give choice to someone in their own home rather than in residential care, where the organisation has to provide a healthy and popular diet for a number of people under budget restrictions. Even in an individual's own home, the shopping may need to be purchased carefully as individuals could be managing on a limited income. However, it is more likely that the food provided will have been purchased with their likes and dislikes taken into account, therefore you can be more sure that the choices you offer will be something that they usually enjoy.

Having said that, you are likely to come across some people who really do not want to eat any of the food choices on offer that day and would prefer something else! So how are you going to respond?

It is important that you:

- ❏ remain calm and unruffled
- ❏ go through the choices available
- ❏ explain reasons why food and drink choices may not be available (medical reasons, cost etc)
- ❏ offer alternatives as far as possible
- ❏ offer choices that could be met on another day if possible.

It is not easy to meet the choices of all the individuals that you work with. Always take the steps necessary to meet choice, but recognise that there may be occasions when you simply cannot meet the request being made. At this point, your role changes into one of helping your service user to accept that fact and move forward towards resolution.

A balanced diet for your service users

When providing food and drink for individuals, remember that everyone needs to eat a well-balanced, healthy diet. To assist you with your meal planning, a section on the five major food groups is included, to help you during the planning phase of providing food and drink to your service users.

There are five major food groups.

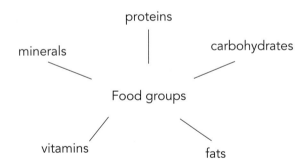

Dietary fibre (roughage) is also extremely important.

A balanced diet should contain two to three portions of meat, fish or a suitable alternative per day, five portions of fruit and vegetables, two to three portions of milk and dairy foods, as well as bread, cereals and potatoes which should make up half of the daily calorie intake.

Water

In addition, it is important to make sure that our service users are drinking sufficient water. Water is vital to the healthy

NUTRIENT	WHERE FOUND	PURPOSE
Proteins	meat, fish, eggs, cheese and milk, nuts, cereals, quorn, tofu and beans	Provide the building blocks for growth and repair of cells. They should be eaten every day, as the body cannot store proteins.
Carbohydrates	bread, potatoes, some root vegetables (eg yams, sweet potatoe), rice, cereals, pasta and all products which are sugar-related	Provide most of the energy and heat to the body, and consist of sugar and starches. They are essential for energy, but if eaten to excess they will be stored as fat.
Fats	butter, cheese, cream, cooking oil, dripping, meat fat, milk and egg yolks	Very concentrated source of heat and energy. If they are eaten to excess they will be stored by the body, in the adipose layer under the skin.
Vitamin A	liver, fish oils, milk, butter, eggs and cheese; vitamin A-forming substances are also found in dark green, orange and yellow vegetables	Important for growth, strong bones and teeth, as well as healthy eyes, skin, nails and hair.
Vitamin B group (there are several)	cereals, liver, yeast and nuts	A large group of complex vitamins, all of which are essential for maintaining good skin. Lack of vitamin B may be responsible for some diseases of the nervous system.
Vitamin C	citrus fruits, strawberries, potatoes and some green vegetables	Vitamin C cannot be stored so it must be taken each day. A lack of vitamin C can cause scurvy, a disease which affects gums and causes bleeding. People with a vitamin C deficiency are more likely to be affected by viral infections and coughs and colds.
Vitamin D	eggs and fish oils, and made by the body when the skin is exposed to sunlight	Enables calcium to be absorbed to strengthen and develop bones and teeth. A severe shortage of vitamin D will lead to rickets, a disease where bones do not develop adequately.
Vitamin E	wheat germ, cereals, egg yolks, liver and milk	This helps to prevent cell damage and degeneration.

NUTRIENT	WHERE FOUND	PURPOSE
Minerals, eg iron, calcium, sodium	a wide range of minerals, essential to health, are found in eggs, cocoa, liver, baked beans, cheese and milk	Important for the formation of red blood cells. A lack of iron can lead to anaemia. Calcium is used for developing firm bones. Sodium is important for maintaining the fluid balance of the body. An excess of sodium can be a contributory cause of oedema (fluid retention).
Roughage (fibre)	Wholemeal cereals and flour, root vegetables, nuts and fruit	The part of the food which cannot be digested and absorbed to produce energy, considered to be helpful in the prevention of such diseases as diverticulosis and constipation.

maintenance of the human body; in fact, our bodies are mostly made of water. Water helps to regulate blood pressure, keeps the kidneys healthy and aids the flushing out of waste products. It is interesting to note that drinking plenty of water also aids fluid retention by preventing the body from storing unnecessary fluids. Everyone should drink at least two litres of fluid a day. This can include tea and coffee, but we need to remember that both of these can act as diuretics and help the body to retain water. If you work in a residential establishment suggest that jugs of water or fruit juice are in place around the building where individuals can help themselves to drinks in between those times when drinks are served. In an individual's own home, make up some fruit juice or water and make it available to your service user when they are on their own.

Fig 8.4 Make sure your service users are eating a well-balanced diet.

A healthy diet balances the amounts of different nutrients which are consumed each day. The amounts eaten will depend mainly on the individual, as we have previously discussed. It is also important to remember that people's appetites may vary with the state of their health. However, it is important to balance the nutrients correctly, regardless of the quantity of food being served.

Sometimes you may have a situation where for medical reasons an individual will have been advised to follow a specific diet. Sometimes the individual may refuse to follow the diet and continue to eat things that they have been advised against. For example, an individual who has diabetes which can be controlled through food planning, may insist on eating anything and

REMEMBER

Unless the choice of menu you offer is varied, your service user might not feel like eating the food on offer. It can be argued that a choice of two is not a choice at all.

CASE STUDY

You are going to a restaurant for a meal. When you arrive you ask for the menu, but the waiter tells you that it has been a busy evening and the only things left are fish pie and smoked salmon. You have never liked fish, so you choose to leave. However, you are hungry and feel the service is unacceptable, so you make a complaint to the manager as you leave. You then go to another restaurant and enjoy a meal from a menu which offers many different options for you to choose from.

- Think about these two experiences, what opinions have you formed about the restaurants?

- What would you tell others about your experiences?

- What effect do you think it might have on the business?

CASE STUDY

Joan has been attending your day-care establishment for a number of years. She has always been independent and able to make her own choices. Joan was fully involved in her care plan and the reviews which followed. Her care plan clearly states that she is a vegetarian but that she does eat fish and eggs. Over the last six months, there has been deterioration in Joan's mental condition and she has been diagnosed with dementia. At lunchtime you notice that one of the other carers has given Joan the meat alternative for lunch. Joan appears to be enjoying her meal so you go and ask the carer if she knows that Joan is a vegetarian; she tells you that she does, but there was not enough of the other option left, and after all it does not matter as she cannot remember what she has chosen.

- What issues does this raise about the care that is being given to Joan?

- What would you do about it?

everything. Your role as carer requires you to advise the individual as to why they should follow their prescribed diet and the benefits they can expect, but you cannot force the diet upon them. In situations such as this it would be expected that you:

❑ inform your line manager of the situation

❑ make notes on the care plan for other carers

❑ support your service user as far as possible to make changes.

Prepare and serve food and drink

To help you meet the requirements for this section of the unit you will need to know and understand:

❑ basic food hygiene

❑ infection control

❑ how to present food to encourage individuals to eat

❑ assistance which may be required

When preparing food and drink for ourselves and other individuals, it is important to follow good food hygiene routines to ensure continued health and wellbeing. You may have studied for a food hygiene certificate as part of your ongoing training, or perhaps you are going to complete such an award as part of this course. Whatever applies to you, there is no harm in refreshing your knowledge about the subject at this point.

Basic food hygiene

Good food hygiene means taking the necessary measures to ensure the safety of food and the health and wellbeing of all individuals who come into contact with the product, from raw and uncooked, through to supplying the consumer with a meal.

Poor food hygiene can have serious consequences, especially for the young and older, frail people. Food poisoning is an acute illness brought on by eating contaminated or poisoned food. This is usually connected with symptoms of pain, diarrhoea and vomiting. It has been suggested that as many as 300 people die each year from food poisoning.

The food hazards associated with poor food hygiene can be divided into three main types of contamination. These can be classified as:

1 microbiological

2 physical

3 chemical.

REFLECT

What are the food choices like where you work? Would you be happy to choose from this menu for the next six months? If not, what needs to be changed? How might your service users feel about the menu on offer to them? Have you asked them what they think of the menu?

CARE VALUES

Whether working in residential care or in the community, you have a duty of care to your service user group. It would not be appropriate for you to dismiss poor food choices (or even a lack or unwillingness to eat) as 'their choice'; you must look to redress the issue. Find out what they used to like eating, try to involve individuals in meal planning, seek help from other key people and if necessary involve a doctor or health visitor.

Fig 8.5 Common sources of food contamination.

☑ ACTION

Find out more about the ways in which food can be contaminated by bacteria, moulds and fungi.

REFLECT

When you are preparing food for an individual that comes from a can or a packet, do you always check the contents for foreign bodies?

REFLECT

Where are the cleaning fluids kept in your place of work? Are they near food products? If so, what action do you need to take to ensure the safety of your service users?

Microbiological

Examples of this kind of contamination are bacteria, mould, viruses, and yeast. Bacteria can occur in all foods but especially in foods that are raw or have not been cooked properly. Contamination of food can occur in many different ways.

Physical

Examples are glass, metal and other foreign bodies. You may have read the stories that reach the national press about pieces of glass that end up in baby foods, or dead insects (or animal droppings) found in pre-packaged foods. These are all examples of how food can be contaminated before you have even purchased it! These contaminants can get into food during food preparation, or during the storage stage if inadequate hygiene practice takes place. Clearly, not only do these products have the potential to lead to poisoning situations, but they could also cause choking and other physical injury

Chemicals

Examples of this kind of contamination are pesticides, cleaning fluids and grease. These can all be transferred to food during the growing stage (eg through pesticides) and during storage or, if inadequate food preparation takes place. It can be too easy for this kind of contamination to take place, especially if food storage cupboards double up with household cleaning products.

Food poisoning bacteria

It is useful to know about the bacteria involved in food poisoning, so that you can take every precaution to protect your service users from food-related harm.

Salmonella

This can be present in animals including household pets, raw poultry, eggs, untreated milk and processed foods. Individuals may experience nausea, vomiting, diarrhoea, abdominal pain and fever. This illness can prove fatal, especially in the old and very young.

Clostridium perfringens

Present in soil, dust, raw meat and animal and human faeces. Individuals may suffer from abdominal pain, nausea and diarrhoea.

Clostridium botulinum

This is also present in soil, raw fish, tinned fish, meat and vegetables. Sufferers can experience breathing difficulties, dizziness, headache, slurred speech and muscle paralysis, which can lead to death.

Staphylococcus aureus

Always present on the human skin, and nose, in the mouth and throat, and in infected cuts and boils. It is also found in milk. Individuals who have been infected with this will experience abdominal cramps and vomiting.

Bacillus cereus

This is present in soil, dust, rice, cereals and cereal products. Sufferers may experience abdominal pain, vomiting and diarrhoea.

Food-borne diseases

Listeria monocytogenes

The bacteria are present in paté, salads, cheeses made with unpasteurised milk, chilled ready meals and soft cheeses. Individuals will experience flu-like symptoms. It has been known to cause miscarriage in pregnant women or illness in the fetus; it can also cause death.

FIND OUT

More about each of the food poisoning bacteria listed.

REFLECT

If you were working in the community and one of your service users was taken ill with suspected food poisoning, what action would you take?

FIND OUT

If there is a food poisoning policy in your workplace. If not, what information would you want to include in such a policy.

Shigella (bacillary dysentery)

This is found in salads, milk and water. Sufferers will experience abdominal pain, vomiting and diarrhoea which may also be bloodstained. It is likely that these symptoms will also be accompanied by a high temperature.

Escherichia coli (E-coli)

This is found in raw meat, human and animal gut, and sewage. Sufferers will experience abdominal pain, vomiting and diarrhoea, a high temperature and kidney damage or failure. This can also cause death.

Campylobacter jejuni

This is found in raw poultry, raw meat, milk, offal and animals. Individuals may experience abdominal pain, nausea, high temperature, headache and diarrhoea with blood.

Most workplaces where food is served will have a policy on the action to take if food poisoning is suspected. The same should apply to those organisations that serve food elsewhere, eg meals on wheels, and service in the home.

Hygiene rules

When providing meals for individuals either in a residential or a domiciliary care setting, we have to ensure that all recommended steps are taken to provide the correct storage, preparation and cooking of food. Here are some hints and tips for keeping food safe.

Rules of the fridge

1 Keep at the correct temperature (1–4°C recommended).

2 Check the temperature three times a day and record the results.

3 Do not overload the shelves and storage sections.

4 Do not put hot food into the fridge. It will raise the temperature of food already stored in there.

5 Do not open the door for longer than necessary.

6 Separate high-risk foods: raw food should always be stored below cooked foods and below salad and vegetables.

7 Keep the fridge clean and disinfected.

8 Protect salad, vegetables etc from dripping blood.

9 Food should be covered, labelled and dated where appropriate.

10 Do not keep open cans in the fridge.

11 Maintain door seals to keep the door closed firmly.

REMEMBER

The most effective way of reducing cross-contamination is to wash your hands between all activities that you carry out in your workplace.

Rules of food preparation

1 Ensure that all food preparation areas are cleaned to a high standard.

2 Do not cross-contaminate foods by using shared surfaces or utensils on raw and cooked foods.

3 Follow instructions regarding defrosting and cooking temperatures, and required times of cooking.

REFLECT

In a residential establishment which is inspected by the environmental health officer, the utensils used in food preparation will be colour-coded. However, this is unlikely to be the case in someone's home. Care will need to be taken that cross-contamination does not take place. What action would you need to take?

REMEMBER

The use-by date on perishable foods means:

❑ considered unfit to eat after the date shown

❑ It is an offence to contravene (sell after the date shown)

❑ It is an offence to change the date shown.

The best-before date means:

❑ no offence to sell after the date if it is still fit for consumption

❑ manufacturer guarantees quality to this date only.

Rules for cooking food

1 Cook at the correct temperature. The core temperature of the product should be 75°C; this means that food should be cooked at or reheated to this temperature.

2 Food which is not being eaten hot should be cooled quickly and then stored in the fridge.

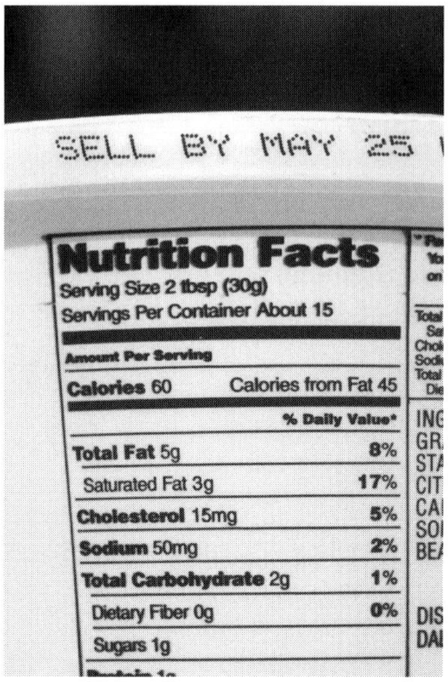

Fig 8.6 Make yourself familiar with food labelling – know what you are looking for.

FIND OUT

. . . what your organisation's policy is on visitors bringing food into your establishment, or taking food into an individual's home.

CASE STUDY

Mary is a respite service user who has come to stay in your care home for a month while her family are on holiday. Mary is feeling unsettled and has not been eating well. A family friend tells you that Mary is very fond of chicken broth, and on her next visit brings a container of the broth for you to give to Mary.

- What food hygiene issues does this raise?
- What action will you take?

Preparing the environment for eating

We have already mentioned that mealtimes are social occasions. If individuals look forward to mealtimes they will be encouraged to eat, which in turn will improve their quality of life.

Choice

When looking after someone in their own home, it can be easier to give them the choice of where they want to eat, what they want to eat and what time they want to eat. On the other hand, in residential care settings you may find it more challenging to build some flexibility into the times of meals and choice of seating available.

REFLECT

If you were working in your service user's home and they asked you to prepare some packed beef broth, which is out of date by two weeks what would you do?
What health issues does this raise for your service user?

Where possible:

- ❏ offer the individual a choice of seating
- ❏ if individuals have a preferred place to eat, try to maintain this
- ❏ keep to the individual's normal meal routines.

Location

Individuals may be eating at a dining table, on a comfortable chair in front of the television, sitting up in bed, or even propped up in bed. It is important to make sure that the area is properly prepared, and that individuals are assisted and if necessary supported in their personal preparations prior to eating. The type of support to be provided will depend on the individual and their setting.

The area where the food is to be eaten needs to be scrupulously clean. This will help to prevent any food-related illnesses, as well as enhancing the look of the area. The dining room setting should be light and bright; tables and chairs should be at appropriate heights, clean and comfortable, taking into consideration the needs of individuals. Where possible add a table decoration (perhaps some flowers), to create interest and stimulation.

If individuals are remaining in bed or in an armchair, a table with adjustable heights should be used, or a suitable, stable tray. You can still use a tablecloth or teacloth to make the tray/table look more attractive for the service user. Food that is served in or on a clean and attractive surface always looks more appetising and tempting.

Hygiene

The utensils to be used for eating should be scrupulously clean and laid out properly. Piling cutlery in the centre of a table does not look professional or welcoming!

Individuals should be encouraged to use the toileting facilities and wash their hands before lunch, to avoid disrupting the meal as this can upset eating patterns. For individuals with dementia, once they have left the table to go to the toilet, they may think they have finished their meal. This could create conflict when being returned to the table.

Supporting individuals

Different individuals will need different levels of support in the dining room. You need to establish with each person the level of

Fig 8.7 Food and drink aids should be readily available to those individuals who need them.

assistance required, while encouraging them to be as independent as possible. You may need to help them to:

- ❏ move into the dining area
- ❏ move using wheelchairs and transferring them into dining room chairs which can be more comfortable for eating (using appropriate moving and handling techniques)
- ❏ protect their clothes with napkins
- ❏ move into a sitting position in bed.

For some individuals with physical problems, you may be required to provide specialist equipment to enable them to manage on their own. Chunky handled cutlery is easier to hold, and special feeding cups can avoid spillage. For partially-sighted individuals you might set out food in separate portions on the plate and describe its positioning to them.

Presentation

Food also needs to look interesting. No one wants to eat the same things day after day, or eat badly cooked food that looks unappetising. Presentation of food is as important as its taste and nutritional value, as this will encourage people to eat. You may enjoy steamed fish, mashed potato and cauliflower, but served together on one plate it will not look appealing, nor will it taste that exciting!

Carer Hygiene

Any carer who is assisting in the dining room should also pay attention to their own personal hygiene and good food serving routines.

- ❏ Hands should be washed thoroughly.

REFLECT

When you are caring for someone in their own home, their care plan will identify where they want to eat their meals, and when they want to have their main meal. When looking after someone in residential care, people will not necessarily want to eat at the same time; some may choose to eat their meal in front of the television, or they might want to have their main meal at a different time than everyone else. Always discuss preferences with the individual and fulfil them whenever possible. If it is not possible, explain why and try to reach a compromise.

❑ Any cuts should be covered with a waterproof dressing.

❑ Protective clothing used elsewhere should be removed and disposed of correctly.

❑ Always use serving utensils to distribute the food.

❑ Interaction between individuals should be encouraged (this means that any background music should not be loud, and should be relaxing).

❑ When asking service users what they would like to eat, do not shout across distances. Walk up to the person and quietly find out what it is they would like to eat or drink. Make sure that everything they need is on the dining table (or tray), and within easy reach.

> **CARE VALUES**
>
> Individuals should be encouraged to be as independent as possible. Their dignity should be maintained and we should consider their wishes as far as possible.

When serving food to your service users, follow their care plan. Some individuals may require their food to be cut up into manageable sized pieces. Carry this task out carefully without disturbing the rest of the food on the plate, otherwise the food may look unappealing.

> **CARE VALUES**
>
> When providing food and drink for individuals, think about how you like your meals to be served. Presentation is very important, and you should not provide less than you would expect yourself.

Remember to think about portion sizes (overloading plates can intimidate people), and of course always allow individuals to eat at their own pace. However, you will need to be aware that for individuals suffering from dementia, prompting may be required throughout the meal to enable them to finish it.

Providing people with napkins helps to protect their clothes and maintain dignity. However, napkins do not prevent food or drink from being dropped or spilt during a meal. You should support your service users and encourage them to clean themselves when finished. Without drawing attention to them, encourage them to clean their hands and face with wipes. If clothing is marked, encourage them to go and change providing any assistance that is required.

Clear away when individuals have finished eating and drinking

To help you meet the requirements for this section of the unit you will need to know and understand:

❑ the importance of waiting until people have finished eating before cleaning away

❑ how to dispose of waste food correctly

❑ how to record and complete records of food and fluid intake

Support individuals

As we have already discussed, individuals will all want to eat their meals at different paces. The clearing away process can therefore be quite challenging. You will need to:

❑ ask individuals if they have finished with their food and drink

❑ sensitively encourage those individuals who find eating and drinking difficult to eat more

❑ demonstrate patience when an individual is taking a long time

❑ provide reassurance to those people who eat slowly.

As part of this process, it is important to make sure that all service users sitting together on a table, have finished eating before you start to remove utensils and crockery. You may have experienced the upset caused in a restaurant by the waiter taking away plates while others are still eating! Therefore, you need to be aware of the eating patterns of the service users so that you do not cause anxiety or upset to those people still finishing their food.

When individuals have finished their meal, it is important to assist those who need help in washing their hands or cleaning themselves, before helping them to return to their chosen place. You should then start to clear away the used cutlery and crockery.

Fig 8.8 Avoid 'hovering' in the background. It can cause anxiety in some individuals.

CASE STUDY

Mary, Jane, Ann and Edith have been residents at Green Meadows for some years. They are all good friends and have chosen to sit at the same dining table. Mary is quite outspoken and tends to speak for the others, who have always been happy for her to do so.

Over the last few months, Edith has become frailer and quieter, and you notice that her clothes are starting to hang loose. You report this to your manager who asks you to set up a chart to record what Edith is having to eat. You inform the rest of the staff team and record this in the service user's care-plan. On observing Edith at the dining table over the next few days, you realise that Mary is deciding for Edith what she wants to eat, and is hurrying her along to finish at the same time as everyone else. This results in Edith leaving a lot of food on her plate.

- What do you think you should do in this situation?

- How could you help to resolve the issues?

CASE STUDY

You are looking after Mrs Jones who is still living at home. You have been given half an hour to prepare lunch, but when you arrive, Mrs Jones tells you that she has already eaten. When you ask her what she has had, she tells you she ate some stew that a neighbour had prepared the night before. You record this on the care-plan and then move on to your next service user. The next time you visit Mrs Jones, you notice the same thing happening. You read the care plan and notice that another carer has also found the same.

- How would you now proceed?

- What concerns may need to be raised with your manager?

Individuals who are mobile and more independent may want to help in the clearing away process as this can give them feelings of wellbeing and control. For many older people, feeling useful is important to their sense of self-esteem. Where this is the case, provide encouragement while at the same time making sure the tasks involved are manageable. For example, break tasks down into 'bitesized chunks' someone may not be capable of carrying plates to the kitchen, but if you provided a small trolley that they could push, they could collect crockery together and then it could be taken to the kitchen. Once the clearing away process is completed once again provide further help to any individual needing assistance with hand washing or cleaning themselves.

REFLECT

How do your service users like to contribute to meal times?

Procedure for clearing away

When disposing of leftover food, it is important to follow your organisation's policies and procedures.

Fig 8.9 *Make sure that you dispose of waste food correctly. Don't leave it lying around!*

REMEMBER 😊

Following your organisation's policies and procedures protects yourself and the people you are caring for. If anyone becomes ill with food poisoning, an investigation will have to take place. This can have serious consequences for yourself and your organisation if breaches in policy and procedures have occurred.

REFLECT

Why should waste food not be left lying around the kitchen or dining room

Once tables have been cleared they should be cleaned, again following your organisation's guidelines. It is likely that your organisation's policy and procedures will include most if not all of the following:

- ❑ Crumbs and spillages should be removed from the tables and chairs.

- ❑ Clean tables (and if necessary chairs) with antibacterial spray and a damp cloth.

- ❑ Floor areas should be swept and left clean.

- ❑ All utensils and crockery should be rinsed, stacked and washed in dishwashers with high temperatures to ensure that they are as clean as possible.

- ❑ When dry, they should be returned to their normal storage areas.

- ❑ All food preparation/serving surfaces including sinks should be cleaned using suitable cleaning materials.

❑ When you have completed the tasks, your hands should be thoroughly washed and your clothing checked to ensure you have not spilled any waste food or drink over yourself.

Legislation

In a health care environment, you have responsibilities under the Food Safety Act 1990. Under this legislation, food handlers (including those carers who handle food) must:

- Wear suitable, clean, washable protective clothing
- keep themselves and the workplace clean (this includes thorough hand washing)
- protect food from contamination
- dispose of waste appropriately
- follow recommended temperature controls for cooking and storing food
- inform their employer if they have food poisoning symptoms or symptoms of illnesses
- not work with food if they have food poisoning symptoms or symptoms of other illnesses until their doctor tells them it is safe to do so.

Avoiding cross-infection/contamination

When preparing and providing food for other people, the opportunities for cross-infection or contamination of food are endless. Every effort should be made to minimise these risks. There are both legal and moral reasons for doing this. As a health care worker, you must recognise the importance of following strict infection control. Cross-infection happens if people do not take care when following procedures relating to the tasks that they are carrying out in the workplace, such as:

❑ moving between work areas without washing hands

❑ poor waste control

CARE VALUES

We all have a duty of care towards our service users, and protecting them from illness and infection is one of those duties. Infection can cause pain and discomfort, and it can increase the use of medication. Time and resources may be used in investigating the causes of infection, and there may be legal implications. Following your organisation's infection control policy will greatly enhance the care you give your service users.

CASE STUDY

It is lunchtime at Holly House, where you work as a health care assistant. You are busy assisting two individuals to access the toilet facilities, when your manager asks you to go to the kitchen and assist the cook (the kitchen assistant has had to leave the building for an appointment). As you arrive in the kitchen, the cook cuts her finger on a knife and asks you to take over preparing and cooking the food.

- Identify where you would put infection control precautions in place, and what precautions you would actually take.

❑   not wearing protective clothing correctly and disposing of it inappropriately

❑   poor cleaning schedules.

Monitoring individuals' food and drink

As a care worker in daily contact with individuals, you are often the best person to establish whether or not an individual is eating properly. At all times you should watch for signs of poor diet or appetite, food allergies or a general reluctance to eat. Sometimes you may be required to monitor and record an individual's food and drink intake.

If you notice that an individual is eating a poor diet (eg no fruit or vegetables), you should first discuss this with the individual involved and try to establish the reasons for this. It may be that they do not like the way the food is cooked, or the variety on offer; it may be that they wear dentures and cannot manage to eat what is being offered. Once you have established the reasons, you can then look to provide solutions to the difficulties and overcome the food barriers.

If it is simply the case that the service user just does not want to eat certain foods, you need to find ways of discussing the implications of a restricted diet with the individual. Sometimes talking about the need for food and drink to preserve independence can be helpful!

Fig 8.10 Encouraging service users to eat can be challenging – ask experienced colleagues for hints and tips that you could use.

If you notice that your service user has a general reluctance to eat, you may need to discuss the reasons for this with them. There could be an underlying medical problem, or an eating disorder, or quite simply they do not like the food being offered to them. You will need to take note of a person's mood, eg are they unhappy or depressed? The way we feel can affect the appetite.

You may also need to discuss situations such as these with the rest of the care team, to see if there are any particular eating patterns developing. It is possible that changed eating patterns can reflect or act as a symptom of something more serious; eg loss of appetite can be one indication of abuse.

You need to be aware that there could even be occasions when a service user has an allergic reaction to the food and drink they are consuming. When (and if) this happens, you need to act quickly and get medical assistance fast.

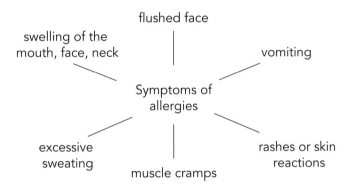

If any of these reactions are immediate, you should summon help immediately. Inform the medical assistance of the food that have been eaten and the quantity, and keep the remainder of the food for analysis. If a reaction develops later, it may be more difficult to relate the reaction to a specific food. However, any suspected food allergy should be recorded in the individual's care plan.

If you are required to record a service user's food intake, your organisation will have specific forms for you to complete. They are likely to reflect the information included on the example shown here.

FOOD AND FLUID INTAKE CHART

NAME _____ **WEIGHT** _____

WEEK COMMENCING

	SUN	MON	TUES	WED	THURS	FRI	SAT
B/FAST UP TO LUNCH							
LUNCH UP UNTIL TEA							
TEA UNTIL BEDTIME							
BEDTIME UNTIL BREAKFAST							

ALL STAFF PLEASE RECORD ALL FOOD AND FLUID INTAKE DURING THE PERIODS SHOWN. PLEASE WEIGH SERVICE USERS AT THE START OF THE WEEK.

Fig 8.11 Compare this chart with a similar one used in your organisation.

☑ **ACTION**

Find a copy of your organisation's form for recording food and fluid intake. Does it record the information needed? Can you improve on it?

Following the care values

Your organisation has legal requirements and duties to observe equality, diversity, discrimination and individual rights legislation when preparing, serving and clearing away food and drink. This means that you should be aware of the different needs of your service users and their cultures, to ensure that you meet their individual requirements for food and drink.

Personal beliefs and preferences

As already discussed, different cultures view types of food in different ways. However, individuals may also require their food and drink to be cooked in a particular way, and served according to their moral or religious requirements. Many individuals need to observe specific hygiene routines prior to eating. You should know your service user's requirements.

For many older people, their religious and cultural requirements places them in a vulnerable position. They are not always able to speak up for themselves, and it is often all too easy for care workers to treat everyone the same. Care plans are in place to protect the rights of service users, as well as providing guidance on physical care needs. The care plan informs you of the individuality of the person you are caring for. As a carer, you must act as the advocate for your service user, providing the best, most culturally acceptable care that you can.

CASE STUDY

Mr Bilgrani has been admitted to Oak House for respite stay for one week. The home brochure states that Oak House will provide specific diets respecting the diversity and culture of all, which was one of the reasons why he chose this care home. You consult with Mr Bilgrani and he informs you that he is a Muslim; he does not eat pork and any other meat he eats must be halal. He also informs you that he will eat vegetarian meals, and particularly likes the use of herbs and spices in his food.

You give this information to the cook and ask her to work out a menu for Mr Bilgrani. Later in the week you ask Mr Bilgrani if everything is alright, and he tells you that he is unhappy with the meals provided. When you ask him why, he tells you he has only had vegetarian meals provided since his arrival and they are bland and boring.

When you discuss this situation with the cook, he tells you that he does not know where to purchase halal meat. He also tells you that he feels he has provided an adequate diet as he has given Mr Bilgrani vegetarian meals as stated in his care plan.

- How could this situation be improved for Mr Bilgrani?
- How might the organisation support the cook in meeting the diverse needs of the service users?

Personal Values

When working in an environment which provides care to a range of individuals with varying needs, you may find that there are differences in the way in which individuals conduct their personal hygiene routines both before and after eating. Their standards and values may be different to your own. As a carer, you must respect these differences while working to resolve hygiene and any potential cross-infection issues. What you must not do is to ignore any risks based on service user choice; your job is to try and resolve any potential conflicts between culture, hygiene and the protection of all individuals involved.

Choice and Time

When providing food at mealtimes, you should take care that you give service users time to respond to any questions. Take care not to remove choice by deciding for individuals what you think they would like to eat and drink. Make sure that sufficient time is given to enable individuals to finish their meal at their own pace.

Confidentiality

Any concerns that you have regarding an individual's diet should be recorded on your organisation's appropriate paperwork. Risk assessments should be completed for activities carried out by yourself and other care workers in relation to food preparation and serving.

Make sure that your paperwork is completed promptly and in accordance with confidentiality agreements. As a care worker, you may be able to access files which will inform you of your service user's needs, any risk assessments in place and any dietary requirements.

High-fibre diets

Constipation is a common problem for the older person. It can cause feelings of fullness, nausea and general distress which often leads to a poor appetite. A high-fibre diet can help prevent constipation; when dietary fibre is eaten it absorbs water, making the faeces soft and easier to pass. If individuals are on high-fibre diets, it is important for them to drink plenty of fluids. You should not give raw bran (sprinkled on meals) to older people as it interferes with the absorption of iron, calcium and other minerals.

Weight-reducing diets

In older people, obesity can aggravate arthritis and lead to mobility problems. Weight gain occurs when more food is eaten than the body needs; extra calories are stored as fat. To lose this body fat, the individual has to eat less than the body uses, so that fat stores are used up. It is however still important for individuals to be given a well-balanced diet. Weight reduction in older people may be difficult as they are often unable to exercise.

Diabetic diets

Diabetes is a disorder in which the body is unable to control the amount of sugar in the blood. For the body to function properly, the amount of sugar present needs to be regulated. One of the symptoms of diabetes is passing water in excessive amounts throughout the day and night. As water is lost, the body

> **REFLECT**
>
> When was the last time you carried out a risk assessment for food preparation in your place of work or in an individual's home.

Fig 8.12 Only appropriately qualified staff should advise on diets.

becomes dehydrated; this causes extreme thirst. Sugar present in the urine is food for bacteria and can lead to urine infections. There are also more serious side effects to diabetes, such as blindness, poor tissue repair, circulatory problems that can lead to amputations and even death if the diabetes is not controlled properly.

There are three forms of treatment for diabetes:

1 diet alone

2 diet and tablets

3 diet and insulin injections.

Only qualified medical personnel should recommend specific diets for service users. If you think someone has gained or lost weight you need to follow the correct procedures as outlined in your organisational policies. The individual's own doctor should see them and if necessary a health check will be carried out to see if there are any underlying causes.

The medical practitioner may then refer the individual to see a dietician. Dieticians are nutritional experts. They can assess the needs of people with a wide variety of illnesses, and identify any specific nutritional concerns, plan appropriate intervention and monitor clinical progress.

Managing illness

Illness can have a great impact on an individual's appetite. When illness occurs, you may need to:

❑ encourage the individual to eat small, frequent meals throughout the day

❑ encourage the consumption of high-protein foods

CARE VALUES

When preparing meals for service users, you need some knowledge of the different ways of preparing and cooking food. When working in residential care or a day-care centre, there is usually a cook present and you may only be expected to help serve or clear away after meals. However, when providing the same service for someone in the community, you need to take other things into consideration. Environmental and social factors affect food choice and eating habits. Some of these are:

• money available to spend on food

• distance to the shops and the time allocated to do the shopping

• types of shops available

• food storage facilities

• cooking facilities and equipment

• time allocated to cook, serve and clear away the meal.

You should ensure that you discuss and plan food details with your service user and plan menus, which you will be able to cook taking into account all of the above. It is impossible to cook a roast dinner in half an hour!

- offer milky drinks instead of tea or coffee

- avoid giving large portions as this can intimidate people when they have a poor appetite

- seek advice about the provision of dietary supplements, as these can be a useful way of adding extra nourishment to the diet.

As people become older, they may experience swallowing difficulties (dysphagia). Swallowing is a very complex procedure; muscles of the face and mouth must be in full working order to swallow properly and easily. Swallowing difficulties can be caused by a variety of disorders such as:

- stroke

- Parkinson's disease

- multiple sclerosis

- head injury.

Any degree of dysphagia can be uncomfortable and frightening for the individual concerned. There are ways of helping people who experience difficulties in swallowing. It is important to follow any guidelines that you may have regarding your service user. Ignoring given guidelines will put individuals at risk of choking or chest infections.

For individuals with dysphagia, the desire to eat and drink will be affected, as will their ability to chew and swallow their food. You may need to prepare food to a specific consistency, or their drinks may need to be thickened to make them easier to swallow. Each service user will need an assessment, and the speech and language therapist will give advice. Care should always be taken to sit people in an upright position to eat, and you should watch for any signs of choking while they are eating and drinking. Do not leave them alone.

CARE VALUES

For some people with swallowing difficulties, food needs to be liquidised.
This can look very unappealing on a plate, and it will be difficult to experience all the flavours.

Liquidise each separate food group, and place as attractively as possible on the plate. Your service user will then be able to recognise and taste the different food groups.

REMEMBER ☺

All mealtimes should be times of enjoyment, and service users should be able to look forward to well-planned meals that take into account their wishes and preferences. You should have an understanding of what healthy eating is and the specialised diets that your service users may require, but unless the food is appetising and served in the right environment, it will not have the optimum effect. A positive attitude from you can help to make mealtimes interesting and increase the likelihood of the individual achieving a good nutritional intake.

Summary

This chapter has looked at ways of ensuring that food and drink are provided in a healthy and pleasing manner to the individual. To demonstrate best practice, make sure that you:

- ❏ identify the individual's wishes and preferences relating to food and drink

- ❏ identify factors which may affect their choice

- ❏ support individuals to understand which food and drink is available

- ❏ offer suitable alternatives when options do not meet wishes and preferences

- ❏ evaluate and change menus to support service user choice

- ❏ prepare the environment so that eating and drinking is enjoyable and individuals can interact with each other

- ❏ support individuals to consume their chosen food and drink

- ❏ respect individuals' religious and cultural beliefs

- ❏ understand why diet is important to good health

- ❏ record individuals' intake and complete records according to their requirements.

Index